GOD'S POTTERS

PULPIT & PEW

Jackson W. Carroll, series editor

Pulpit & Pew is a major research project whose purpose is to describe as comprehensively as possible the state of Protestant and Catholic pastoral leadership in the U.S. What are the trends, and what issues do clergy face? The project also aims to contribute to an understanding of excellent pastoral leadership and how it can be called forth and supported. Undertaken by Duke University Divinity School, the project is supported by a grant from Lilly Endowment, Inc. For further information, see *www.pulpitandpew.duke.edu*.

GOD'S POTTERS

Pastoral Leadership
and the Shaping of Congregations

Jackson W. Carroll

With the assistance of
Becky R. McMillan

WILLIAM B. EERDMANS PUBLISHING COMPANY
GRAND RAPIDS, MICHIGAN / CAMBRIDGE, U.K.

Wm. B. Eerdmans Publishing Co.
2140 Oak Industrial Drive N.E., Grand Rapids, Michigan 49505 /
P.O. Box 163, Cambridge CB3 9PU U.K.

Printed in the United States of America

11 10 09 08 07 06   8 7 6 5 4 3 2

Library of Congress Cataloging-in-Publication Data

Carroll, Jackson W.
God's potters: pastoral leadership and the shaping of congregations /
Jackson W. Carroll; with the assistance of Becky R. McMillan.
p.   cm.
Includes bibliographical references and index.
ISBN-10 0-8028-6320-5 / ISBN-13 0-8028-6320-1 (pbk.: alk. paper)
1. Pastoral theology. 2. Christian leadership.
I. McMillan, Becky R. II. Title.

BV4011.3.C37   2006

253 — dc22

2005034137

www.eerdmans.com

Contents

Contents

List of Tables and Figures

Tables

Figures

Preface

This book is a primary fruit of a large research project on pastoral leadership in the United States. The project, *Pulpit & Pew,* has been designed to take stock of the state of pastoral leadership in the United States, both Catholic and Protestant: Who are America's clergy? What do they do? How are they faring? What does excellent ministry by a congregation and its pastor(s) look like? And what can be done to nurture and sustain excellence? Supported by generous grants from Lilly Endowment, Inc., we have brought together a wide variety of scholars, denominational leaders, clergy, and laity to attempt to gain purchase on these issues from various perspectives. Ten research reports and seven books relate what has been learned.[1]

As an attempt to provide answers to the research questions, this book is mostly descriptive rather than prescriptive. I write from my perspective

1. The ten reports, plus a number of articles on various topics, are available at no cost from the *Pulpit & Pew* Web site (www.pulpitandpew.duke.edu) or from *Pulpit & Pew,* Duke University Divinity School, Box 90983, Durham, N.C. 27708. Two previous books focused on Catholic priests (Hoge 2002 and Hoge and Wenger 2003) and were published by Liturgical Press in cooperation with the National Federation of Priests' Councils. William B. Eerdmans Publishing Company is publishing the remaining five books as a *Pulpit & Pew* series. In addition to this book, they include a study of clergy who have left pastoral ministry either to take another type of church-related position or to leave ministry altogether (Hoge and Wenger 2005); a study reporting in-depth interviews with six pastors about how they and their congregations seek to engage in public ministry in their local communities (Constantine 2005); a theological reflection on the meaning of excellence in ministry (Jones and Armstrong 2006); and a history of pastoral leadership in America (Holifield, forthcoming).

as a social scientist and also an ordained minister. Although I try to present the findings as objectively and fairly as possible, I do not avoid making normative and evaluative judgments when I believe they are warranted; however, I try to be clear when I am doing so. My aim has been to paint a broad, descriptive portrait of today's clergy as opposed to the more detailed look that in-depth case studies of individual pastors might provide.[2] My hope, in sacrificing depth for breadth, is that the portrait that I paint will be helpful to a wide range of clergy by holding up a mirror of the profession by which they might look at their own ministry. I hope too that seminary students and others who may be wrestling with a call to ministry will find the book helpful. I especially hope that the book will be of interest to laity, helping them to understand better what it is that pastors do and experience, and the role that they can play in supporting and encouraging pastors to provide excellent leadership.

Data for the book come from several sources that are described in greater detail in Appendix A. One is a major national telephone survey of clergy that was conducted for *Pulpit & Pew* by the National Opinion Research Center (hereafter NORC) of the University of Chicago in the spring and summer of 2001. Using a sampling technique called hypernetwork sampling (described in Appendix A), 1,231 senior or solo pastoral leaders were selected, a number of whom were in very small denominations or independent congregations. The latter pastors are often missed when samples are drawn from denominational lists. Regrettably, we were unable to include assistant and associate pastors or other clergy serving on church staffs. Interviewers were able to conduct forty-five minute telephone interviews with 883 of the pastors, a completion rate of 72 percent. The data have been weighted statistically to reflect more accurately the size of congregations in which clergy serve. Although this is by no means the largest survey of senior or solo pastoral leaders ever undertaken, it is arguably the most representative. Those interviewed represent over eighty-one denominations and faith traditions. A small number of leaders were from several religious traditions other than Christian. Because of their small number, we have omitted their responses in what follows. Rather, we have focused

---

2. For a rich description of pastoral life, see Richard Lischer's memoir of his first parish, a small rural Lutheran congregation in southern Illinois (Lischer 2001). Also Marilynne Robinson's novel *Gilead* (Robinson 2004) presents a compelling portrait of pastoral life — its highs and lows — as the central character, John Ames, reflects on his long tenure as a Congregational pastor as he faces his impending death.

entirely on Christian clergy, both Catholic and Protestant. A tabulation of responses to the interview questions can be found in Appendix B.

A second data source is information from twenty-three focus groups with a diverse set of participants — pastors from congregations of various size and locations, laity, and denominational leaders. The focus groups were conducted in seven regional sites across the country: Alabama, North Carolina, the District of Columbia, Indiana, Illinois, Texas, and southern California. The groups provide insight into some of the issues and puzzles that our survey data raised for us, and we were able to listen to the stories and insights of the participants as they reflected on their understanding and experience of pastoral leadership. The focus group methodology is also described in Appendix A.

A third source of data comes from a national survey of congregations also funded by Lilly Endowment: the U.S. Congregational Life Survey conducted by Cynthia Woolever (now of Hartford Seminary) and Deborah Bruce of the Research Services Office of the Presbyterian Church (USA). We were able to coordinate our telephone survey with theirs, using the same sample of congregations served by the clergy who were interviewed for us by the NORC. Of the 434 congregations that took part in their survey, we have telephone interviews with 351 of their pastoral leaders. Thus, I have been able, for some purposes, to compare the clergy's comments with those of their lay constituents.

One further note on method: Because there are too few clergy in the survey from most denominations to do separate denominational analyses, and because doing so would also be extremely tedious, I have grouped the denominations into four traditions: Catholic, mainline Protestant, conservative Protestant, and historic black churches. These are classifications of denominations that the research team has made and not self-definitions of the clergy we surveyed. The classifications follow closely those of Wade Clark Roof and William McKinney in their book *American Mainline Religion* (1987), although we collapsed their liberal and moderate Protestant categories into a single mainline Protestant category. Typically these are Protestant denominations that are affiliated with the National Council of Churches of Christ in the U.S.[3]

---

3. Although it is problematic, we included the several clergy who are members of various branches of the Orthodox communion as mainline Protestant. While it can be argued that they should be grouped with Catholics, we wanted to restrict the Catholic analysis to

Conservative Protestants — also often referred to as evangelicals — encompass a number of large and small denominations as well as independent congregations. Our conservative Protestant category also includes Pentecostal traditions. Many conservative denominations are affiliated with the National Association of Evangelicals.

The historic black denominational category primarily includes the major large denominations that were initially founded by blacks: the African Methodist Episcopal Church (AME), African Methodist Episcopal Church Zion (AMEZ), the Christian Methodist Church (CME), the Church of God in Christ (COGIC), and several large predominantly black Baptist denominations (for example, the National Baptist Convention of the USA and the Progressive National Baptist Convention). Other smaller black denominations are also grouped in the historic black category; however, black clergy who are members of predominantly white mainline or conservative Protestant churches are included within their respective denominations.

Catholics, of course, represent a single tradition. It is important to acknowledge that these four traditions are not monolithic or uniform in perspective. All, including the Catholic Church, reflect considerable diversity.[4] Despite their diversity, these four ways of classifying denominations do represent important streams in American church life with distinctive emphases and practices that provide interpretive frameworks for their leaders and members.

A number of organizations and individuals have helped to make this work possible. I especially wish to acknowledge the support of Lilly Endowment, both in the planning stage and in the five years that it took to bring the project to completion. Chris Coble, the program officer at the Endowment with whom I worked most directly, and Craig Dykstra, Vice President for Religion, have been both extremely helpful as well as quite patient as the initial four-year project stretched to five. I deeply appreciate

---

Catholic priests. Also, unlike Catholics, Orthodox priests (except for bishops) may marry, and members of the Orthodox communion hold membership in the National Council of Churches.

4. For analysis of internal diversity among Catholics, see D'Antonio et al. (2001) and Hoge & Wenger (2003). See Balmer (1989), Dayton and Johnston (1991), and Smith (1998) for a discussion of the different streams that make up contemporary conservative Protestantism. Two helpful treatments of the diversity within the African American church tradition are Lincoln and Mamiya (1990) and McRoberts (2003).

their probing questions and the wise counsel that they gave to me and to other project staff. They were regular, active participants in the core advisory group that met twice yearly over the course of the project. It was Craig who asked me to develop the proposal for the research that became *Pulpit & Pew* when I had contacted him about a much more limited project. John Wimmer, who joined the Endowment staff during the course of the project, was a helpful participant in the other key advisory group of church leaders.

I am also deeply grateful to Duke Divinity School administrators and colleagues who gave support and encouragement to the project — especially to Dean L. Gregory Jones, who not only served on the core advisory group but also is coauthor of one of the project's books, a theological exploration of excellence in ministry (Jones and Armstrong 2006). A number of faculty colleagues were important conversation partners during the course of our work.

Early in the project, I was privileged to spend four extraordinary weeks as a visiting scholar at the Rockefeller Foundation's Study and Conference Center in Bellagio, Italy. While there, I was able to begin analysis of the data from the national survey and write a paper with fellow visiting scholar and close friend, Wade Clark Roof, that informed Chapter 2 of this book. Having uninterrupted time for study and reflection in such a lovely setting and sharing ideas with an international group of distinguished scholars from many disciplines are experiences to be treasured.

I have been quite fortunate to have several associates who contributed much to the work. Becky McMillan served as Associate Director of the project for three years. In addition to her theological training, Becky brought her background as a labor economist and expertise as a statistician to our work and played important roles in a number of aspects of the project. Before leaving to move to Oklahoma, she contributed to early drafts of several sections of the book. Her able predecessor in the Associate Director's position was Matthew Price, who left after two years to take a research position with the Church Pension Group of the Episcopal Church. Matthew was of great help in planning for the overall project, reviewing previous research on ordained ministry, and assisting with the design and pretest of the interview protocol for the national survey. McMillan and Price co-authored an important and much-cited *Pulpit & Pew* report on clergy compensation (McMillan and Price 2003).

From the outset of the project planning through its completion,

John James has served ably as project coordinator. He has managed mountains of paperwork, overseen the budget and the project's Web site, handled the logistics for some twenty-plus project consultations and advisory group meetings, and has taken care of many other administrative duties to keep the project on track. Brooke Pike has provided valuable assistance as staff associate, making sure that requests for payment were handled in a timely manner, responding to phone calls, overseeing the mailing of reports, and generally assisting with the project's clerical tasks. Bob Wells of the Divinity School's Communications Office has served as communications director for the project, managed news releases and our electronic newsletter, and shepherded project reports into publication. David Reid and Jon Goldstein of the Communications Office have also been quite helpful. Finally, Stephen Berry served ably as graduate assistant, including day-to-day management of the project Web site, transcribing and coding focus group interviews, and assisting with literature searches.

As I have noted, we were able from the start of the project to coordinate our work with the U.S. Congregational Life Survey. I am grateful to Cynthia Woolever and Deborah Bruce and others on their staff for their cooperation and support as well as their sense of humor in the face of the typical snafus that large research projects often encounter.

We also owe a debt of gratitude to the staff of the National Opinion Research Center, especially to Alma Kuby, NORC Project Director, Asma Ali, the project's Survey Specialist, and a number of others at NORC, including the able interviewers who took great interest in their work for our project.

To assist with our focus group process, we enlisted the services of Professor Richard Kruger of the University of Minnesota. His expertise in the design and conduct of such groups prevented many mistakes and helped us to gain quality information. Focus group moderators included Kevin Armstrong, Diana Butler Bass, Scott Cormode, Michael Jinkins, Deborah Kapp, and Penny Long Marler. Ruth Moore, Joe Sicking, Genie Cormode, Alison Riemersma, Tim Weddle, and Kristen Curtis assisted them.

Throughout the project, we relied heavily on the insights and discussions of two advisory groups. Our core advisory group met twice yearly for three days each time. Members read and discussed the works of other research and reflection on ministry, reviewed our planning, and made many helpful suggestions to keep the project on course. Members of the group included Daniel Aleshire, Dorothy Bass, Anthony Brown, Kenneth Carder,

Mark Chaves, David Daniels, Douglas Hicks, Brooks Holifield, Gregory Jones, Clarence Newsome, Stephanie Paulsell, Katarina Schuth, Joseph Small, Robert Silva, Barbara Wheeler, Melissa Wiginton, and James Wind.

A second group of advisors were church leaders — denominational and seminary officials and pastors — from over twenty denominations who met twice yearly for two days over the course of the project. They helped to shape the various research reports in discussion with their authors and became the first audience to review them when complete. They also helped to strategize ways of getting the findings noticed within their various constituencies. Members included Philip Amerson, Wilbur Brannon, Elise Brown, Deborah Clemens, William Craddock, Robert Dale, John Dever, Wayde Goodall, Chad Hall, Bruce Hartung, Joe Harvard, Edwin Hernandez, Chris Hobgood, Samuel Hogan, Steve Holt, Thomas Hoyt, Gerald Kicanas, Cletus Kiley, Robert Kohler, Steven Land, Louis Lotz, Clayton Matthews, James Meek, Albert Meyer, Martha Grace Reese, Rollin Russell, Craig Settlage, Clay Smith, C. Jeff Woods, and McKinley Young. Joseph Small served as coordinator/facilitator of this group. Two members of this group, Craddock and Matthews, hosted a meeting with Daniel Conaway and Phyllis Tickle, to help us think through communication issues, including naming the project.

The two groups of advisors met jointly near the project's end and read and commented on a portion of this book. Additionally, Mark Chaves, Dean Hoge, and Chris Coble read the completed manuscript and gave very helpful feedback. During the course of the project, I was also helped by several conversations with Howard Gardner.

I also wish to acknowledge my considerable indebtedness to the late Samuel W. Blizzard, my graduate school mentor and a pioneer in the study of American clergy. It was Sam who encouraged me to become a "clergy watcher," a focus that has characterized much of my work, and for that I am grateful.

I could not have completed this project without the support of my wife, Anne Ewing Carroll. Her patience was often tried as I continued to work on the project and this book for several years beyond my retirement from teaching. For her love, encouragement, and sometimes more than gentle prodding when the writing seemed to be taking an inordinate amount of time, I am deeply grateful. She and I also share a love of pottery, especially from the rich tradition of North Carolina, which has contributed to my choice of the book's title.

Finally, I dedicate this book to my two daughters and their spouses: Susan Carroll Whitcomb and her late husband, Giles M. Whitcomb, whose untimely death during the course of the project has left a deep void in our lives; and Frances Carroll Strumph and her husband, Paul S. Strumph. They and their children bring more joy to my life than anyone deserves.

Chapter 1

Pastoral Leadership
at the Beginning of the 21st Century

"But we have this treasure in clay jars so that it may be clear that this extraordinary power belongs to God and does not come from us."

St. Paul (2 Corinthians 4:7)

"There is no dearer treasure, no nobler thing on earth or in this life than a good and faithful pastor and preacher."

Martin Luther[1]

In his second letter to the Corinthian Christians, the Apostle Paul uses a pottery metaphor to describe congregations. He calls them "clay jars," or, as earlier translations expressed it, "earthen vessels," through which the extraordinary power of God may be experienced. This is a startling claim! Paul is saying that in their congregational life — in their beliefs, practices, relationships, and the witness of their daily lives — God is revealed. How startling his claim actually is becomes particularly evident when one re-members that the Corinthian Christians were far from being "cardboard saints." Their individual behavior was not always exemplary, and their life together, from Paul's description, was often conflicted. Some have inter-

---

1. From "A Sermon on Keeping Children in School" (Willimon 2002b).

1

preted this image as implying that congregations are at best neutral or empty human vessels that contain and often obscure God's power. To be sure, Paul's words emphasize the humanity — the "earthen" dimensions — of congregations. Also, it is clear that congregations often do obscure rather than reveal God by their behavior; yet Paul's words suggest that it is through these human qualities — a congregation's life together and its witness in the world — that God's extraordinary power is visible and experienced. In their very humanity, congregations are revelatory agents — for good or for ill.

If we extend Paul's metaphor, if congregations can be thought of as clay jars, then we can think of the clergy who lead them as potters — God's potters — whose work is shaping, glazing and firing those congregational clay jars so that they reveal rather than hide God's power in their life and practices. Later in this chapter, I will draw on insights from cultural sociologists to flesh out this point about the work of a pastor, describing pastors as producers of culture, primary agents in constructing and forming their congregation's culture, its beliefs and practices — not, of course, by themselves, but with the active engagement of laypeople as together they wrestle with the implications of Scripture and church tradition and the challenges of the world in which they live. "Shaping congregational clay jars" and "producing congregational culture" are complementary ways of thinking about the work to which pastors are called.[2]

Being a pastor is a tough, demanding job, one that is not always very well understood or appreciated. Pastoral work is more complex than that which transpires in the hour or so a week that many lay people see the pastor in action as she or he leads worship and preaches. What happens during this time is surely central to clergy and their parishioners, but it is not the only important thing that clergy do. Thus, as I indicated in the Preface, the aim of this book is to ask what God's potters do in their work in today's church. Who are they? How they are faring? What does excellence in the craft of ministry look like? And how can it be nurtured and supported?

As a start toward addressing these questions and as a way of emphasizing the considerable diversity of both pastors and congregations, consider the following four vignettes (note that no real names are used):

2. Throughout the book, I mostly use the term "congregation" to speak of local religious assemblies, whether Protestant or Catholic. Sometimes I use the term "parish" instead, although I do not use it with its traditional territorial connotation, as has been the case in Catholic and some other traditions.

• Father William, a sixty-nine-year-old Catholic priest, is pastor of a rapidly growing suburban parish in North Carolina, once a solidly Protestant enclave. With many "transplants" from other parts of the United States, the parish has over nine thousand parishioners. Hispanics, who have moved into the state in large numbers, are also a growing constituency. Two priests serve as associate pastors along with two lay ecclesial ministers[3] and several other paid lay staff. Together they assist Father William in the leadership of the parish and its parochial school.

A major responsibility of the three priests is leadership of the multiple celebrations of the Eucharist each week — five each weekend (one of which is in Spanish), plus daily masses Monday through Friday. Some 4,500 worshippers take part in the services in an average week. In addition, the priests and lay ecclesial ministers share the teaching in the parish's religious education program, provide pastoral counseling and spiritual direction to parishioners, visit sick and infirm members, and give support and guidance to the numerous other programs and activities of the busy parish. Father William also serves on several boards and committees in the larger community beyond the parish, and as the pastor, he has overall administrative responsibility for the work of the parish and school, assisted by a lay parish council.

His is a complex and demanding job in this growing parish, one that will become even more daunting in the months ahead as one of his associates is being transferred and not replaced because of the Catholic Church's severe shortage of priests. "As it is already, I go to bed tired and wake up still tired," Father William commented as he contemplated the increased work load facing him with one less priest on the staff. Furthermore, the growing number of Hispanic congregants calls for an expansion of the parish's programs in response to the special needs and concerns of this new constituency, including offering programs in Spanish. Recruiting lay leaders fluent in Spanish is an increasing challenge.

• Pastor James is the founding pastor of a small, independent Baptist

---

3. The term "lay ecclesial minister" defines a Catholic or vowed religious working at least twenty hours per week in a paid position as a member of a parish pastoral staff (Murnion and DeLambo 1999: 5).

congregation on the edge of a city in California. The congregation, with 135 mostly blue-collar members, is unapologetically fundamentalist in its theology and conservative in the lifestyle it promotes for its members. Though the congregation encourages separation from many aspects of the surrounding society, it supports the agenda of the religious right — especially on pro-life and anti-gay/lesbian issues. Members have fairly often taken part in picketing Planned Parenthood clinics and have handed out anti-abortion literature in shopping centers. Disdainful of the secular education offered in the local public schools, members hope someday to establish their own Christian school.

Pastor James, a graduate of a nearby Bible college, understands his role to be the teaching minister of the congregation. Most of his sermons at the two Sunday services (morning and evening) are careful expositions of scriptural passages interspersed with applications to contemporary life. He uses an overhead projector to outline his points, and members take notes in space provided in their worship programs. Wednesdays provide another teaching opportunity, as he works his way chapter by chapter through the books of the Bible. His wife teaches in the congregation's Sunday school and also serves as one of the counselors of the youth program. Much of James's time, when he is not studying Scripture in preparation for his teaching ministry, is spent counseling his members and doing evangelistic calling. This latter task entails visiting prospective members who live in surrounding neighborhoods, speaking with them about their faith, and inviting them to the church — a task in which he often experiences rejection. A twelve-member deacon's board, under James's strong leadership, governs the life of the congregation. Deacons also assist him in the congregation's evangelistic outreach. Because the congregation is small and has no affluent members, finances are always a major issue. As much as James and his deacons would like to start their school, they struggle just to meet current operating expenses.

• A forty-one-year-old United Methodist pastor, Reverend Susan is not only one of an increasing number of women serving as pastors, but she is also typical of a growing population of clergy who are in ministry as a second career. She was first a public school teacher and then a stay-at-home mother before feeling called to ordained ministry. She is in the second year of her first pastoral appointment since seminary. Located in the Midwest, her appointment is what Methodists call a two-point charge — that is, she serves two congregations located near each other. The larger of the two, mostly rural congregations has eighty-five regular participants of various ages, and shortly before Susan arrived it experienced serious conflict over the ouster of a longtime volunteer choir director who had regularly clashed with a succession of pastors. Although many in the congregation supported Susan's predecessor when he removed the choir director, others did not, and the acrimony that resulted led members to ask the bishop for a change of pastors. The smaller congregation, some fifteen miles away, has thirty-five participants, many of whom are members of two extended families.

Susan, her husband, and their two older teenaged children, live in a parsonage adjacent to the larger of the two churches and thirty miles from the nearest large city. Her husband makes a daily commute to the city for his work. Every Sunday morning Susan preaches at both churches, hurrying between them to reach the second service on time. Along with lay volunteers, she and her husband also work with the combined youth fellowship of the two congregations, and he teaches an adult Sunday school class in the larger congregation.

On Wednesdays, Susan leads a Bible study, also combined for the two congregations and alternating in location between them. Afternoons and many other evenings are given over to parish visiting — shut-ins, members in hospitals, and others needing pastoral attention — and to meetings of each congregation's administrative council where, in the larger congregation, she has attempted to help heal the conflict that she inherited. Susan also is required to participate in her denomination's mentoring program for those who, like her, are new to pastoral ministry. Added to this is that she serves as her own secretary and often finds herself taking on some of the janitorial tasks of the congregations when the lay volunteers fail to show up. Despite being so busy, she enjoys her work immensely, and the congregations are responding positively to her leadership.

• Pastor Donald is the founding pastor of a four-thousand-member, predominantly African American congregation in a large Texas city. The congregation is one of a growing number of megachurches in Protestantism. Although it has no formal denominational affiliation, it is Baptist in its organization and beliefs. Donald, however, encourages members to engage in Pentecostal practices — for example, speaking in tongues, holy dancing, and upbeat gospel singing — that are increasingly typical of many African American megachurches. Members, especially newer ones, are overwhelmingly in their mid-thirties to early fifties — Baby Boomers and Generation Xers. Most of the newer members are in professional and managerial occupations, and some have advanced degrees. A staff of two full-time associate pastors and a full-time music director assists Donald. Five other ordained ministers who work full-time in other occupations but help out in various aspects of the church's work join them on the leadership team.

On most Sundays, Pastor Donald preaches at the congregation's two lively morning worship services that are necessary to accommodate the large number of worshippers. Two choirs and a praise band — drums, guitars, and a keyboard — provide music and accompaniment for the congregational singing. Donald and one of the associates share leadership of the congregation's Sunday evening worship, which is especially geared toward youth. Leadership of the congregation's other programs is shared among the staff, though Donald takes on a heavy load of teaching, including classes on marriage and parenting. He is also heavily involved in local community affairs, currently serving as an elected member of the city's school board. Meanwhile, he works with his board of deacons to govern the congregation's life.

Until recently, Donald's leadership style has been rather autocratic. As founding pastor, he developed the vision for the congregation and made most decisions about programs. But as the congregation has grown, especially as the membership became increasingly middle class and professional in makeup, he has experienced some discontent about his top-down leadership style. Members who are used to sharing in decision-making in their work and family life are pressing for a greater voice in the congregation. Some have brought a petition to the deacons asking for a revision of the congregation's by-laws to increase lay members' voice in church affairs.

William, James, Susan, and Donald are God's potters, engaged in making congregational clay jars. They represent but four of the large number of clergy whose work is also shaping faithful clay jars as they lead the estimated 350,000 congregations in the United States. Most U.S. religious leaders, like them, are Christians, but their number also includes rabbis and an increasing number of imams, Hindu priests, and Buddhist priests who lead America's growing religious mosaic.

Even if one only considers Christian clergy — the focus of this book — these four examples barely begin to scratch the surface of the considerable diversity that exists among America's pastors. Some are full-time; others are part-time. Some have been ordained; others are laity commissioned by their denomination to provide pastoral services for congregations unable to afford an ordained pastor, especially one who is able to work full time. In the Catholic case, the shortage of priests has meant that some priests serve as pastor of more than one parish or that deacons or nuns lead some smaller parishes and do everything in the congregation that a pastor would do except celebrate the sacraments — a role left to a circuit-riding priest who comes occasionally to perform sacramental duties. Some clergy are seminary trained; others, like Pastor James, are graduates of Bible colleges or institutes or have no formal training. Most are men, but a growing number, like Susan, are women. Some are in ministry as their first career; others, also like Susan, have come into ministry as a second career. Some are representatives of a particular denomination; others, like Donald and James, started their own churches and are denominationally unaffiliated. Yet these clergy, diverse as they are, are called to form their congregational "clay jars" so that the congregations reveal God's extraordinary power through their life and ministry. That, to put it mildly, is a daunting task!

Martin Luther, author of the second epigraph for this chapter, may perhaps be forgiven for a bit of hyperbole in his words about pastors as dear and noble treasures; yet, in light of the church's calling to reveal God's power in its life and ministry, he was generally on target in recognizing the singular importance of "good and faithful" pastoral leadership in shaping a congregation's life. Few congregations will find it possible to exhibit vitality and excellence in the face of poor pastoral leadership. Several centuries before Luther, the church father and theologian Gregory the Great wrote, "When the head languishes, the members have no vigor. It is in vain that an army, seeking contact with the enemy, hurries behind its leader, if he has lost the way" (Gregory the Great 1950: 69). Neither Gregory's nor Luther's insight is any less true today.

Although congregations are not the only settings in which ordained

7

clergy work, and although the work that clergy do in other settings is certainly important, this book is about those approximately 365,000 who lead congregations and make up the majority of ordained clergy.[4] In the remainder of this chapter, I will address several issues that help to frame the ensuing report: overall characteristics and aim of the work that clergy do in the quite diverse congregations in which they serve; changing aspects of the profession that have led at times to unsettledness; and ways of defining the work of clergy, including, as noted above, thinking of their role in producing congregational culture.

Pastoral Leadership and Congregational Diversity

Over 90 percent of U.S. congregations, whether large or small, Christian or otherwise, have a primary full- or part-time formal clergy leader (Chaves 2004). Although the clergy's leadership role differs according to the congregation's tradition, as we will see, because congregations share a common organizational field, certain core tasks of clergy are relatively similar across traditions — not only for Christians but for non-Christians as well.[5] Almost all clergy lead their congregations in worship and other ritual activities, whether those be baptisms, confirmation rites, communion or Eucharist, weddings, or funerals. Most also preach as a part of their worship leadership, and they may teach in the congregation's religious education program. Additionally, most clergy provide pastoral care — for example, counseling with participants about personal and spiritual mat-

---

4. Of the 365,000 serving as pastors in congregations, some are associate or assistant ministers. The total number of clergy is estimated to be almost 600,000. The latter figure, however, includes retired clergy; chaplains in hospitals, prisons, or the military; and those who teach in colleges, universities, and theological schools. Still others serve as ministers on college and university campuses, and some on the staff of pastoral counseling centers. Denominational boards and agencies also employ many ordained clergy on their staffs (Lindner 2004).

5. DiMaggio and Powell (1983) refer to this as "institutional isomorphism" to indicate the way in which organizations that share a common organizational field (e.g., religious congregations) come to resemble each other in form or substance even when they differ significantly in their normative agendas. As we will discuss in Chapter 2, institutional isomorphism is also evident in the movement of most American congregations, regardless of religious tradition or formal polity, toward what has been called "de facto congregationalism" (Warner 1994).

ters and visiting sick and shut-in members. Some also have major responsibility for administering the affairs of the congregation and leading it in planning and carrying out its work. And some play important roles in the broader community as participants or leaders in community organizations. If their congregation is a member of a denomination or other larger religious organization, clergy may also be called on to take part in that body's regional or national work.

At the same time, however, different traditions have different priorities. Protestant clergy, especially those heavily influenced by the Reformers such as Martin Luther and John Calvin, give priority to preaching and teaching. Catholics and those in the Orthodox communion, in contrast, focus more on the clergy's priestly role — especially as celebrant of the sacrament of the Eucharist, which is at the heart of Catholic and Orthodox life. A priest's preaching and teaching are important but secondary tasks in these traditions. Rabbis, even more so than Protestant clergy, are expected to be teachers of the faith.

In addition to these differing priorities, another kind of diversity can be seen in the social and personal characteristics of those engaged in pastoral leadership. As is clear from the examples of William, James, Susan, and Donald, clergy differ in age, gender, ethnicity, educational background, and preparation for ministry. Thus it is difficult, if not impossible, to make facile generalizations that apply to all clergy as if all were somehow alike. The differences, especially when they exist within the same denomination, also make it evident that clergy are not "interchangeable parts." Not all have similar gifts for ministry, nor do they necessarily have the social or personal characteristics that make them able to lead in every type of congregation or context. The match between clergy and congregation — or at least the capacity of clergy to adapt their ministry to differing congregations — is a theme to which we will return at several points in this book.

This leads to a third very important kind of diversity: congregational size and context. Most congregations that clergy serve are small — some have been so throughout their history; others were once large but have lost members over the years. A recent nationally representative study of U.S. congregations found that the median congregation has only 75 participants (including children and adults) and only 50 regularly participating adults (Chaves 2004: 19). Small size, as we shall see, is especially characteristic of Protestant congregations. Only a few Protestant megachurches may have as many as 2,500 or more worshippers at several services on a given weekend. Catholic parishes, in contrast, are typically much larger, including even most "small" Catholic parishes such as those that lay pastoral administrators lead. The average U.S. Catholic parish has 3,000 members. Nonetheless, despite variations in congregational size, the majority of U.S. *churchgoers* — almost 90 percent of Catholics and Protestants alike — participate in larger congregations. Half of the church-going population worship in congregations that average 400 weekly participants. The difference between the size of the typical U.S. congregation — especially Protestant — and the size of the congregations in which most Americans worship is an important one, as we shall note at several points in subsequent chapters. These different-sized congregations, in turn, are located in considerably varied types of social and cultural landscapes — urban, suburban, small town, and rural — each with its own challenges and dynamics.

Why Are Congregations and Their Leaders So Important?

Why is it important to focus on congregations and pastoral leaders as I do in this book? There are both a sociological and theological answer to this question. First, the sociological: I have already called attention to both the pervasiveness and social significance of congregations in our nation's life and thus the importance of those who lead them. In his book *Bowling Alone,* political scientist Robert Putnam writes that "Faith communities in which people worship together are arguably the single most important repository of social capital in America" (Putnam 2000: 66). By "social capital" Putman means "connections among individuals, social networks and norms of reciprocity and trustworthiness that arise from them" (2000: 19). Religious involvement not only provides occasions for such connections to happen in worship services, Sunday school classes, coffee hours, and potluck suppers, but it also gives members opportunity to develop civic skills: leading groups, running meetings, giving speeches, and learning how to manage disagreements. Involvement also encourages participants to give greater attention to the needs of others in and outside the congregation. Beyond their contribution to social capital, congregations and the networks of organizations that they support are also increasingly called to deliver needed social services in their communities, so called "faith-based initiatives" — food pantries, homeless shelters, drug and alcohol counseling services, ministries to those suffering from AIDS, and so forth. These social contributions are significant enough on their own to highlight the sociological importance of congregations and their leaders.

Yet, as important as these sociological contributions are, congregations' principal significance is theological. As I have emphasized using Paul's image, they are the clay jars through which God's extraordinary power is revealed and experienced. Put differently, Christians understand congregations to be a primary mode — arguably *the* primary mode — through which the Christian gospel is organizationally embodied and made visible. They are settings in which people encounter the meaning of the gospel in word and sacrament, grow in their understanding and commitment to it, experience the community and support of fellow believers, and are empowered to participate in the church's ministry and mission.

In addition to the clay jar metaphor in his correspondence with the church at Corinth, Paul also referred to the Corinthian congregation as the "body of Christ." (1 Cor. 12:27). This is an equally extraordinary claim: that in the common life and witness of these quite ordinary and often wayward Christians at Corinth, Christ was present. They were not simply Christ's emissaries or representatives, but his very body, charged with continuing his ministry of reconciliation in the world, calling others to accept God's gift of salvation and be reconciled one to another. As such, they were to be both a present sign as well as a foretaste of God's coming reign in which all human divisions will be healed. By extension Paul's words apply also to Christian congregations gathered elsewhere; whether in his time or ours; whether in Rome, Athens, or Philippi, or in Seattle, Bombay, or Cape Town; whether in one of the world's megacities or in a crossroads community in rural Nebraska. They are clay jars that make Christ present to the world, and as such, they and their leaders have a significance that is both sociological and theological.

Difficult Congregations and Ambivalent Clergy

Despite their importance, however, we should not romanticize congregations. As clay jars, they are sometimes poorly formed, cracked, and imperfectly glazed. In other words, they are not always happy or faithful communities, and the face that they present to the world is not always an attractive one. Paul found this to be true not only in Corinth, but also in other congregations that he helped to establish; and it continues to be true today, as

11

some of our data will suggest. Some congregations struggle with inadequate finances; others face uncertain futures as their members age and no younger cohorts are readily available to replace them; others have a difficult time understanding and adapting to the changing social and cultural contexts in which they exist; and many are mired in internal conflict, either between members or with their pastor. As important as congregations are both sociologically and theologically, they are frequently difficult places in which to serve as a pastoral leader today.

The clergyman and hymn writer John Newton once commented that being a pastor is at one and the same time "the worst of all jobs and the best of all callings."[6] Newton's words, though written in the nineteenth century, probably resonate with many present-day pastors. Some would affirm both halves of Newton's statement; others might stress one half over the other. They might concur that being a pastor *could be* the best of all callings were it not for the job that the pastor is required to do or the particular congregation he or she is currently serving. As one pastor put it, "There are . . . a lot of smelly jobs in the pastoral ministry. . . . The pastor . . . has to fire unproductive staff, meet with chronic complainers, wade into conflicts between leaders, and represent the unpopular changes being proposed by the church board. . . . [S]omeone has to do [these jobs], and often that someone is the person who is being paid to come to church" (Barnes 2004).

Comments that we heard from two clergy illustrate the ambivalence that some pastors have about their calling. One commented effusively that "I can think of no more exciting work than the opportunity that the ministry gives me to participate in God's work in the world." In sharp contrast, the other complained that "The pastor is kind of a 'fifth wheel,' an employee of an institution that is comforting to have around but far removed from the real issues of the world." Some laity also express the same ambivalence about ordained ministry as an attractive occupational choice. In an interview conducted for another research project, the researchers were told by a Catholic laywoman that she had great admiration for her current priest and for the priesthood generally. Yet, when reflecting on the Church's current shortage of priests, she had this to say: "People just aren't becoming priests. I mean it's not a popular occupation. Nobody wants to be a priest. It's not a real attractive job. No pay, no marriage, no fun, just a lot of work" (Carroll and Roof 2002: 167-8).

6. Cited in Miller (2001).

A widely cited study of pastors in the Lutheran Church — Missouri Synod (Klaas and Klaas 1999) also found ambivalence. The authors reported that about 30 percent of the clergy expressed substantial joy and satisfaction with their work. They described their ministries as tough, challenging, and fulfilling, with a constant demand for creativity and flexibility. They thrive on these challenges. Another 30 percent expressed mixed feelings about their work but were moderately satisfied. For them ministry is "a roller coaster of highs and lows," "a balancing act of extremes of fulfillment and frustration." Of the remaining 40 percent, the researchers described half of them as moderately depressed and approaching burnout. The other half, representing as many as one thousand pastors, were severely depressed and in advanced stages of burnout. Comments such as, "The joy is gone. I can't take the crap anymore," or "I cannot encourage others into this," or "Young people see this and say, 'No way!'" were typical. Some of the most negative criticisms of ordained ministry came in interviews with spouses and children of current and former pastors.

The authors of the Lutheran study gave their survey findings a generally negative interpretation, choosing to highlight the dissatisfaction that clergy and their families experience. One can, however, read their findings more positively by emphasizing the 30 percent who experienced joy and satisfaction and the additional 30 percent who were moderately satisfied, experiencing highs along with lows. As we shall see in Chapter 6, many clergy are highly satisfied with their work life and find great fulfillment in ordained ministry as a calling.

In the last analysis, both readings of clergy satisfaction are probably correct. There are a substantial number of clergy who find the job difficult to the point of despair and are prime candidates for dropping out. But they also have their opposites who are deeply fulfilled in their work and would never consider leaving. And there are those in the middle, experiencing the roller coaster of highs and lows that the Klaases describe.

An Occupation in Flux

Whatever interpretation one may decide to give to ordained ministry today does not alter the fact that the pastor's job is not an easy one, as Newton recognized long ago. Moreover, as one considers the role of clergy in today's church, it is clear that there is unsettledness about it. It is a job in flux, as several of the comments imply. It is made increasingly difficult by rapid changes in the pastor's work environment, including the broader culture in which pastoral work is done — the topic of the next chapter. There and in subsequent chapters I will consider a number of changes that have created a sense of an occupation in flux, including the following:

First, a major redefinition of clergy and lay roles has taken place since the 1960s. For Catholics, it came as the result of the Second Vatican Council, which taught that the church — including both clergy and laity — is the "people of God." An understanding of shared ministry replaced the older cultic model that had put the priest on a pedestal and left laity as mostly passive followers.[7] For Protestants, a similar change occurred in the 1950s and '60s with a "rediscovery" of and new emphasis on the Reformation doctrine of "the priesthood of all believers." For both traditions, the change has led to a greater sense of mutuality in ministry between pastors and laypeople, but it has also blurred distinctions between them and left some clergy wondering what their distinctive role is.

Second, the opening of ordination to women in many Protestant denominations in the mid-1970s is, arguably, one of the most important changes ever to affect ordained ministry. Although the Catholic Church and many conservative Protestant denominations still do not ordain women as pastors, the growing number of clergywomen in mainline Protestant denominations is changing ordained ministry from a "sacredly male calling" to one that now incorporates both genders, and women are now bringing their distinctive gifts to the pastorate.

Third, Catholics and Protestants currently face a growing shortage of clergy. For reasons somewhat different from those experienced by Protestants, since the late 1960s, Catholics have faced a declining number of candidates for the priesthood, accompanied by many resignations of existing priests — so much so that Catholic researchers project that by 2015, the number of active priests will have declined by 46 percent since 1966 (Young 1998). Some Protestant denominations, having experienced an

---

7. The changed relation between clergy and laity was symbolized quite dramatically when, almost overnight in 1965, altars in Catholic churches were turned around, the priest said Mass facing the congregation, and the laity became active participants in the service. It is almost impossible for non-Catholics to imagine the impact of this and other Council decisions on priests and laity alike, especially since many were ill-prepared in advance for the sweeping changes that took place. See Andrew Greeley (2004) and Robert Orsi (2005) for a discussion of the suddenness of the Council's changes and the confusion that they wrought.

oversupply of clergy in the 1980s and 90s, now find themselves also facing something of a shortage, brought on in large part, as we shall see, by the difficulty of filling the many small, often rural congregations that are increasingly unable to afford or attract full-time, seminary-trained pastoral leadership.

Fourth, a sharp increase in recent years has occurred in both the number and proportion of older, second- (and even third-) career entrants to ministry and what appears to be a declining interest among younger seminary students in becoming pastors of congregations. Why these changes? Has pastoral ministry lost its attraction for younger men and women? And what are the consequences, positive and negative, of second-career clergy?

A final issue that has been an especially important contributor to clergy unsettledness is one that, for the most part, became a highly publicized national scandal after we had conducted much of the research for this project. I refer to the issue of clergy moral failures, exemplified especially by widespread charges of priestly pedophilia. Since I do not treat this issue separately elsewhere, it deserves some further comment here.

For much of American history, clergy have been held in high social esteem. But this high esteem has been waning in recent years for various reasons and not just because of moral failures on the part of clergy. In public opinion polls taken between 1973 and 1997, the public's confidence in religious leaders and religious institutions dropped for all age groups, with the largest overall decline over the total period — just over 20 percent — coming in the fifty-five to sixty-four-year-old group. By 1997, however, it was young and middle aged Americans — groups between twenty-five and fifty-four — who were least likely to express confidence in clergy and churches. Twenty-four percent or less of these age groups expressed a great deal of confidence (Smith 2000).[8] These polls were mostly conducted prior to the time that the pedophilia scandal and the Catholic hierarchy's often tepid response (in some cases appearing like nothing so much as an attempt at cover-up) became national headlines. But these events have now further eroded public confidence in clergy, especially priests. A 2004

8. It should be noted that confidence in most institutions, and not just in clergy and churches, was falling during this period. Major exceptions (for most age groups) were confidence in the Supreme Court and the armed forces. For most age groups, the percentage expressing a great deal of confidence in these two institutions increased.

Gallup poll found that 56 percent of the population rated clergy as "very high" or "high" in terms of their honesty and ethical standards. Although the percentage may seem to be relatively high, it is considerably lower than that for nurses (79 percent), military officers (72 percent) and physicians (67 percent) (Moore 2004). The scandal is also having a major depressing effect on recruitment to the priesthood and on the morale of priests not involved in the scandal. Though less so than Catholic priests, Protestant clergy — and not just a few high-profile Protestant televangelists — have also had their share of high-profile moral failures, including financial improprieties and sexual abuse. This, too, has no doubt contributed to the public's diminishing confidence in clergy as well as lowering clergy's own self-esteem. Such moral failures are by no means new, but their current prominence contributes to the unsettledness and flux that the profession is experiencing.

Defining an Occupation in Flux: Three Models of Ministry

Both the diversity of types of ministry and the current flux that present-day pastoral leadership represents raise a question about ordained ministry as an occupation. Just what kind of occupation is it? A brief look at three efforts to define the occupation — three models of ministry — will provide a perspective for the portrait of contemporary clergy that I present in the chapters that follow.[9] The models, as I will argue, are not mutually exclusive; each, however, focuses on a particular characteristic or quality of pastoral leadership that its proponents have felt to be its defining characteristic, and in each, there are tensions with the other models.

Pastoral Leadership as an Office

One answer that goes back to the early history of the Christian church is understanding pastoral leadership as an *office*, a formal position in the

9. An important recent book that considers changing understandings of ministry is William Willimon's *Pastor: The Theology and Practice of Ordained Ministry* (Willimon 2002a) and its companion volume, *Pastor: A Reader for Ordained Ministry* (Willimon 2002b). Also, E. Brooks Holifield is currently writing a history of pastoral leadership in America to be published as part of the *Pulpit and Pew* book series (forthcoming 2007).

church with specified "official" duties and recognized by ordination, either by a congregation or a denomination. In this office, the pastoral leader stands as the inheritor and communicator of the church's tradition that stretches back to the first Apostles.

In the earliest Christian communities as we see them reflected in the Gospels, especially that of John, and in Paul's letters to various congregations, there do not seem to have been formal offices to which individuals were ordained, but rather various functional tasks or roles that particular individuals were called to undertake for the community. Such roles were based on recognized *charisms* or gifts of the Holy Spirit. Writing to the Corinthian church, Paul emphasized that every member, by virtue of his or her baptism, has a spiritual gift to be used for the good of the whole. Every member participates equally in the Body of Christ. But he acknowledged that some have gifts for exercising particular leadership roles in the community — as apostles, prophets, teachers, healers, and so forth (1 Cor. 12:28).

As the young churches grew and expanded geographically, they encountered new challenges, especially the threat of movements such as Gnosticism, and they found it necessary to establish more formal offices — bishops or presbyters and deacons — that would guard the apostolic teachings and practices of the church against teaching and practice deemed to be heretical. In sociological lingo, they "institutionalized" or regularized these roles into official positions or offices. The writer of the pastoral letters to Timothy, claiming the authority of the apostle Paul, counseled Timothy to "Hold to the standard of sound teaching that you have heard from me, in the faith and love that are in Christ Jesus. Guard the good treasure entrusted to you, with the help of the Holy Spirit living in us" (2 Tim. 1:13-14). To insure faithfulness to the tradition, he also laid down guidelines for those who hold the various offices. As Raymond Brown (1984: 39) has written, "Already the 'Paul' of the Pastorals had divined that the best response to a plethora of views claiming to be revealed and even traditional was a pedigreed tradition, involving a link between the apostolic era and approved church officials."

Early in the church's life, rites of ordination were established through which the pastoral office was conferred by the church on those considered to have the requisite gifts to lead congregations. Presiding at the Eucharist, communicating the Word through preaching and teaching, and overseeing the life of the congregation came to be the primary tasks of the ordained officeholder. By committing these pastoral tasks to the officeholder, the church emphasized that the Gospel the pastor was to preach and teach is the tradition received from the apostles, however much its communication may bear the stamp of the individual pastor.

The history of ordination — how it has been variously understood and practiced in diverse Christian traditions — is much too complex to be considered here. The Catholic tradition — including the Roman Catholic Church, various expressions of Orthodoxy, and the Anglican communion — has emphasized the sacramental nature of ordination. A special priestly character, a special gift of grace, is conferred on the ordinand who now becomes "a priest for life" and a representative minister for the whole church. For Roman Catholics, by the fifth century, ordination was understood to stamp the priest with an "indelible character," allowing his work to be efficacious despite any personal failings on his part. Ordination, in the Catholic tradition, also links the priest to the apostles and their teachings through the laying on of hands by a bishop who himself stands in the apostolic succession. This perspective has obviously been affected by the Second Vatican Council's emphasis on laity and clergy sharing in ministry as the "people of God," but in many ways it still persists.

In sharp contrast to the Catholic tradition, the Free Church tradition (for example, Baptists and Congregationalists) has emphasized the functional nature of ordination. The pastorate is still considered to be an office, but it is one that grows out of the recognition by a particular congregation of its need for certain functions to be undertaken for the good of the whole, and its acknowledgement by means of ordination that a particular candidate has the necessary gifts to carry out these functions. This person, however, is no different from other baptized members of the community, who also have spiritual gifts to be exercised on behalf of the community. In some churches in the Free Church tradition, recognition of ordination does not extend beyond the particular congregation doing the ordaining: when the office holders leave the community, their ordination does not go with them; or when the congregation no longer deems the function to be needed, the office ceases to exist.

The Catholic tradition, with its sacramental and hierarchical view of ordination, and the Free Church tradition, with its functional and egalitarian one, constitute two ends of a spectrum of views on ordination and the pastoral office. A variety of other interpretations fall in between them, sometimes taking other factors into account — such as, for example, the need for the state to recognize ordination in countries where there is a state church.[10] (Of course, the states also recognize clergy's ordination in the U.S. when it comes to officiating at weddings, a recognition that is being increasingly trivialized by the number of weddings performed by persons ordained via the Internet.[11])

Despite differences, however, each Christian body emphasizes in its own way that pastoral leadership is an office, recognized in ordination by the community that gives "officialness" to the ordained person's activities. She or he is set apart through ordination by a community — a denomination or a local congregation — to administer the sacraments, preach and teach, and give oversight to a congregation's life. Thus one way of thinking about ordained ministry is that it is the office that defines the core work of clergy and is the constant amidst the flux that the occupation is currently experiencing. Yet, as we will shortly see, this way of thinking about ordained ministry has at times stood in tension, if not open conflict, with other understandings of ministry.

Ordained Ministry as a Profession

Few ways of defining ordained ministry as an occupation have created such controversy in recent years as has the understanding of it as a *profession*. I will not rehearse the controversy in any detail;[12] rather, I simply note that the emphasis on clergy as a profession has been an important one in shaping contemporary understandings of the clergy role. My use of the term — others emphasize other meanings — is to imply an educated or learned clergy, competent largely by virtue of that education to engage in the core tasks of the pastoral office.

The professional model as we have come to know it today is mostly a

10. A more extreme view than that of the Free Church tradition is to be found, for example, among Quakers. They abolished the office of clergy altogether and believed that all Christians equally have access to the power and leading of the Spirit.

11. The Universal Life Church, one of several Internet sites offering ordination online, claims to have ordained (for free) more than 400,000 people since its founding in 1959, maintaining "We strongly believe in the rights of all people to practice their beliefs, regardless of what those beliefs are" (Bahari 2005).

12. Carroll (1985) reviews many of the arguments for and against the professional model and argues that the model needs reconceiving if it is to be helpful in defining the role and task of ordained ministry.

product of the nineteenth century. Early in that century clergy began, though not frequently, to refer to themselves as professionals.[13] Prior to that time, both in Great Britain and the United States, the professions, especially lawyers, doctors, and clergy, had been more social statuses to which one belonged in a hierarchically ordered society than self-conscious occupational groups. With urbanization and industrialization, the older "status professions" and other occupations came to be transformed into modern professions and organized occupationally in order to meet the specialized needs for knowledge and services in the new society (Bledstein 1976; Larson 1977; Russell 1980). It was important for the older and emerging professions to demonstrate that their practice was grounded in sound knowledge and skills for addressing important human problems. A number of universities and professional schools, including theological seminaries, trace their origin to this push to provide education for both the older and newer professions.

It is probably true that a major impetus for professionalization, both for clergy and for other occupations, was to establish control or jurisdiction of a particular body of knowledge and practice. To quote historian Donald Scott (1978: 155) regarding the clergy: "Its character as a profession enhanced the clergy's collective legitimacy as the overall guardian and definer of God's word and presence in society. Under the culture of professionalism, monopoly . . . properly belonged to the collective body of certified practitioners, those who had gone through the rituals and training (which only those already through them could define and control) that made one a 'professional' rather than a layman or amateur." There is truth in this assertion. Knowledge, especially that not generally available save through extensive education, creates social distance between the one who has it and those who do not. Whether intended or not, this clearly has been a consequence of the emphasis on an educated clergy that professionalization represented, and it is one of the legitimate criticisms of the professional model of ministry.

The concern for an educated clergy, however, long preceded the professional model. Early in the history of the church, predating anything resembling seminary formation, "ministerial 'know-how' was passed on by informal instruction, example, and apprenticeship. Thus in addition to [passing on] the apostolic tradition in the strictest and narrowest sense,

---

13. I am indebted to Brooks Holifield for this information.

there would have been episcopal traditions of preaching, liturgical ceremony, catechetical formation, and community organization" (Cooke 1975: 415). Still, the lack of formal education and lax oversight of clergy persisted throughout the Middle Ages and led to numerous complaints about the low state of education and morals of diocesan clergy. Clergy occupied the office of ministry, but in the eyes of many the clergy's low moral standards and lack of education tarnished the office considerably. The Protestant reformers were especially concerned to change this picture. By elevating preaching to the center of the clergy's task, for example, they brought the need for clergy education to the fore. As a historian expressed it, writing about sixteenth-century England, "In a Catholic or sub-Catholic church, where the visual and the ceremonial dominated the verbal and intellectual, it scarcely mattered if the priest was well qualified; he was simply the conduit for divine meaning. But in a proper, pure reformed church, the minister needed to be, more than anything else, an effective preacher of the word, not a mere 'dumme dogge,' as the phrase went at the time — it came from Isaiah — who would go through the motions and convey nothing of the intellectual spirit of reformed Christianity" (Nicolson 2003: 35).

Catholics soon responded to the threat of the Reformation by requiring, at the Council of Trent, that every diocese establish a seminary for the education of aspiring priests in ecclesiastical studies and spiritual formation. For both Protestants and Catholics, reform of the church depended heavily on an educated clergy, an emphasis that was strongly reinforced in the nineteenth century by the emphasis on ministry as a profession. From that time on at least through the mid-1960s, the image of a professionally educated clergy was dominant, if not universal, for Catholics and most Protestant traditions. Even today, critics of the professional model speak positively about the ideal of a "learned" clergy even as they decry how reality fails to live up to the ideal. Moreover, as I noted earlier, in a society that so strongly values education, laity have come to insist on an educated pastor. Few will willingly settle for one that is poorly educated. And this is one of the positive meanings of ministry as a profession. If considering ordained ministry as an office emphasizes the "officialness" of the world of the pastor, viewing ministry as a profession emphasizes the competence that is needed for carrying out the tasks of the pastoral office. The two need not be mutually exclusive.

Ministry as Calling

Although office and profession are two ways of defining the work of the ministry, Christians have also expected that the person ordained to the pastoral office must exhibit not only learning but also spiritual depth and character. These are qualities associated with ministry as a *calling*. Ordination recognizes that God has called the ordinand to this office.

The recent renewed emphasis in many circles of Christianity on what is variously termed the "ministry of the laity" or "priesthood of all believers" reminds us that all Christians, both clergy and laity, through their baptism, are called to ministry. H. Richard Niebuhr (1957: 64) referred to this as the *call to be a Christian*, to follow Jesus Christ as a disciple. Yet, Niebuhr noted, there were three other types of call especially relevant to clergy. These include the *providential call*, "the invitation to assume the work of ministry which comes through the equipment of a person with the talents necessary for the work of the office" — what I implied in the discussion of an educated or professional ministry. Niebuhr also spoke of the *ecclesiastical call*, the invitation extended to a person by some community or institution of the church to engage in the work of ministry. The ecclesiastical call gives the ministry its "officialness." It is a call to the office of ministry.

But another type of call is also essential to ordained ministry: what Niebuhr referred to as the *secret call*. The secret call is "that inner persuasion or experience whereby a person feels himself [or herself] directly summoned or invited by God to take up the work of the ministry." John Calvin described the secret call as "the honest testimony of our heart that we accept the office offered to us, not from ambition or avarice, or any other unlawful motive, but from a sincere fear of God" (quoted in Christopherson 1994: 219). It is this latter, secret call that critics of ordained ministry — typically from within the church — have sometimes felt to be lacking. An individual may be installed into the office and have the necessary educational grounding to be a pastor and still lack the inward call from God that shapes one's character and gives spiritual depth to one's practice.

In seventeenth-century England, for example, a number of dissenting Protestant movements such as Baptists and Quakers "excoriated the parish clergy . . . because of their educational pretensions. [They] declared that a call from God was the sole qualification for the exercise of the preaching office, and they dismissed the parish clergy as 'hireling priests' who lacked the Spirit-filled power of a divine call" (Holifield 2002: 46).

True ministry, some argued, needed no human help or learning but was solely a gift from God. Similarly, in the United States in the eighteenth century, supporters of the Great Awakening, led by Gilbert Tennent, clashed with those from the Philadelphia Presbytery who opposed the revival. At the heart of their conflict was the question of the qualifications needed for pastoral ministry. Was it a sufficient guarantee of a candidate's worthiness that the candidate had received ministerial training, as the anti-revivalists generally maintained? Or should the church insist on an inward call from God? Tennent's clear position was expressed in his sermon, "The Danger of an Unconverted Ministry," where, among other things, he compared an unconverted minister with "a man who would learn others to swim before he'd learned it himself, and so is drowned in the Act and dies like a fool . . ." (Smith et al. 1960: 326).

Tennent's argument for a "special call" has continued to find expression through the years, especially among evangelical Protestants, including leaders of what are now called "new paradigm" congregations. In a study of these churches, Donald Miller (2003: 20) reported a conversation with Chuck Smith, founder of the Calvary Chapel association of congregations: "God does not call those who are qualified," Smith said, "but qualifies those who are called." Miller continues, "The questions guiding selection of leaders in these new paradigm congregations have very little to do with formal credentials. They include the following: Does the individual have a passionate commitment to God? Does he or she have a vision for transforming people and the world around them? Does the person manifest a Spirit-filled life? If these qualities are in place, then God will give them the skills to carry out the task to which they have been called, regardless of formal training. After all, they say, Jesus used a group of fisherman to establish his kingdom."

For Catholics, too, concern for the spirituality of the priest has been emphasized in various ways, though somewhat differently from Protestant evangelicals. Priestly spirituality was at the center of the reforms introduced in the Council of Trent in the sixteenth century. As I noted earlier, from the fifth century on, official Catholic teaching had viewed the sacrament of ordination as stamping the priest with an "indelible character" that made his work as priest efficacious even if he himself exhibited moral and spiritual failings. The Tridentine Fathers sought to rectify the abuses that this view of priesthood had wrought. Thus, the Council not only pushed for the intellectual reform of the clergy through education, but the seminaries (from the Latin *seminarium,* meaning "seed plot") that the Council established were especially to be "seed plots" where a candidate's vocation could be nourished and protected from the negative influences of a sinful and indifferent society.[14] Given the Catholic understanding of the priest's role as mediating God's presence through the sacraments, the priest's personal sanctity helps to make him an instrument for the sanctification of the laity. Thus the Church's concern about the spirituality of the priest is not totally unlike that of the Protestant Gilbert Tennent. Indeed, in recent years, especially in light of the pedophilia crisis, Catholics have placed renewed emphasis on nurturing the vocation of their candidates, forming their spirituality and character.

It is true that in the Catholic or sacramental tradition, in contrast to evangelical Protestants, the emphasis is not so much on the individual piety of the priest as it is on the priest's role as bearer of the sacred within the worshipping community.[15] Nonetheless, the font of the priest's spirituality is, like the Protestant clergy's, rooted in what Niebuhr understood as the special call, the summons from God to take up the work of ministry. In addition to being the ground of pastoral spirituality, the special call also provides the frame through which clergy make sense of their experience: It functions as "a kind of moral compass to guide the 'called' through the changing landscape of modern society" (Christopherson 1994: 222).

This look at these three different models or ways of understanding ordained ministry, brief though it is, can be helpful as we think about pastoral leadership today, especially in light of some of the changes that we considered. Positively speaking, each is a way of protecting some attribute or quality that churches or clergy themselves have felt to be important. Giving each of them emphasis in the face of the current flux reminds us of

14. See Lee and Putz (1965) and Wagoner (1966) for discussion of the significance of spiritual formation in Catholic theological education since Trent. Wagoner comments that, in contrast to Protestants, Catholics have understood their seminaries, not primarily as the intellectual center of the church's life, but *"primarily as that place, those years, wherein the seminarians are helped to devotional and spiritual maturity"* (1966: 24-5, emphasis in the original).

15. The Episcopal theologian Urban Holmes, a persistent critic of the professional model of ministry, described the priest as a "sacramental person," a *theotokos* or "God-bearer," a "mystagogue." He viewed the priest's calling as leading "people into the mystery that surrounds our life . . . deepening humanity's understanding of itself by word and action, by the very nature of the priest's presence" (Holmes 1978: 67).

what clergy are called to be and do. It is true that each can be, and sometimes has been, a way of protecting the clergy's status vis-à-vis laity,
whether as an office, a learned profession, or one specially called by God. It
is also true that in practice the three emphases have at times become un-
hinged from one other, and diverse traditions within the church have differed in the emphasis they have given to one or another of the three defini-
tions. My perspective, however, is to consider each of the emphases as
essential for a holistic view of ministry. Each is best kept in dynamic relationship to the others. Emphasis on one without the other two, or on two
without the third, is to end with a truncated, incomplete, and, in my opinion, inadequate view of ordained ministry. This holistic view informs my
analysis in subsequent chapters.

Clergy as Producers of Culture

As one additional way of thinking about the work of ministry, let me return to and elaborate the perspective that views clergy as producers of culture. This is not a model of ministry in the same way that office, profession
and calling are models; rather it is a way of thinking about the work of ordained ministry — as office, profession, and calling — in the particular
congregation and environment in which that work takes place. As I noted
previously, it resonates with the image of clergy as "God's potters."

As producers of congregational culture, clergy give shape to a congregation's particular way of being a congregation — that is, to the beliefs
and practices characteristic of a particular community's life and ministry.
Strange though the image may seem, it offers a helpful way of describing a
pastor's core work, which obviously is undertaken in interaction with
congregational participants and in a particular time and place. Through
the core work of the pastoral office — preaching, leading worship, teaching, providing pastoral care, and giving leadership in congregational life
— a pastor helps to "produce" or at least decisively shape a congregation's
culture.[16] As clergy preach, lead worship, teach, and counsel, they draw on

16. In his book, *American Congregations,* Mark Chaves views congregations' primary
work to be cultural production, "expressing and transmitting religious meanings" through
worship and religious education (Chaves 2004: 8). A similar emphasis on cultural production in and by congregations informs Nancy Tatom Ammerman's recent study of congregations, *Pillars of Faith: American Congregations and Their Partners* (2005).

beliefs, symbols, stories, and practices from the Christian tradition to construct narratives and interpretive frameworks that help members locate themselves and find meaning and perspective for dealing with issues in their daily lives. Through their leadership and support of congregational gatherings, programs, and organizations pastors help to build community and supportive relationships — social capital — among members. In turn, members are helped to engage in their own ministry beyond the congregation in their family, work, and community life. It is through this kind of cultural production — or shaping clay jars, to keep the pottery metaphor — that pastors fulfill the demands of their calling to the pastoral office, using their God-given gifts for ministry and the knowledge and practical wisdom gained through their professional training and experience.

I have found sociologist Wendy Griswold's (1994: 14) "cultural diamond" helpful for thinking about what is involved in cultural production. The diamond has four elements: the *cultural creator* (in our case, the pastor); the *receiver* (the congregation's participants); *cultural objects* (the church's traditions — Scripture, liturgies, hymns, symbols, doctrines, ritual practices — as well as models of ministry such as office, profession, and calling); and the *social world* (the broader social and cultural context, both local and global, in which the pastor and congregation are embedded). These four elements, led by the pastor or "cultural creator," interact to produce the congregation's culture. Figure 1.1, based on Griswold and adapted to clergy and congregations, shows the four elements and their relationships. Each element is connected to the others interactively, as the lines between them suggest. The pastor's calling is to use her or his gifts and training to help members discover how biblical teachings and the church's traditions and practices apply to their lives and help them to face the challenges of the social and cultural context in which they live. In this process, members are not a passive audience but rather active meaning makers themselves as they respond to the pastor's leading, or resist doing so as the case may be. And both pastor and congregation are anchored in a particular social world that influences how they create meaning together out of the cultural objects (biblical teachings, church traditions, shared practices, models of ministry, and so forth). Indeed, it is often the case that parishioners' location in the social world leads them to hold different interpretations of the cultural objects from that of the pastor.

Figure 1.1 The Cultural Diamond

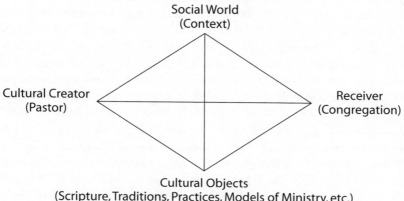

Social World
(Context)

Cultural Creator
(Pastor)

Receiver
(Congregation)

Cultural Objects
(Scripture, Traditions, Practices, Models of Ministry, etc.)

Another sociologist of culture, Ann Swidler (1986), provides an additional helpful image in thinking about the pastor's role as a producer of culture. She describes what Griswold refers to as "cultural objects" as a kind of cultural "tool kit," a kit containing a treasure of symbols, stories, rituals, and worldviews that one can draw from and use to create strategies of action or practices for meeting both the day-to-day issues that arise in the course of our lives and, especially, the challenges that come during times of rapid personal and social change. It is in unsettled times — times of flux like that which I have described — that people, leaders especially, can draw on the cultural tools available in their "tool kits" to construct new strategies of action.[17]

These perspectives remind us that the work of clergy is never static nor is it undertaken apart from interaction with others. As office, profession, and calling, it takes place in a dynamic interactive field that is constantly challenged by the gospel as embodied in the various cultural objects of one's "tool kit"; by the social world in which pastor and congregation are embedded; and by the perspectives, questions, and issues that members bring to the congregation.

17. In an earlier book (Carroll 2000), I found Swidler's tool kit metaphor to be particularly apt for describing innovations in church life and practices — small groups, Basic Christian Communities, the Womenchurch movement, megachurches, congregations designed for specific generations, and so forth — that have come into prominence in recent years.

To come back once more to the pottery metaphor, the interaction that occurs between the points of the cultural diamond is not too different from what occurs as a potter makes clay jars. The potter brings the knowledge and skills of her craft — her "tool kit" — that she has acquired through apprenticeship, study, and observation. But before she starts to turn, she must decide what she is aiming to make. Is it a utilitarian jar in a traditional form that others before her have made? Or does she want to use her knowledge and skills to make a piece of art pottery in a new form of her own design? What kind of clay will she need to get the desired results? What glaze will give her the colors she wants? What kind of kiln will be best for her project? At what temperature will she fire the kiln to bring out the colors desired from the glaze? All of these issues and more go into the process of producing clay jars. And, even with the most careful preparation, potters get surprises: broken or misshapen pots, pots that meld with one another in the kiln, glaze colors that run together or turn out differently from what was intended. Try as she might, the potter never has full control over the jar that is produced. Clay, glaze chemistry, kiln temperature, her own knowledge and skills all play their part in the finished product. Sometimes these surprises disappoint. At other times they thrill with their beauty. So it also goes with clergy as they work to produce congregational clay jars that reveal God's extraordinary power.

Plan of This Book

Following this introductory chapter, I look, in Chapter 2, at the setting in which pastoral leadership takes place today — the "social world" point of the cultural diamond. Believing that pastoral work and the congregation's response to it do not occur in a vacuum, I discuss several characteristics of the social world, including social and religious trends, that are especially important for understanding some of the challenges and opportunities that pastors and their congregations face today and that influence their life and work.

In Chapter 3, I ask who is doing the work of ministry today and how, if at all, this has changed over time. Here I draw heavily on responses to our survey to consider such issues as where today's clergy work as well as their age, gender, ethnicity, and other social characteristics. I also look at types of clergy — for example, full- and part-time pastors and those who are bivocational, and, where possible, I compare the characteristics of those in our survey with surveys of clergy in the past, permitting some assessment of continuity and change over time. I conclude the chapter by considering how congregants view their pastors.

Chapter 4 provides a look at the work of clergy as producers of culture. What are the core tasks of the pastoral office? How do pastors divide their time among the various tasks? Have there been changes over the years in the amount of time that clergy spend on various core tasks? Are there differences in the way that current clergy spend their time? What are the areas of their core work that clergy feel that they do best? Where do they hope to improve? How do they spend their non-work time? And, finally, how are they compensated for their work, especially in comparison to other occupations and professions?

In Chapter 5, the focus turns to pastoral leadership. "Providing pastoral leadership" is an overarching way of summarizing the clergy's core culture-producing work, and it is especially important for shaping good and faithful congregational clay jars. What leadership styles do clergy practice? How do the clergy's preferred styles relate to the way that lay members view their leadership? Do clergy's leadership style and practices make a difference in the culture that is produced in the congregation — in the way that members experience meaning, belonging, and empowerment? What do clergy believe legitimates their leadership in the eyes of members? Is it ordination to the pastoral office? Their educational credentials as professionals? Their calling from God?

I turn in Chapter 6 to the important question of how clergy are faring. Because being a pastor is a difficult, if often rewarding calling, what does this mean for individual pastors' commitment to ordained ministry and their satisfaction with various aspects of pastoral work? What stresses do they face, including congregational demands and conflict? How do clergy balance their private life with the demands of their work? How do they spend their time in non-work activities? How, in general, are they faring emotionally and physically? What is the impact of their work on their family?

I then move on to address one of central questions of the *Pulpit & Pew* project. Using what has been learned from the survey and focus groups, in Chapter 7 I ask what excellent ministry looks like, both the congregation's and the pastoral leader's. What are some of the primary marks of good and faithful ministry? The answers are both normative and contextual in character.

Finally, in Chapter 8 I focus on what can be done to strengthen pastoral leadership and nurture and sustain pastoral excellence in the years to come, given what has been learned about the practice of ministry today. What will this mean for congregations, theological seminaries, the denominations and their agencies, and for pastors themselves? What is required to support God's potters in pursuing their craft with excellence so that the congregational clay jars that they shape reveal God's extraordinary power?

Chapter 2

The Social and Cultural Context
in Which Clergy Work

"Birmingham is in the same location that it's been in for over one hundred years. They haven't moved Birmingham, but the way to get to Birmingham has changed. The road leading to Birmingham has changed, so [our] methods must change."

An African American pastor in Alabama

"A modern Christian theology . . . is the Gospel taking the age seriously, with a real, sympathetic, and informed effort to understand it, in the interest of no confession, but always keeping a historic and positive salvation in the front and refusing everything in any age that is incompatible with it."

P. T. Forsyth

Forming congregational clay jars that reveal God's extraordinary power has never been easy, and this is especially true in today's world. In this chapter, we begin our look at clergy as producers of congregational culture by focusing on the social world — one point in the cultural diamond (see Fig. 1.1 on p. 27) — that affects their work in important ways. Beginning at this point reminds us that ministry never takes place in a vacuum. Try as we might, we cannot build a protective shield around our churches. They are not hermetically sealed off from the world in which their clergy and

31

members live and breathe. As part of our research for this book, we asked pastors about a number of daily problems that they face; the one that they reported as their greatest challenge was reaching people with the gospel in today's world. Seventy-four percent overall said that this was a problem they faced on a day-to-day basis. The Alabama pastor's comment in the first epigraph above acknowledges an important insight about the social world: although the church's purpose may not have changed — it still aims to reach people with the gospel — the setting in which it seeks to do so has changed, considerably so in the last half century, and this affects how ministry is carried out.

The importance of the context for one's work is not just an issue for clergy. In an endeavor known as the GoodWork Project, Harvard University psychologist Howard Gardner and two colleagues have studied a number of professions, asking what makes it possible for persons to do good work. By "good work," they mean work that combines both excellence and ethics, work done expertly that is also socially responsible. They argue that those most able to do good work are those whose work is well aligned with forces in the larger context in which they work, especially with the values and expectations of primary stakeholders in their work (Gardner et al. 2001). The opposite is also true: those whose work is in some way misaligned with forces in the larger context and with the values and expectations of primary stakeholders have a difficult time doing good work.[1] The pastors' response to our question about the problems they face suggests that they fall more into the latter category, experiencing misalignment between the world and the gospel. Although this is nothing new — the gospel in its very essence is countercultural — it nonetheless makes the work of a pastor a difficult one that has to be addressed in every time and place. It is a perennial challenge.

In this chapter's second epigraph, the theologian P. T. Forsyth (1907: 19) described that challenge as "taking the age seriously," that is, understanding and addressing it, yet without compromising the gospel message. The age, however, is not static. It is always changing. "It's a kind of floating

1. In their book, *Good Work*, these authors compare geneticists with journalists. They found that the values of geneticists as a profession are generally well aligned with their relevant stakeholders. All want the same thing — longer and healthier lives. In contrast, they found journalism to be poorly aligned. What journalists consider as excellent and ethical journalism is often at odds with the financial interests of corporate media owners and with the low-level taste of much of their audience. They conclude that few if any geneticists but quite a few journalists would like to leave their respective professions.

target," as an Indiana pastor in one of our focus groups put it. For this reason, good ministry, in the words of another pastor, requires "the wisdom of both pastoral leaders and parish leaders to understand what 'chapter' they happen to be in, in terms of the larger picture of ministry in which the congregation is set." If it is to be faithful, each congregation must figure out what chapter it is in, how it differs from that of its predecessors, and what the new chapter demands.

Although I must be highly selective, I want to point to several characteristics of the current social world that are of special importance for the work of pastors and congregations. In some cases they create opportunities for reaching people with the gospel; in others they make it difficult for leaders to lead and for the church to pursue its purpose. I highlight the following characteristics:

- Selected demographic changes that are having an impact on church life and clergy functioning;
- The general religious climate in which the church does its work today, which is, for the most part, supportive of religion and religious institutions;
- The considerable increase of religious diversity that new immigrants are bringing, both within and between faiths;
- The growth of religious conflict due to the prevalence of special interest groups;
- The impact of consumerism and choice on churches and church involvement; and,
- Implications of what has been called "de facto congregationalism" on religious participation and the clergy's work.

In considering these characteristics, I must paint with a rather broad brush. Each of them by itself could be the subject of an extended essay.

Demographic Changes

A number of broad changes in characteristics of the population are affecting pastoral ministry and congregational life today. First, at the beginning of the twentieth century, the United States shifted from being a rural society to being an urban one; this helped to depopulate the countryside and left many small congregations struggling to survive, a struggle that many continue to face. This trend toward urbanization was followed around mid-century with the rapid growth of suburbs, especially during the 1950s. This time it was inner city churches that were the victims of the shift, while denominations struggled to meet the challenges of suburban growth. Currently exurbs are rapidly expanding as families and businesses move further from city centers and older suburbs. Exurban growth poses an opportunity for small churches in these formerly rural areas, but only if they can muster the will and imagination to welcome the newcomers.[2]

Second, African Americans who fled the rural South in droves during the first half of the twentieth century left many small, struggling rural churches and spawned a host of urban congregations in the cities where they moved. In the 1970s, however, a gradual reverse migration began as both older and college-educated blacks moved back to the South, attracted by improved race relations, economic prospects, and cultural and family ties. These trends have created a positive context for black churches in the South, but they also pose new challenges to churches as increasingly well-educated constituents demand an educated black clergy.[3]

This challenge is a particular example of a third more general demographic trend affecting not only black but also white churches and pastors: the overall rise in the educational level of the U.S. population over the past half-century that has leveled the "playing field" between clergy and laity. Until quite recently, many (though not all) clergy have been better educated than most of their lay members. This was especially true for Catholic priests and pastors in mainline Protestant denominations, who were generally expected to have both college and seminary training. Educational differences, however, have been dramatically reduced over the past half-century as an increasing number of Americans have earned college and graduate degrees. In 1950, 6.2 percent of the U.S. population had completed four or more years of college; by 2000, over 25 percent had done so. This represents a 181-percent increase in the number receiving bachelor's degrees. For those earning doctorates during this time, the increase was a striking 567 percent — a significant change even when we take into ac-

---

2. See Eiesland (2000) for a study of the ways in which several churches responded, successfully and unsuccessfully, to exurban development.

3. The implications of this reverse migration for black churches is discussed in greater detail in the *Pulpit & Pew* report by Lawrence Mamiya (2006).

count that approximately one in four of these doctoral graduates were nonresident aliens (Russell 2000: 77, 96). In denominations that have not previously emphasized clergy education, the rising tide of educated laity has had what might be called a "push-up" effect on clergy, with an educated laity pushing for better-educated pastors. Simply put, educated laity generally expect more of their pastors. This has become an especially important dynamic in African American congregations (Mamiya 2006); however, it applies to all traditions. Educated laity expect more thoughtful preaching and teaching and a greater sharing in congregational leadership.

A fourth trend of importance is the rather dramatic increase in life expectancy over the past century. In 1900, the average life expectancy was forty-seven years; in 1950, it was sixty-eight years; by 2000, it had reached seventy-seven years (National Vital Statistics Reports 2004: 33). What does this trend have to do with clergy? It is very likely one of the important factors contributing to the growth in the number of second-career clergy. Increased longevity has dramatically boosted the average number of years that most Americans spend in the workforce, making career changes over the course of life much more likely and feasible. The increase in longevity is also a contributor to the greatly expanded elderly population, many of whom are active members of congregations. Their presence in significant numbers, along with Baby Boomers and members of Generations X and Y, creates important and sometimes conflict-laden dynamics in congregational life. Differences between older and younger members in preferred worship and music styles, congregational priorities, and decision-making often foster conflict, as we shall see.[4] Recognition of these differences in generational cultures has spurred entrepreneurial clergy to start new congregations that target specific generations — first the Baby Boomers, but increasingly the younger generations, leaving many older congregations to serve an increasingly aging membership.

The growth in number of young adults ages eighteen to forty-four deserves special mention as we consider demographic trends. This group (who make up Generations X and Y) numbered over 113,000,000 in 2003 — almost twice the number of Baby Boomers in the population (that is, those who are ages forty-five to sixty-four). These young adults have their own unique social and religious characteristics that will be important for

---

4. For a discussion of ways that generational differences affect congregational life, see Carroll and Roof (2002).

clergy and congregations to understand if they are to involve them in congregational life.[5]

Another important demographic trend, the sharp increase in the number of women in the labor force, has also significantly affected congregations and clergy. In 1900, 20.6 percent of women over age sixteen were in the U.S. labor force. By 1950, the number had grown to 31.4 percent, and by 2000, 59.9 were in the labor force, an increase of just over 39 percent for the century. The percentage change for married women working (excluding widows and divorcees) is even more dramatic: there was an increase of 5.6 percent in 1900, 24.8 percent in 1950, and 61.1 percent in 2000 (U.S. Census 2003: 52-3). This trend has had an obvious and profound effect on reducing the availability of women for church work. Women have historically filled the many volunteer roles needed in congregational life, from serving on altar guilds to teaching Sunday school. Women's organizations in congregations have also suffered a severe decline in participation. Additionally, for Protestants, the trend has often meant the loss of an unpaid and unofficial "assistant pastor": the pastor's wife. As pastors' wives join other women in the work force — something that is often necessary to supplement their husbands' relatively meager salaries — they are no longer available to meet the unstated but often real expectations that many congregations have had for them to function as their husbands' assistants. The increase of working clergy spouses (male and female) has also made pastoral deployment more difficult. Pastors are often unwilling or unable to consider a call or pastoral appointment that might jeopardize their spouse's job, especially if that spouse is the primary wage earner.

These examples by no means exhaust demographic changes that are having an important impact on both congregational life and the work of pastors.[6] They were, however, often mentioned in focus groups and other

5. In a February 2005 lecture at Princeton Theological Seminary, Robert Wuthnow called this group of young adults the "next wave," and he described some of their personal and social characteristics — e.g., longer life expectancy, delayed marriage, delayed child rearing, uncertainties in work and money, and changing social relationships. He also speculated about their religious profile — e.g., believing though not always belonging, revising their orthodox religious beliefs to accommodate religious diversity, church shopping and hopping, and an experiential, intuitive spirituality.

6. For example, I have not noted the impact of population movement to the Sunbelt states, a trend that has affected church life in both the sending (Northeast and Midwest) and receiving (South and West) regions. An article in the May 2005 issue of *America* (Harris

project conversations when we discussed aspects of the social environment affecting clergy and their work.

A General Receptivity to Religion

Despite demographic trends that often create difficulties for clergy and congregations, it is important to acknowledge that the overall religious climate in the United States appears to present a more receptive environment for religion and pastoral leadership than in other advanced industrial or post-industrial societies.

As an example, Figure 2.1, based on Gallup surveys taken during 2003, compares U.S. respondents and their counterparts in Canada and Great Britain when asked about the importance of religion in their lives. The figures for the U.S. and Great Britain are almost mirror opposites, with 60 percent in the U.S. saying that religion is very important in their

Figure 2.1
Importance of Religion in the U.S., Canada, and Great Britain

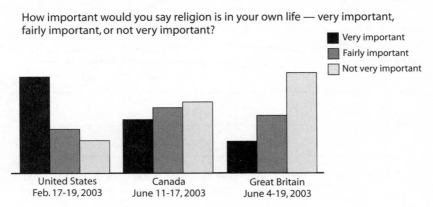

How important would you say religion is in your own life — very important, fairly important, or not very important?

Very important
Fairly important
Not very important

United States
Feb. 17-19, 2003

Canada
June 11-17, 2003

Great Britain
June 4-19, 2003

Source: The Gallup Organization (Ray 2003)

2005) examines the impact of this population shift (and also the growth of immigrants from Latin America) on Catholic parishes. These shifts have also likely contributed to the growth of religious and political conservatism and their "marriage" that was evident in the 2004 national elections and in ongoing controversies over such issues as abortion, same sex marriages, and stem cell research.

lives and 52 percent of those in Britain saying that it is not very important. Canadians fall in a middle position, but are more closely akin to Britain than to their U.S. neighbors. Measures of worship service attendance taken at the same time reveal a similar pattern, with over twice as many (38 percent) in the U.S. reporting that in the past seven days they attended a church or synagogue service than did so in Britain (17 percent). Again, Canada is in a middle position (26 percent).[7]

In tracking U.S. poll responses over time to questions about the importance of religion, church attendance, and self-reported church membership, we can see considerable stability over time (Figure 2.2). Although ups and downs in the trend lines are evident, they are, in general, remarkably stable.

Figure 2.2
Trends in Three Measures of Religion

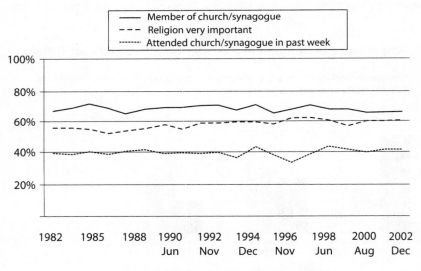

Source: The Gallup Organization (Saad 2003)

7. Several sociologists have questioned the Gallup figures based on counts of actual attendance at churches in a sample of U.S. counties. They estimate that attendance has dropped from about 40 percent in the 1960s to about 25 percent in the 1990s. See Hadaway et al. (1993), Chaves and Cavendish (1994), Hadaway and Marler (1998) and the Symposium on Surveys of Church Attendance in the *American Sociological Review*, February 1998.

Of course, were we to look in greater detail at trends in particular denominations or denominational families, the picture would be considerably more varied. We would see the membership declines that began among mainline Protestants in the 1960s and inspired considerable distress and hand-wringing for many denominational leaders and parish clergy. Mainline declines have slowed or plateaued since their nadir in the 1970s, but the average age of mainline members has increased considerably (to the upper 50s) as younger generations have, so far, been much less likely to participate in mainline churches than their elders. Conservative Protestant growth rates have also slowed since their rapid rise in the 1960s and '70s, although conservatives have had greater success in attracting, and holding younger generations than have mainline Protestants. Membership in Catholic churches has continued to grow, but primarily as a result of immigration, especially from Latin America. Mass attendance among Catholics has declined over time, especially in recent years since the priest pedophilia scandal. At the end of 2002, 28 percent of Catholics reported attending at least weekly, down from 44 percent in 2000.

One other noteworthy statistic that partly dampens the assessment of a positive religious climate is the growth in the number of religious "nones" — that is, the growth of adults (age 25-74) who claim no religious affiliation. Responses to the General Social Survey show a doubling in "nones" from 7 percent in 1973 to 14 percent in 2000. Extrapolated to the total U.S. population, this represents approximately 25 million adults!

Despite the decline that some denominations have experienced in membership and attendance and the growth in those claiming no affiliation, the overall picture, especially that presented in the poll data, suggests that the religious climate of the United States is not hostile or indifferent to religion, especially in comparison to other similar nations. It may be headed in that direction, but if so, the rate of change is quite slow and not uniformly experienced. Congregations and the clergy who lead them should, in principle, experience less misalignment than would be the case in other national contexts.

On the other hand, it may be true, as some have argued, that it is precisely *because* of the favorable climate towards religion in the U.S. that clergy report difficulty in reaching people with the gospel: that a high degree of religiosity is not the same as commitment, that it fosters a kind of complacency that may even serve as an inoculation against serious religious commitment and involvement in church life. The Danish theologian and philosopher Søren Kierkegaard once wrote, "It is easier to become a Christian if one is not a Christian than to become a Christian if one is already supposed to be" (Kierkegaard 1999: 216). When almost everyone professes to be Christian, regardless of whether they are committed and involved in a church, it may be difficult to know what commitment actually means. This, in fact, may be what the survey data reflect, and the clergy's response about the difficulty of reaching people with the gospel suggests that it is.

Growing Religious and Ethnic Diversity

A sharp growth in religious and ethnic diversity is another characteristic of the current social and cultural world that is having an impact on American church life and mission. A Chicago-area associate pastor in one of our focus groups commented that "We're much more aware of the diversity in our world, of different kinds of faith. Unfortunately," she continued, "Christianity in our country has often bludgeoned people, . . . thinking that it's the only way to God, to salvation." If one rejects such a negative response to religious diversity, the question becomes, as another pastor put it, "How do we value each other without devaluing one's own culture and experience? . . . That is the challenge," she said.

Religious diversity is not new in the United States. The Constitution guarantees individuals' right to free exercise of religion and prohibits the establishment of any national religion, meaning that the U.S. has been, in principle, a religiously diverse nation almost from the start. Yet, for much of that history, down to the early twentieth century, Christianity — or more precisely Protestant Christianity — generally defined the shape of the culture and established the rules of engagement. By the 1950s, the U.S. had become essentially a Protestant-Catholic-Jewish nation (Herberg 1955), and the term "Judeo-Christian ethic" came into use to indicate that reality.

This tripartite religious identity underwent a dramatic change beginning in the mid-1960s, when the U.S. Congress liberalized the nation's immigration policy through the Immigration and Nationality Act Amendments, with the effect of eliminating the national quotas that had favored European immigration. With this change, immigration became open to people from around the world. As a result, the nation has experienced an enormous expansion in global cultures and religions — by some estimates an average of a million new immigrants each year, primarily from Asia, the Middle East, and Latin America, with the majority concentrated in the Southwest and West, especially Texas and California. Houston, to give just one example, traditionally a Bible Belt stronghold, is now one of the most religiously and ethnically diverse cities in the United States, a gateway city for a host of new immigrants. Now almost anywhere one goes in the U.S., one is aware of the presence of world religions, with Muslims, Buddhists, Hindus, and Sikhs taking their place alongside Christians and Jews.

There is little doubt that interreligious diversity has increased considerably since the change in immigration laws. In her book *A New Religious America: How a "Christian Country" Has Now Become the World's Most Religiously Diverse Nation,* religion scholar Diana Eck (2001) argues that interreligious diversity is now the dominant characteristic of American religion. Although Eck probably overstates the degree of *inter*religious diversity (as I will note below), religious diversity has sharply increased in recent years with important implications for Christian congregations and clergy.

A 2002 poll found that most Americans viewed themselves tolerant of other religions: 81 percent of Christians say that they are "very" or "somewhat" tolerant of peoples of other faiths, though only 54 percent of non-Christians share this opinion about Christians. Most also say that they do not think of their own religion as the only true religion, though most admit that they do not know a member of another religion nor do many profess knowledge of the beliefs of other religions (Survey Results: Exploring Religious America 2002). Not all, however, are so tolerant; perhaps they do not "bludgeon" others with exclusivist beliefs, as the focus group pastor put it, but nonetheless they are not willing to concede truth to other religions. For example, a New York City pastor, a leader in the Lutheran Church — Missouri Synod, was initially suspended from his duties for taking part in an interfaith service in the aftermath of the September 11th attacks. His offense, participating in a prayer service with representatives of other religions that gave the impression that there might be more than one God or more than one path to God, was considered quite serious by denominational officials. Although an appeals court of the denomination subsequently overturned his suspension, tensions remained high over the incident.

For many Americans, especially those taking a more tolerant stance, pluralism appears to mandate an increasing privatization of faith and a somewhat uncritical acceptance of the assumption that public life should be shaped by secular, or at the very least, religiously neutral values. We can see an example of these arguments at play in the calls for religious neutrality that are increasingly made regarding public celebration of religious holidays such as Christmas and Easter. Given the multiplicity of religious perspectives in our society, religion becomes a private matter, one of personal belief, mostly divorced from public aspects of life. Interestingly, not only do many representatives of the non-Christian traditions find this to be strange, but new Christian immigrants from the Southern Hemisphere also find it bizarre that American Christians can so easily privatize religion and isolate it from the rest of life.

In this shift of religion to the sphere of the private and personal, many experience what sociologist Peter Berger (1992: 67) has called "pluralization." In other words, the religious pluralism of the broader culture is internalized by the individual, becoming "a set of options present in his [or her] mind." Like the majority of Christians in the poll cited above, people in whom this shift has taken place find it difficult to claim that theirs is the only true faith. Instead, they come to believe that other religions are equally valid paths to or expressions of truth. Thus, as Berger comments, "the very phrase, 'religious preference,' perfectly catches this fact."

With the ease of contact with diverse religious traditions, it is also not surprising that some people develop hybrid religious identities, incorporating elements of various religions into their sense of self. Princeton sociologist Robert Wuthnow tells of a twenty-six-year-old woman he interviewed, the daughter of a Methodist minister, who describes herself as a "Methodist Taoist Native American Quaker Russian Orthodox Buddhist Jew."[8]

Religious diversity also increases the likelihood that interfaith marriage will be an issue that any given clergy and congregation must face. Needless to say, today's interfaith marriages mean something quite different from what they meant in the past. In the essentially Protestant world of the small South Carolina town in which I grew up around the time of the Second World War, for example, eyebrows were raised when a Presbyterian married a Baptist or a Methodist married an Episcopalian. It was almost unheard of for a Protestant to marry a Catholic or for a Christian to marry a Jew. Now, however, the possible combinations of differing faith tradi-

8. Cited in Brooks (2000: 242).

tions through intermarriage are significantly greater, and clergy must know much more about the religions of the world if they are to minister to mixed-faith families or to those with hybrid religious identities such as the young woman described above.

Not only must clergy know more about other religions, they must know how to work cooperatively with other religious leaders in this expanded context. Broader, more inclusive ecumenical networks are replacing old-style clergy associations. The public arena also becomes much more contested, given that the players — Buddhists, Hindus, Muslims, Sikhs, Native American traditionalists, Jews, and Christians — share fewer common beliefs and practices. They jockey with one another to exert influence, and new networks and alliances emerge among disparate groups to advance common causes. Christian clergy often find themselves ill-prepared to deal with this expanded number of players. Skills of negotiation and cooperation in public ministry are called for at a level hitherto unknown within the American civic arena.

Another — and arguably more important — story about current religious diversity also needs to be acknowledged: Although it is the case, as Eck and others argue, that *interreligious* diversity — the growth of non-Christian religions — is a real and important fruit of immigration, it is not its primary consequence, at least not yet. Rather than being non-Christians, the majority of new immigrants to the U.S. are themselves Christians who have come from a variety of cultures: from Latin America (Mexico is the largest single sending country); from various African nations; from China, South Korea, and Vietnam; from India and Pakistan; from Israel and the Palestinian West Bank. These are regions where Christianity is flourishing — in general contrast to the West, especially Europe. The Christianity that these new immigrants bring with them, however, is considerably different from the European version brought by immigrants who came in large numbers in the late nineteenth and early twentieth centuries. R. Stephen Warner argues (against Eck) that we are not witnessing the de-Christianization of American society but the de-Europeanization of American Christianity. He estimates that "within a reasonable range of error, the poll data tell a consistent story: two thirds or more of new immigrants are Christian, no more than one fifth affirm any non-Christian faith, and as many as one sixth claim no religious identity at all" (Warner 2004: 21). The new immigrants bring with them a Christian faith and practice that is deeply imbued with their own culture — language, traditions, rituals, foods, and music. Much of it is Pentecostal in character because, notes Warner, of Pentecostalism's capacity to absorb and express local cultures.[9]

Therefore even if Americans share with their new immigrant neighbors a common commitment to Christianity, most of them bring with them a much more conservative brand of Christianity in both theology and personal morality than is true for many mainline Protestants and Catholics. Yet, in contrast to many white evangelical Protestants (but like many African American Christians), these new immigrants combine conservative theology and morality with a strong concern for social and economic justice. These commitments are having an important impact on denominational debates over such issues as abortion, homosexuality, and war.[10]

Furthermore, newcomers also bring to congregational life their own non-European culture — traditions, symbols, rituals, music, and language — which have been inculturated into the version of Christianity they encountered, often through the work of American or European missionaries. Mariachi bands, brought by Mexican immigrants, are increasingly present in Catholic and Pentecostal worship; healing rituals to cure possession by demonic spirits are a part of the practice of congregations of African immigrants and Native American congregations; Buddhist traditions are often incorporated into Chinese Christian practices, even when sharply discouraged by Chinese pastors. Hymns and praise songs from Latin America, Africa, and Asia have found their way into hymnals of historically European denominations. Ethnic foods are now part of the fare of church potluck suppers. In these and many other ways, immigrants are bringing aspects of Latin or African or Asian cultures into the Christianity they learned and are creating new, non-European expres-

9. The growth as well as the Pentecostal flavor of global Christianity, especially in the Southern Hemisphere, have been increasingly noticed in recent works. See, for example, Philip Jenkins, *The Next Christendom: The Coming of Global Christianity* (2002) and an essay by Sara Miller, "Global Gospel: Christianity Is Alive and Well in the Southern Hemisphere" (2002), in which she reviews several interpretations of global religious trends. In a report for *Pulpit & Pew*, Donald Miller (2003) has described a similar Pentecostal flavor to pastoral leadership and congregational life in several Southern Hemisphere megacongregations.

10. The furor of Anglican Christians in Africa over the ordination of Eugene Robinson as a bishop in the U.S. Episcopal Church is an example, as is also the strong support given by African and other non-western church leaders to the United Methodist Church's ban on the ordination of openly gay and lesbian clergy.

sions of Christianity. This process of inculturation is not at all different from what happened as enslaved Africans created a distinctly African American style of being Christian that persists today and is one of the reasons, in addition to persisting racism, that black and white congregations remain mostly separate.

American Christians, especially pastors in their role as interpreters of the faith, are challenged to understand these cultural differences that are de-Europeanizing Christianity. This is particularly true for pastors serving multi-racial or multi-ethnic congregations or parishes where new immigrant groups join existing congregations, adding their beliefs and practices to the mix. Their desire to express their faith through their accustomed practices and, for some, their need to do so in their native language, create quite a challenge, as one Chicago pastor said of his experience: "I have to be able to honor [the diverse cultures] in my congregation without trying to water down the differences or pretend they don't exist."[11] Finding pastoral leaders able to serve the needs of such congregations is a distinct challenge.

Because they are more truly a global church and also because of the continuing, if weakened, strength of geographically defined parishes, Catholic parishes are more likely than most Protestant congregations to be multicultural in their makeup. But Catholics are also facing a different multicultural challenge. The shortage of priests has led bishops to import foreign-born priests to serve U.S. congregations (a kind of "outsourcing" of jobs); a priest from Africa or India or Vietnam may be appointed to serve as pastor of an all-Anglo parish in Minnesota or Georgia. Such priests bring practices and interpretations of Catholic teachings from their home cultures, some of which may be at odds with those of the Anglo parish to which they are appointed. Language also becomes a significant barrier: "My mother, who lives in Michigan, called last week to complain that she couldn't understand a word of her Vietnamese priest's homily," a Catholic priest told us.

In ways large and small, then, it is evident that immigration, whether of persons of other faiths or of Christians from other cultures, is an important fact of the social world in which today's clergy live and work.

---

11. A recent work on multiracial and multiethnic congregations, *United by Faith* (DeYoung et al. 2003), discusses the promise that such congregations hold, but the authors also provide an honest look at the difficulties encountered in trying to establish such congregations.

Special Interest Groups and the Increase in Conflict

Since the 1960s, we have witnessed another significant trend: the considerable growth in the number of groups organized around a particular issue or concern and actively attempting to sway public opinion — what Robert Wuthnow has called "special purpose groups" (Wuthnow 1987) and what we often hear referred to in the news and on television as "special interest groups." Such groups focus on a wide array of political and ethical issues: abortion, feminism, the environment, stem cell research, taxes, and so forth. Literally hundreds of such advocacy groups exist, actively bombarding Americans through mass mailings, advertisements, and Internet networking. Many people became especially aware of them during the 2004 presidential election and the subsequent debates over same-sex marriage and judicial appointments.

A great number of these groups, both conservative and liberal, appeal to Americans' religious convictions. However, they often do so by what amounts to a selective retrieval of religious symbols and beliefs favoring a particular interpretation of religious tradition. Hence we can find, for example, feminist Catholic nuns appealing to one interpretation of Catholic doctrine and history, and traditionalist ones appealing to a different interpretation — both claiming to represent Catholicism. In response to the consecration of an openly gay bishop in New Hampshire in 2003, one group of Anglicans appealed to Scripture and tradition in opposing the bishop's consecration, while the bishop's supporters appealed to different parts of Scripture and tradition in favor of it. Similarly, the Confessing Movement, a socially conservative United Methodist group, issued its Memphis Declaration in 1992, which included the following statement on marriage: "We affirm marriage as the God-ordained pattern of relationship between men and women. God created us male and female, and the natural order of creation and procreation is the union of male and female as husband and wife. . . . We challenge the Church to be unequivocal in support of the Christian family, the sanctity of human life, and Christian sexual morality: fidelity in marriage and celibacy in singleness" (Memphis Declaration 2003). A critic of the group, however, drew on another part of the tradition, noting that "the declaration ignores Jesus' explicit prohibition against divorce on which there is much compromise among Christians" (Howell 2003: 30).

Examples like these are interesting within the broader context of the impact of modernity on religion because they suggest a change in the relationship that religious groups have with tradition. Rather than being enveloped and rooted within a commonly accepted interpretation of Scripture and tradition, as the examples illustrate, individuals and groups see Scripture and tradition as resources to be contested and used — almost like weapons — in advancing one or another interpretive stance.

Fundamentalist and evangelical Christians foster one set of special interest groups, while their liberal and progressive counterparts spawn competing groups. Clergy, like many Americans, feel pulled in one direction or another on these issues, and they are often caught in the middle of competing points of view in their denominations and congregations. In just about any congregation today there are members who feel more aligned on some issue or another with members of other congregations, either of the same or different faith tradition, than they do with people in their own congregation or denomination. Congregations, by turn, have become increasingly contentious and even polarized, making training in conflict management as important for clergy as homiletics or pastoral counseling.

Congregational conflicts, however, are not only on the "big issues" that trouble denominations; they also are about more localized and at times mundane issues. In our survey, we asked pastors about the extent of congregational conflict and what these conflicts were about. Over 20 percent of the clergy reported that their congregation had experienced a significant conflict during the past two years, many of sufficient magnitude so as to result in leaders or members leaving. From one perspective, 20 percent may appear to be a relatively low number of congregations with significant or major conflicts — until we recall that this represents one of every five congregations! Additionally, another 50 percent of the pastors said that their congregation has experienced one or more minor conflicts during this time. Congregations experiencing conflict most often disagreed about money, staffing, buildings, different visions of congregational mission, use of inclusive language, liturgical and music styles, and especially pastoral leadership. I will return to the issue of congregational conflict in a later chapter. I simply note here that both the increasing tensions caused by special interest groups, as well as the more local issues that create congregational conflict, make it clear that the present is not an easy time to lead a congregation as a pastor.

Heightened conflict adds to the difficulty of reaching people with the gospel. A Chicago pastor sees this as creating one of "the biggest obstacles for people to understand the gospel. . . . [P]eople who are spiritually hungry are told that the place you can find nurture is the church, and then they come into the congregation and . . . find all the internal politics and dynamics. And . . . it's really hard [for them] to get through to where the gospel is in all of this."

Consumerism and a Culture Of Choice

A fourth broad trend that contributes to misalignment with those of the larger culture, making it difficult for pastors and congregations to reach people with the gospel, is the emergence of what might be called a "culture of choice" and the consumption-oriented mentality that accompanies it, both of which affect religion as well as many other aspects of American society. Consumerism encourages people to view religion as a commodity like any other, from which they can pick and choose those elements that best suits their sense of self or identity.[12]

While contemporary consumerism is one of the fruits of America's heritage of individualism, the available options from which consumers may choose in almost every area of life have increased exponentially over the past half-century. Educational and occupational choices have exploded, especially for women, who, prior to World War II, had a very limited array of choices available to them: teacher, nurse, social worker, secretary, or sales clerk. Areas of life such as entertainment also illustrate the growth of choice: contrast the single-screen motion picture theater that some remember from their childhoods with today's multiplex theaters at which one can choose from among fifteen or more films. When television came on the scene, there were only three, or at most four, channels from which to choose. Now there are hundreds, if one has the right equipment to receive them.

In his analysis of consumerism and religion, Vincent Miller (2004) argues that the emergence of the single family home is the single most important factor in the development of consumerism. It reduces, if not elimi-

---

12. For an extensive theological analysis and critique of the development of consumer culture and its impact on religion, see Vincent J. Miller's *Consuming Religion: Christian Faith and Practice in a Consumer Culture* (2004).

nates, the effect of the extended family on the transmission of traditional beliefs and practices as it removes children from the strong influence of matriarchs and patriarchs. And as children grow up and themselves become heads of households at a younger age, the influence of their parents is also reduced. He writes, "The smaller and more volatile social unit of the single family home accelerates cultural change. Each generation is freer to make its own choices regarding cultural and religious practices from the options they encounter. These choices of culture are increasingly drawn from commercial offerings as consumption becomes a means of establishing and expressing identity" (Miller 2004: 52-53).

In short, we live in a culture where having multiple options is the norm, and this fosters a consumerist mentality as the various options bombard us with advertisements and pleas for us to give them our attention and loyalty. We pick and choose those that we believe best fit or express our identity or sense of self. Given these broader changes, it should not be surprising that religion has also been affected.

Even as recently as the 1950s, most people's religious identity was more likely to be an ascribed one; that is, whether one was Methodist, Baptist, Episcopalian, Italian or Irish Catholic, Russian or German Jew, or had no religious affiliation was something that was mostly inherited from one's family or ethnic community. Individuals rarely changed their affiliation over the course of life. In contrast, religious identity today is much more likely to be viewed as something achieved or chosen. Parents are often uncomfortable with playing a strong role in forming their children's religious identity, wanting instead to expose them to a variety of options so that they can decide for themselves. As a result, many, especially those generations born since World War II, choose how and whether they will define themselves religiously. They self-author their religious identity, drawing from the multiple options open to them, sometimes creating hybrid identities like the young woman described earlier in the chapter. Self-authoring is also evident from responses to a study of generations and religious involvement in which Wade Clark Roof and I surveyed a large random sample of residents of North Carolina and California. Seventy-three percent of Generation-Xers, 64 percent of the Baby Boomers, and 59 percent of those born prior to World War II agreed with the statement that "an individual should arrive at his or her own religious beliefs independent of any church or religious group" (Carroll and Roof 2002).

Although denominations have obviously not withered away, they are much less salient than they once were, for older generations as well as for ones that are younger. The attractiveness of the programs and ministries of particular local congregations is more significant in the religious choices that most people make than those congregations' denominational labels. People choose to participate if the congregation meets their needs. And they look elsewhere if it does not — regardless of their family or ethnic heritage or the place where they live.

In response to this self-authoring, new forms of church have literally been invented for spiritual "seekers" — for example, small groups that meet to discuss a wide range of topics; worship practices that avoid use of traditional symbols and forms; praise and worship services employing music written in popular contemporary genres — all designed to appeal to religious seekers.[13] In these ways, choices are multiplied and offered for religious consumption. In response, many seeker participants come to the churches as consumers, approaching them with the same frameworks that they would use in choosing which film to see, what music to listen to, or which car to purchase: Will I enjoy this? How does it fit my personal tastes? How well does it meet my needs? The picking and choosing among congregations that goes on today is not entirely for the worse, however. It allows individuals to find congregations that speak to their particular personal and religious needs. And it allows congregations to shape their programs and practices to address the needs of particular contexts.[14] I will return to this issue in Chapter 5.

Additionally, in our consumerist society, a spirituality industry has arisen outside the churches as a reflection of the increase of religious choices. Retreat centers present weekend seminars and lectures; medical schools offer courses on the role of prayer and meditation in healing; major corporations hire consultants to conduct workshops that use aspects of spirituality to deal with stress and other workplace issues; there are telephone lines and Web sites to which one can turn for spiritual guidance. (One Web site offers a virtual Eucharist, complete with do-it-yourself instructions for celebration in the privacy of one's home!) To varying de-

13. Carroll (2000) describes these new forms of church life, which he calls "local ecclesiologies," as a response to detraditionalization.

14. Anthony Healy addresses these issues helpfully in a recent book, *The Postindustrial Promise: Vital Religious Community in the 21st Century* (2005). He emphasizes the need of many individuals to "re-root" their religious and social narratives in a disordered society.

grees, these options unhinge religion and spirituality from communities of shared beliefs and practices where commitments are made and a common vision of life as God's people is formed and sustained.

All of this has encroached fairly far onto turf that congregations and clergy have traditionally claimed as their own. Churches no longer have a monopoly on religion or spirituality. Pastors compete with such cultural intermediaries as Dr. Phil, Oprah, Dr. Laura, and James Dobson in helping people make life choices about sexuality, child rearing, the search for meaning, and so forth (Miller 2004: 100-101).[15] Indeed, ministry itself has been transformed into a commodity, a service to be purchased. United Methodist Bishop Kenneth Carder laments that "congregations see themselves as consumers of ministry and the pastor as the dispenser of the religious wares. . . . Laity choose churches on the basis of need fulfillment rather than as a context for being in ministry. Failure to fulfill the [laity's] needs will result in a request for a new pastor, or a shopping trip to a nearby religious outlet. . . . In a market-shaped church, all activities are optional and depend on 'what the market will bear'" (Carder 2001). An example of this came recently on a postcard that I received inviting recipients to a new United Methodist church about to begin offering services. The card read: "A warm cup of gourmet coffee; listening to great music; laughing with friends. These are some of the things that make our lives rich, full, and rewarding. Church can be that kind of experience!" The only overtly religious message was a closing wish for "Peace and joy in Christ."

A pastor in one of our focus groups summed it up well: "The dominant [consumerist] culture is so strong with all the golden calves out there that it is difficult for churches to resist. [Christians] have an alternative vision, but it is a minority report to this culture." It is little wonder that many pastors lament the difficulty of reaching people with the gospel today. It is a different religious world than that in which many thought they were called to minister.

15. This situation recalls the experience of immigrant Jews from Eastern Europe on coming to America. Used to turning to the village rabbi for advice, they found their clergy to be as confused by the new world as they were and unable to be of much help. They turned instead to the editors of the Jewish newspapers. The editors, they assumed, were sufficiently knowledgeable about life in America to be able to give helpful advice. They were the immigrants' cultural intermediaries.

De Facto Congregationalism

One need not look outside the church to find other characteristics of the social world in which clergy work that can lead to misalignment, nor are they necessarily of recent origin. Especially important is the voluntary character of American religious life, a characteristic that living in a culture of choice greatly exacerbates. American religious participation, as I have implied, is mostly a matter of voluntary choice. It is true that ascribed characteristics, especially ethnicity, still define religious belonging for some people. But for most Americans, religious involvement is a choice, a voluntary activity in which they are free to engage or not.

This particular characteristic of American religious life has had its impact on almost all American religious communities. To varying degrees they all have come to adopt the voluntary principle. Almost all practice what sociologist R. Stephen Warner has called "de facto congregationalism," an organizational pattern that more or less follows the model of the Reformed Protestant tradition that defines the congregation as a voluntarily gathered community (Warner 1994: 54). In Warner's words, "To say that the congregation is a *voluntary* community is to say that mobilization of members must rely on idealism or personal persuasion, rather than coercion or material incentives, but *voluntary* also signifies, particularly in the U.S., that the congregation cannot assume the loyal adherence of its members as if it were all part of the same tribe; it must actively recruit them" (63).

To be sure, not all American religious communities are officially congregational in their polity or pattern of governance — that is, not all give lay members in local congregations the final say about some issues. Indeed, some are distinctly non-congregational officially — for example, Catholics with their hierarchy of decision-making that typically moves from the top downward, from pope to bishops to priests. Only since Vatican II have lay Catholics had much voice at all in decision-making.

Denominations with "connectional" polities — chief among them the various Methodist denominations that have grown out of the Wesleyan tradition — officially emphasize the importance of decisions by and connections among regional and national bodies. Such bodies include but transcend local congregations and have varying degrees of authority over congregations. Methodist bishops, for example, appoint pastors to congregations rather than permitting congregations to select and call their pastors.

In contrast, many other denominations are officially "congregational" in polity. These include the various Baptist groups, denominations growing out of the Congregational tradition — for example, the United Church of Christ — and the several Christian bodies that owe their origins to Alexander Campbell and Barton Stone, such as the Disciples of Christ and the Churches of Christ. Although several of these groups have national and regional bodies to whom congregations look to for resources, guidance, and at least a partial sense of identity, decision-making authority, even for such major issues as calling pastors, resides fully in the local congregation.

Another group of denominations is mixed in polity, having some characteristics that are congregational and others that are connectional. These include, for example, the various Presbyterian and Lutheran denominations as well as the Episcopal Church. Congregations in these traditions call their own pastors, for example, but only with the approval of their presbytery or bishop; and they are more closely "connected" to their regional and national bodies than those with a congregational polity.[16] In later chapters I take note of important differences in these various polities in their implications for pastoral leadership; nonetheless, I also agree with Warner that, despite these official differences, there is an unofficial or popular convergence toward de facto congregationalism in all U.S. religious bodies, and that this has important implications for pastoral leadership in their work of producing religious culture.

For one thing, because participation is a voluntary activity as far as laity are concerned — one of several activities or networks in which they may be involved — they often bring perspectives from these other networks that are different from those of the clergy, for whom the church and its mission are the central focus of life. This affects the religious culture that is produced in the congregation. It is shaped by the interaction between clergy and lay perspectives. Clergy tend to network with other clergy, forming a kind of closed system that reinforces their allegiance to their core commitments about Christian beliefs and practices. Laity, however, are more likely to experience cross-pressures from their networks outside the church — cross-pressures that can bring them into conflict

---

16. The connection between national and regional denominational bodies and local congregations is explored in some detail in Nancy Ammerman's book *Pillars of Faith: American Congregations and Their Partners* (2005).

with their pastor when he or she calls on the congregation to challenge some aspect of the broader culture in service of the church's mission. We can see this clearly when we recall the 1960s, when civil rights activism by many church leaders led to considerable conflict in many congregations and denominations. One sociologist at the time described these conflicting perspectives as "a gathering storm in the churches."[17]

Another, related implication concerns perceptions about clergy authority, which I will consider in more detail in a later chapter. Suffice it to say here that the trend toward de facto congregationalism or voluntarism has meant that the clergy's authority of office, given to them in ordination, often seems of less importance in terms of exercising leadership than does their personal authority, their capacity for persuasion and influence. Sometimes it is the pastor's personal competence that is critical; sometimes it is his or her personality or "likability"; sometimes it is the pastor's spirituality or personal piety; most often it is some combination of these personal attributes. While authority of office is important in all traditions, it has been more so in hierarchical or connectional denominations, and personal authority has often assumed greater importance in traditions with congregational polities; however, de facto congregationalism has made personal authority increasingly important generally, and it is often accompanied by a recognition of the importance of shared decision making between laity and clergy, blurring boundaries between them.

De facto congregationalism also has an impact on how clergy are viewed and evaluated. When taken to extremes, congregationalism can lead to clergy being viewed solely as employees of the congregation, there to do the congregation's bidding. Of course, this is nothing new; the eighteenth-century Frenchman Michel-Guillaume-Jean de Crèvecoeur noted it in his well-known description of American life, *Letters from an American Farmer.* He noted that the typical American "conceives no other idea of a clergyman than that of a hired man; if he does his work he will pay him the stipulated sum; if not he will dismiss him, and do without his sermons, and let his church be shut up for years"[18] A contemporary version of this sentiment was expressed by Edgar Bronfman, past president of the World

17. The "gathering storm" metaphor is from Hadden (1968). Another study of controversies over clergy civil rights activism that takes differences in denominational polity into account is by James Wood (1981).

18. Cited in Mead (1956: 217).

Jewish Congress, who urged any Jewish congregation dissatisfied with its rabbi's teachings "to rise up and fire the rabbi and get one who will do its bidding."[19]

Although these comments represent extreme versions of congregationalism and are somewhat atypical, evaluation of clergy's work is significantly affected by de facto congregationalism, especially given the previously described culture of choice. Because lay participation in congregations is voluntary, unaffected by material incentives or coercion, laity often evaluate clergy in terms of how effectively they recruit, retain, and motivate member participation and financial support; thus membership and financial growth statistics become major barometers that lay leaders, denominational officials, and clergy themselves use to assess effectiveness. Clergy regularly are asked, "How large is your congregation?" Or, "Is your congregation growing? By how much?" To be sure, those in growing congregations may feel that their work is affirmed by such growth, but in situations of stasis or decline, it is more difficult for pastors to feel positive about their work. An Alabama pastor told us that he would like to define good ministry as relational — "walking alongside people on their spiritual journey." But as another focus group participant added, "Society, culture, and the church almost always define good ministry quantitatively, in the success syndrome. So good ministry has big numbers."[20]

It is not that the use of quantitative measures to assess clergy is wholly inappropriate, especially in voluntary religious communities. Rather, it is the importance that they assume when they become primary evaluative criteria. Clergy recognize this and often chafe under it, as a Chi-

19. Cited in Wertheimer (2003: 36).

20. We suspect that, especially for mainline Protestants, the considerable focus on numbers has been encouraged by the substantial membership losses suffered by mainline denominations since the mid-1960s and the consequences of such losses for church budgets. Many conservative Protestant denominations, in contrast, have not suffered such losses. Nevertheless, conservative churches place a high premium on evangelism and church growth and, like their mainline counterparts, give membership and financial statistics considerable evaluative weight. Catholics, who are more concerned with the shortage of priests, probably do not feel these pressures as strongly as Protestants; nonetheless, they too worry about parishes that lose members and especially about parishes whose revenues decline. At the time of this writing, a number of Catholic dioceses — notably the Archdiocese of Boston — are beset with conflict from angry lay members over plans to close a number of parishes over the next few years. Church financial settlements of pedophilia cases have increased the pressure to close parishes that have become financial drains on diocesan funds.

cago pastor said: "Numbers are very deceptive. I think that all of us get caught up in numbers [of members] and how many people come to worship. It's very deceptive. You can get obsessed with it." It is this near obsession with numbers to the exclusion of other criteria that creates the problem, and it is one of the fruits of de facto congregationalism.

Conclusion

In this chapter I have named a number of characteristics of the social world in which clergy and their laity live and work — characteristics that affect how they produce religious culture and give shape to their congregational clay jars. In some cases there is a significant degree of alignment between clergy and culture, but in most there is much misalignment. Of course, not all clergy experience these features of the social world in equal measure, nor do I wish to suggest that clergy and congregations face greater difficulties and misalignment today than in previous generations. Today's social world is not necessarily a more *difficult* one in which to be a pastor. But it is a *different* world, one that offers pastors and congregations challenges peculiar to this time in history and different from the social world in which many pastors and lay Christians first became part of the church. The purposes of the church have not changed, but the way to get there has. Understanding how the way has changed and taking the age seriously are of signal importance for the work that clergy do and for the religious culture that they and their congregations produce.

Chapter 3

Who Are God's Potters Today?

"In this . . . culture, people — if I let them really ask for what [kind of pastor] they want — would tell me they want a nice young man with a family. . . . The majority would still like a young married male who fits the traditional stereotype of thirty years ago."

A United Methodist District Superintendent[1]

Although the church official quoted above may exaggerate somewhat, his observation is not too far off the mark. This image or stereotype of an ideal pastor, however, is considerably different from the actual profile of today's clergy. Nice young men with families continue to become pastors, to be sure, but the pool of clergy has become increasingly diverse. We saw a hint of this diversity in Chapter 1, in the profiles of the four pastors and the list of the variety of other clergy types. This chapter explores this profile in greater detail, highlighting some of the more important characteristics of today's clergy and of the congregations they serve. Doing so lays the groundwork for subsequent chapters as we look at what clergy do and how they are faring.

I remind readers that the survey of pastors from which we have drawn this profile included only solo and senior pastors of local congrega-

1. Cited in Lummis (2003: 17).

tions or parishes. It did not include associate or assistant pastors, youth ministers, counseling ministers, and other ordained persons who may be serving as members of church staffs. Neither did it include the large number of ordained clergy who serve in ministry positions other than as pastors of congregations. Even with this restricted purview, however, the diversity is striking, as we shall see. The aim of the chapter is not to be comprehensive but to place in the foreground several important characteristics of the settings in which clergy serve and, especially, several important characteristics of contemporary clergy that are critical for understanding changes taking place within the profession. The latter include:

- The changing gender composition of the clergy in many traditions;
- The general aging of the clergy that reflects the growth of second-career entrants;
- The continuing and increasing use of bivocational and various forms of lay pastoral leadership.

I have not singled out for separate analysis a fourth major characteristic: the growing racial and ethnic diversity of current pastoral leadership. Unfortunately, our survey did not capture a sufficient number of interviews with Hispanic and Asian American clergy — representatives, in other words, of the two most rapidly growing new immigrant groups — to allow us to single them out for analysis.[2] There were, however, a sufficient number of African American pastors to take note of important issues within that community at various points, both in this chapter and the ones that follow.[3]

In the final two sections of the chapter, I consider the relative fit or

2. Readers are referred to two *Pulpit & Pew* reports, one on Latino pastoral leadership (Hernandez et al. 2005) and another on Asian American and Pacific Islander pastoral leadership (Tseng 2005). These two reports provide rich discussion of the particular challenges facing pastoral leaders in these two communities. Similarly, Lawrence Mamiya (2006) discusses African American pastoral leadership issues in a report prepared for *Pulpit & Pew*. The reports are available at http://www.pulpitandpew.duke.edu.

3. Some African American pastors are members of predominantly white denominations, whether Catholic, mainline Protestant, or conservative Protestant. Or they are pastors of independent congregations that we characterized as conservative Protestant. Their responses are included in these three denominational traditions rather than with pastors of the historic black denominations. For a more detailed discussion of African American pastoral leadership, see Mamiya (2006).

match between pastors and their congregations and conclude with a brief look at how clergy are compensated for their work.

The Settings in Which Clergy Work

First, we need to consider the denominational and religious contexts in which clergy work — both their traditions and their polity. Doing so is necessary for making greater sense of differences among pastors and their work.

Denominational Traditions as Interpretative Frameworks

As I said in the Preface, for both methodological and descriptive purposes, I typically make comparisons among four denominational traditions. Excepting Catholics, these denominational groupings are essentially constructed categories, combining clergy and congregations that belong to similar types of actual denominations. Despite the diversity that they represent, the categories describe distinctive religious or theological frameworks. The frameworks reflect ways of interpreting the Bible, church traditions, shared practices, narratives, and symbols — those things, in our cultural production perspective, that are the cultural objects or "toolkits" — that pastors and laity draw on as they interpret their experiences and practice their faith.[4] These are especially important in unsettled times and in dealing with change. Each of our four traditions and each particular denomination and congregation has such a cultural toolkit from which it can draw.

I noted in the Preface that we weighted our sample so that the data more accurately reflect congregational size. Although Catholics constitute 29 percent of U.S. churchgoers, because Catholic parishes are so much larger than Protestant congregations, there are fewer of them proportionately in the overall universe of U.S. congregations, and this is reflected in the weighted data. Thus, in the weighted sample, 5 percent of the head pas-

---

4. The 2004 national election results highlighted the role that religious frameworks played in voting even if they were only partly reflective of particular denominational traditions.

tors and congregations are Catholic; 37 percent are mainline Protestant, 45 percent are conservative Protestant; and 13 percent are in historic black denominations.[5]

It would take us too far afield to try to demonstrate the differences in the four frameworks. Suffice it to say that while Catholics differ from the other three groups in many important respects — especially in their views of the church and priesthood and the centrality of the Eucharist — they and mainline Protestants share other somewhat similar attitudes. In the lay members' responses to the U.S. Congregational Life Survey, the majority in both traditions take a nonliteral view of Scripture: the Bible is God's Word, but it must be interpreted in light of its historical context and (especially for Catholics) in light of church teaching. Both also view coming to faith as a gradual process rather than as a decisive experience of being "born again"; and both express greater commitment to community involvement and issues of social justice than do conservative Protestants.[6] The majority of conservative Protestants hold to a literal interpretation of Scripture as God's Word. They not only emphasize the importance of a "born again" experience and have higher levels of church activity (worship attendance, Sunday school, small group involvement, and so forth), but they also are more committed to evangelizing. Historic black denominations share something with each side: a progressive commitment to social justice and community ministry with Catholics and mainline Protestants, and a more conservative theology and personal morality with many conservative Protestants. Their ethnicity and shared history also provide them with a distinctive identity and sense of belonging.

On the basis of these differing frameworks, some scholars argue that compared to conservative Protestants, Catholics and mainline Protestants (especially the latter) are lukewarm in their faith commitment and overly accommodating to modern culture. In contrast, evangelical or conserva-

---

5. Actually, 22 percent of the parishes in our unweighted sample were Catholic. Weighting the data inversely proportional to parish size reduces their overrepresentation in the sample. By weighting, the responses of all priests in the survey reflect their proportion in the population of American pastoral leaders. In Mark Chaves's National Congregational Study that used sampling methods similar to ours, after weighting the data Catholic parishes were 6 percent of the total (2004: 222). See Appendix A for further discussion of weighting.

6. It should be noted that in at least some circles conservative Protestants are increasingly becoming involved in issues of social and economic justice, especially those involving the environment. They are not only concerned with individual salvation.

tive Protestants thrive because they adapt without accommodating, creating a strong subculture of beliefs and practices that provide meaning and belonging in the face of a religiously pluralistic society (Smith 1998).[7] Others maintain that the primary difference between the traditions is in what they believe to be important. Nancy Ammerman, for example, describes the religious style of a large percentage of mainline Protestants and Catholics as "Golden Rule Christianity." They value right living — following the Golden Rule and caring about others — more than right believing or getting answers to life's big questions, both primary concerns of conservative Protestants (Ammerman 1997a). It is beyond our concern to try to say which interpretation is correct. Indeed, while the two differ, they are not necessarily mutually exclusive. What is essential to note, for our purposes, is that the interpretive frameworks of the four traditions are critical for understanding the work of today's pastoral leaders and the cultures they produce, as we shall see especially in Chapter 5.

Polity

Chapter 2 called attention to polity differences — differences in patterns of governance — among denominations. As we saw, *congregational* polities lodge decision-making in each local congregation; *connectional* polities (including those that I described as having a mixed polity) vary in the degree of denominational control over congregational practices and decision-making, and view congregations and denominational bodies as connected by mutual obligations to each other; and *hierarchical* polities feature a pattern of authority that moves from the top downward. As I noted, the case has been made that most American congregations practice a kind of de facto congregationalism, regardless of official polity; yet, official patterns of governance cannot be ignored.

When ministers' denominational affiliations are placed into polity categories, almost nine of ten mainline Protestants are in denominations with a connectional polity, while a similar percentage of conservative Protestants are in denominations with a congregational polity. Eight of ten historic black churches are also congregational in polity. Official Catholic polity is obviously the same for all priests, though some parishes give more

7. See also Finke and Stark (1992) for a similar but slightly different perspective.

voice to laity than do others. These various patterns of decision-making are important for numerous aspects of pastoral leadership, especially how pastors are called or assigned to congregations and how they are supported in their ministry. They are, however, so highly correlated with our categories of denominational tradition that the two are practically interchangeable.

Size Matters

Equally as important as denominational tradition and polity for understanding pastoral leadership — perhaps even more so — is congregational size. Size affects both what is expected of the pastor and the resources available to support his or her ministry. We will see this clearly in the next chapter. In Figure 3.1, we see the distribution by size of the congregations in which God's potters do their work.

Except for Catholic priests, a majority of whose parishes are large, *the large percentage of clergy serve in small congregations* — congregations that average fewer than a hundred in attendance at the main weekly worship service. In contrast, however, *the majority of American churchgoers participate in large congregations,* with about half in medium-sized churches and another 25 percent in churches with 351 members or more. A consequence is that the clergy that most laypeople (and, I suspect, many denominational leaders) see regularly on a Sunday morning are those serving larger urban or suburban congregations. Relatively invisible to them are the many pastors leading small congregations that are often in small-town and rural settings or in inner city neighborhoods. Thus, many laity whose vantage point is primarily the large church may fail to appreciate the circumstances in which the majority of Protestant clergy serve or the different challenges for leadership that small congregations pose.

While small churches have numerous strengths, their financial resources are often limited, making it difficult if not impossible for them to provide adequate pastoral support for a full-time pastor. Later in this chapter, we will consider a less costly strategy for meeting leadership needs for small congregations, one that appears to be on the increase: the use of bivocational and lay pastors. Another strategy with a long history, especially in rural areas, has been yoking parishes into circuits, with one pastor serving two or more congregations. The pastor is typically full-time, but serves part-time in each of the yoked churches. Eighteen percent of Catho-

Figure 3.1
Congregational Size (Average Weekly Attendance)
by Denominational Tradition

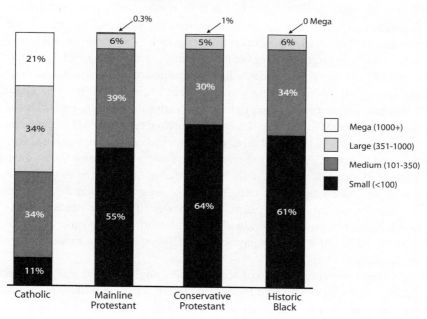

lic priests are "circuit riders," mostly in parishes with less than 350 active parishioners. For such parishes the issue is not one of inadequate finances to support a full-time priest, but the shortage of priests. As I noted in Chapter 1, the circuit-riding priest often provides sacramental ministry while the primary administration of the parish falls to a lay parish administrator — a deacon or a nun, for example. For Protestants, however, the yoking of small congregations has typically been a strategy for piecing together an adequate salary for pastors. In our survey, 15 percent of mainline Protestants, 8 percent of conservative Protestants, and 19 percent of pastors in historic black denominations reported that they serve two or more congregations — the majority of them with fewer than 100 active members. It is impossible to say from the survey whether the number of small congregations is increasing, but from various reports, the number experiencing financial stress is on the rise.

Although the principal story of Figure 3.1 is that of the considerable number of small Protestant congregations, the graph also calls attention to the presence of large congregations — those with active weekly attenders of 350 or more, and what have come to be called megachurches (by our definition, churches with one thousand or more active attenders). In Catholicism, such parishes are in the majority (55 percent); however, their number in Protestant traditions is much smaller — about 6 percent of the total. Yet, these large and mega congregations are the ones in which a majority of U.S. churchgoers, Catholic and Protestant, participate, and their number is increasing, especially in the three Protestant traditions. Many Protestant megachurches tend to be conservative in theology, regardless of their tradition. African American megachurches especially are likely to be Pentecostal or neo-Pentecostal (as some prefer to call themselves) in theology and practice. Although they differ considerably among themselves, Protestant megachurches usually have a strong, often charismatic senior pastor who oversees a large staff. They have programs seven days a week and many small groups and outreach ministries.[8] Their size poses particular challenges of pastoral workload and leadership that are quite different from the difficulties faced by pastors of small congregations, as we shall see in subsequent chapters.

One other important consequence of congregational size deserves mention: The distribution of Protestant churches by size is like a pyramid, with the number of congregations narrowing dramatically as size increases. As a result, a large majority of Protestant clergy will almost inevitably spend their entire ministry in small or medium-sized congregations. While there is nothing intrinsically wrong with this, what makes it an issue is the penchant among clergy, denominational officials, and laity for equating career success with climbing ever higher up the pyramid, serving ever-larger congregations. This is quite simply a goal that most clergy will not reach, if for no other reason than that there are, proportionally, so few large Protestant congregations. Furthermore, bigger is not always better; many Catholic priests might welcome smaller parishes. As will be evident in the next chapter, priests carry quite a heavy administrative load.

8. For a fuller discussion of their characteristics, see the research by Scott Thumma at the Hartford Institute for Religions Research Web site: http://hirr.hartsem.edu/org/faith_megachurches_FACTsummary.html.

A Note about Congregational Location

Another important characteristic of any congregation is its location, whether urban or rural. Some denominations are experiencing difficulty finding pastors to serve small congregations that typically are located in remote rural areas and some distance from major population centers. Unfortunately, we do not have from our survey an entirely satisfactory measure of congregational location. We do, however, have the ZIP code in which each congregation or parish is located, and we used that to attempt to construct a rural-urban measure.[9] By this measure, admittedly imprecise, the majority of all congregations are in low-density areas that would be characterized as rural. This includes six of ten Catholic parishes and slightly more than seven of ten of the other denominational traditions. The Protestant figures are not especially surprising. Protestantism's base has historically been in small town and rural America. We are, however, less certain of the Catholic figures, since Catholicism has been perceived as more urban than rural — especially as a result of the waves of Catholic immigrants who settled in U.S. cities in the late nineteenth and early twentieth centuries. Yet many Catholics also settled in rural areas, especially in the Midwestern and Plains states, so our Catholic estimates may not be entirely wrong.

Taking congregational size into account along with location, there is a somewhat more nuanced picture: Between 40 and 50 percent of large and very large Catholic parishes are in urban locations; more than a third of medium, large, and very large mainline and conservative Protestant congregations are urban, as are more than 40 percent of mid- and large-size black congregations. In contrast, over eight of ten small Protestant congregations are rural by our definition.

9. Following general convention, we designated a congregation as rural if the geographic region surrounding the church has a population density of less than 1,000 persons per square mile, using population figures reported in the 2000 Census. We were able to calculate population density by adding up the total population for all ZIP codes that were within a ten-mile radius from the center of the ZIP code within which the church is located and then dividing that number by pi × 100 (since the area of a circle is pi × radius squared). This is obviously an imprecise estimate, but since it is more likely to overstate the population density, we are probably conservative in categorizing a congregation as located in a rural area. That is, we are less likely to mistakenly designate a congregation as rural if it is near a population center.

With these several characteristics of the congregations in which clergy practice the craft of ministry, we look next at some of the important changes that are reshaping the profile of today's clergy.

How Are America's Clergy Changing?

No Longer "Sacredly Male"

Male clergy have long been and continue to be the overwhelming majority of all Christian clergy, both Protestant and Catholic. Yet, as I have already noted, arguably the most dramatic change in the makeup of America's pastoral leaders and perhaps of clergy generally has been the opening of ordination to women in several denominations. This change, which has been extensively studied by others but nevertheless deserves to be highlighted here,[10] brought an end — at least for many Protestants — to what had been a "sacredly male" image of ministry, one that had persisted down through most of the church's existence. In this section we will take a look at some of the most salient statistics concerning women in ministry.

The "sacredly male" image of ministry is still dominant for Catholics and a number of mostly conservative Protestant denominations. Beginning in the early 1970s, however, in the wake of the civil rights and feminist movements, several major mainline Protestant denominations opened their doors to the ordination of women. Although ordination had been available to women in several denominations prior to this time — in a few cases since the late nineteenth century — only a small number of women had bucked the longstanding tradition of an all-male clergy until the 1970s, and most of these earlier women did not serve as pastors of congregations. It was late in the 1970s that a significant number of women began to graduate from seminary and become ordained. In 1983, women made up approximately 6 percent of the total number of clergy. By 1999, the percentage of women clergy had more than doubled to 14 percent (U.S. Census 2000: 418).

10. For a recent comprehensive look at clergywomen in Protestant denominations, except for the historic black denominations, see Zikmund et al. (1998). See also the *Pulpit & Pew* report by Edward Lehman (2002) in which he reviews six major studies of clergywomen, including Zikmund et al.

Table 3.1
Women Clergy in the Four Denominational Traditions

	Catholic	Mainline Protestant	Conservative Protestant	Historic Black
Male	100%	80%	99%	97%
Female		20%	1%	3%

The distribution of clergywomen across denominations, however, has been and remains uneven. According to 1994 figures (Zikmund et al. 1998: 6, 155), United Methodists had the largest number of clergywomen: 3,003, or 15 percent of the total number of Methodist clergy. The theologically liberal Unitarian Universalist Association and United Church of Christ had the largest denominational percentages of clergywomen: 30 and 25 percent respectively. Presbyterian (PCUSA) clergywomen were 19 percent of the total. The overall figure for women clergy in conservative Protestant denominations was approximately 1 percent. Catholics, who do not ordain women to the priesthood, obviously had none; although, as we noted previously, the priest shortage has led some bishops to appoint nuns as parish administrators, doing everything that a priest would do except celebrating the Eucharist and other sacraments.[11]

As Table 3.1 shows, only mainline Protestants have a significant number of clergywomen: one in five. Women make up only 1 percent of conservative Protestant pastors and just over 3 percent of pastors in the historic black denominations. Recall again that these percentages primarily represent senior or solo pastors, sixteen percent of whom are serving either as co-pastors (typically with their clergy husband) or as interim ministers.[12] The percentages do not include associate pastors, though a relatively large number of clergywomen hold this position, especially during their early

11. See Ruth Wallace (1992) for a discussion of this practice and examples of women parish administrators.

12. Co-pastors are typically clergy couples, both of whom are ordained. Sometimes they share a single position; in other cases, they may each hold a full- or more-than-half-time position in the congregation. Interim pastors are serving in congregations that are in transition between regularly called or appointed pastors — often with the responsibility of preparing the congregation to plan for and receive its new pastor. Interims are especially important for a congregation in which the previous pastor has left as a result of conflict or when he or she has been long-tenured and much-loved.

years in ministry; nor do they include ordained women serving in non-congregational settings. In the study by Zikmund and her colleagues (1998: 61), 28 percent of female clergy were serving as associate or assistant pastors as compared with 11 percent of male clergy. Their numbers would have to be added to those who are solo or senior pastors in order to gain a full portrait of women pastors in today's church.

It is unclear overall how many clergywomen who have been ordained have chosen not to become pastors of congregations, nor is it known how many did so initially and then left for some other type of ministry or left ministry altogether. Zikmund and her colleagues (1998: 86-87) report that 30 percent of women and 17 percent of men enter either a non-parish ministry position or secular work for their first job after ordination. By the third job, the percentages had increased to 37 and 26 percent respectively.[13]

Despite these figures, current enrollment of women in theological schools is high. In 2002, women constituted 32 percent of the students enrolled in Master of Divinity programs in U.S. and Canadian theological schools (ATS 2002-2003: 7), and in some schools women were the majority of those enrolled. But not all of these women will be planning to become local church pastors, and some who do become pastors will leave pastoral ministry after several years, as will some of their male colleagues. Whether this signals a trend cannot be determined from the data; however, reports from Protestant denominational leaders of a growing shortage of seminary graduates willing to serve in small, often rural congregations suggests that the number of graduates choosing not to become local church pastors may be increasing.

Looking at the backgrounds of the ministers in our survey, we found

13. A recent study of United Methodist clergywomen (Wiborg and Collier 1997) found that 82 percent of the women surveyed became local church pastors or associates upon being ordained; yet, nearly one-third of them were not serving as pastors or associate/assistant pastors of local churches at the time of the survey. Some had left to pursue other ministry-related positions such as hospital chaplaincy or campus ministry; others were on leave; others had left ordained ministry altogether. They left for various reasons, most often to pursue another form of ministry; however, a primary complaint was also lack of support from the hierarchical church system in the United Methodist Church. Family responsibilities were another important reason for leaving — especially for those taking a temporary leave. For those who left ministry altogether, the strongest reason given was their inability to maintain integrity in the Methodist system. Although the researchers did not include men in their study, they report a denomination statistic that women leave local church ministry at a 10 percent higher rate than male clergy.

that women were more likely to have had a father in a professional occupation; men, in contrast, were more likely to come from non-professional families. Women and men did not differ significantly in their family's church involvement at age sixteen: the majority had parents who were active churchgoers. Women were more likely than men to have been involved in a church youth group at age sixteen but no more likely to have been youth group leaders. There was also little difference in theological preparation of the two groups, at least among mainline clergy: almost nine in ten, male and female, had graduate-level training — a Master of Divinity degree or above. In contrast, while there were only five clergywomen in our sample who represented conservative denominations, all but one had the Master of Divinity or Doctor of Ministry degrees, something only half their male counterparts did. At the time of our survey, the average age of both clergywomen and men was fifty-two, though when we compare only more recent entrants (those who entered ministry during the past twenty years), the average for men was forty-four and for women it was fifty. The average age of male clergy at the time they were ordained was thirty-one; for women it was thirty-eight.

The large-scale entrance of women into the ministry highlights the tension between ministry and family life that every minister must face. In regard to marital status, clergywomen were significantly more likely than men never to have married (24 percent to 4 percent) or to be divorced or separated (20 percent to 2 percent). Eight of ten men were in their first marriage, while four of ten women were; 10 percent of each group had remarried after a divorce. For women who have children, the desire or need to wait until after rearing their children is often an important reason for late entry into ministry. Far fewer women than men in our survey had children still living with them at home: 26 percent of women versus 42 percent of men.[14]

---

14. In an op-ed article in the *New York Times,* David Brooks (2005) noted that most women who enter a career after college graduation often enter the job market and delay having children until it is often too late. He cites a Gallup poll indicating that the proportion of women over 40 who have no children has nearly doubled over the past 50 years. Many women, he notes, wish that they had reversed the sequence — delaying graduate education and job entry until after childrearing. "But the fact is that right now, there are few social institutions that are friendly to this way of living," he writes. "Social custom flows in the opposite direction." Our data about clergywomen suggest that the church is an exception. It is more friendly to older women and, as we shall note, to second-career clergy generally.

Pastors of both sexes face numerous competing demands and expectations from family and congregations. All the spouses of the married clergywomen in our survey worked outside the home, while 80 percent of the spouses of married clergymen did so. As we have already mentioned, a spouse's job often determines whether or where a pastor may accept a call to serve a particular congregation — especially if the spouse is the family's primary breadwinner. This often makes mobility for clergywomen more difficult than for men. Further, the atypical hours of pastors' work schedules — for example, weekend pastoral responsibilities, many evening meetings, or the need to do pastoral visiting in the evening — often make it difficult for pastors, male or female, to be available at times that many family activities typically occur. Because societal, congregational, and structural expectations differ for men and women, clergymen and clergywomen face different pressures and constraints. For example, the fact that such a large percentage of male pastors' wives work outside the home means, as we said previously, that congregations are no longer likely to find their pastor's wife willing to serve as their unpaid "assistant minister." This is even more true of the husbands of clergywomen, virtually all of whom work outside the home.

Although women are slowly overcoming some of these structural and personal barriers, once they are in ministry they face additional frustrations and confounding factors. One stumbling block may be lower salaries. Pastoral compensation issues are the topic of a later section of this chapter, but it is appropriate to consider gender-based differences in compensation here. Zikmund and her colleagues found that once a pastor's experience, education, and work hours were taken into account, women clergy in 1991 earned on average 91 percent of men's salaries in the same position. However, ten years later, in our *Pulpit & Pew* sample, the majority of men and women solo and senior pastors had comparable salaries. For mainline pastors earning less than $60,000 — who comprise 85 percent of all mainline senior or solo pastors — there was little or no difference in average salaries for men and women with the same education, years of ministry experience, size of congregation, and average income level of laity.[15] The current average salary plus housing for all mainline men and women clergy who have entered ministry since 1980 is virtually identical: $42,000 for men and

15. This conclusion is derived from regression analysis on the restricted sub-sample of mainline pastors earning less than $60,000 in annual salary and housing benefits.

$41,000 for women. From many perspectives, this is good news. The majority of mainline churches appear to provide equal pay for equal work.

It is important to balance these indisputably positive gains with the problems that remain. First, women make up a disproportionately large percentage of associate pastors, and, as Zikmund and her colleagues documented, the gap between senior and associate pastors' salaries is large. Second, while women may receive equal pay for equal work, they may still face unequal access to higher-paying positions. In our survey, comparing men and women who had been in ministry less than ten years, approximately 80 percent of both sexes served small churches. But among mainline clergy in their second decade of ministry, 70 percent of men were serving medium or larger sized churches compared to 37 percent of women. With regard to the top 10 percent of full-time clergy with the highest salaries, women made up only 3 percent of the total, and 10 percent of the total when the top 15 percent of clergy incomes were considered. These figures make it clear that a "glass ceiling" is still in place even if some clergywomen are breaking through.

However, despite the real and often unjust barriers to the success of clergywomen in traditions that now ordain women and continuing resistance to their ordination in other denominations, cautious optimism seems warranted. In a review essay summarizing six recent studies of clergywomen, Edward Lehman (2003) maintains that structural and congregational biases against women in ministry are slowly being ground down by the inherent incompatibility of a practice of exclusion with core Christian values. I agree with his assessment.

A "Graying" Clergy and Second-Career Pastors

If God's potters are no longer all male, neither are they all young people who have proceeded directly from college to seminary to the ministry. In this section we will look at some of the data pertaining to the age of clergy and the increase in second-career entrants.

The median age of clergy has remained stable since 1971. The median age for Catholic priests is fifty-six;[16] for mainline Protestants, it is fifty-

---

16. Priests in our study were slightly younger than in a 2001 priest study that found the average (mean) age of all priests to be 60. Diocesan priests averaged 59 and religious

one; for conservative Protestants, it is fifty; and for clergy in historic black denominations, it is fifty-three. Had our survey included associate pastors, who are likely to be younger, as well as clergy serving in non-parish positions, the overall clergy median age would be lower, as it is, for example, in a 2001 report of the U.S. Bureau of Labor Statistics. There the median age for full-time, graduate-educated clergy was forty-five — within one to two years of the median age for full-time social workers, teachers, doctors, and lawyers with graduate degrees.[17]

With this said, data from our study point to a graying of solo and senior pastors. Figure 3.2 shows the proportions of clergy in several age groups. The figure makes clear that there is a relatively small number of young clergy (those less than 45 years of age) in each of the four denominational traditions. Catholics and the historic black denominations have the fewest.

One can get a sense of how the age distribution has tilted toward older clergy by noting that in 1968, 56 percent of mainline Protestant clergy and 54 percent of conservative Protestants were *less* than forty-five years of age.[18] For Catholics, the average age of all active priests in the U.S. in the period between 1966 and 1969 was 46.8 years (Schoenherr & Young 1993: 179). What this clearly means is that if the desire of many lay search committees is to attract a young pastor, male or female, their hopes are likely to be thwarted. There aren't that many young clergy to go around. This increase in average age is primarily the result of the second-career trend that first began to be noticed in the seminary population during the 1980s,[19] a trend that is one of the indicators of flux or unsettledness in ministry discussed in Chapter 1. From 1962 to 1991, the average age of seminarians in Master of

---

priests averaged 64. While this sample of priests was considerably larger than ours, thus probably more accurate, it also included a large percentage of priests who were in non-parish positions.

17. These data come from Current Population Surveys produced by the Bureau of Labor Statistics between 1976 and 1979.

18. These percentages are from a 1968 salary study by Edgar Mills of some 4000 Protestant clergy from 25 denominations. We have grouped the denominations into mainline and conservative Protestants to make them comparable to our groupings. There were some clergy from historic black denominations in the study but not in sufficient number to show separately. We have grouped them, as appropriate, into the mainline or conservative traditions. Dr. Mills graciously made the survey data available to us for comparison with our own.

19. See Ellis Larsen and James Shropshire (1988).

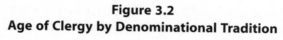

Figure 3.2
Age of Clergy by Denominational Tradition

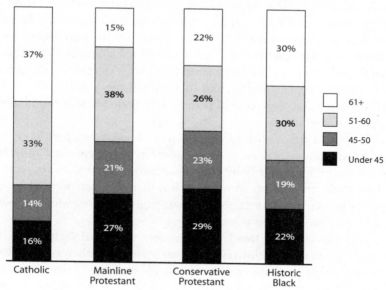

Divinity programs rose from twenty-five to thirty-four years (Larsen 1995: 9-11). The 1999 Auburn Seminary study of entering theological students found the average age to be just over thirty-five (Wheeler 2001). To be sure, young men and women continue to come into ordained ministry, enrolling in seminary shortly after college and going on to pastoral ministry upon graduating. In most theological schools, however, these are the minority rather than majority.[20] Most have had another career before enrolling.

In our survey we asked clergy whether they had worked in an occupation other than ministry prior to being ordained and, if so, for how long. Those who had done so for more than three years were classified as second-career entrants.[21] By this definition, Catholics, at present, appear

20. There are exceptions: Duke Divinity School, to cite one example, has regularly attracted a younger student body, with a median age of entering students ranging from 25 to 27 over the same time period that other schools were experiencing a median of at least 10 years higher. Several other institutions report similar numbers; yet, the overall median age remains high.

21. We opted for this somewhat arbitrary definition, assuming that many young col-

to offer a major exception to the second-career trend — 73 percent of the priests in our survey had chosen ministry as their first career. This is deceptive, however, because most recently-ordained priests are older and had another career prior to becoming priests (Hoge 2002; Hoge and Wenger 2003). But there are considerably fewer of these than there are older priests for whom ministry was the first career — thus the high percentage of first-career priests. For mainline Protestants, first-career clergy are a slight majority (54 percent). In contrast, and surprisingly, two-thirds of conservative Protestants and 78 percent of pastors in historic black denominations are second-career clergy.[22]

In each of the traditions, the number of second-career clergy will continue to increase as the average age at ordination increases. This is the message shown quite clearly in Table 3.2, which illustrates that in each of the four traditions, pastors in ministry less than ten years were older, on average, when they were ordained than was true for pastors who have been in ministry more than ten years.[23]

The second-career trend is attributable to several factors: (1) the opening of ordained ministry to women in a number of mainline Protestant denominations, creating a hitherto untapped reserve of older entrants (73 percent of the women in our sample were second-career compared with 59 percent of the men); (2) the tendency of many women to delay ordination until after child-rearing; (3) the aging of the U.S. population generally, which has reduced the pool of younger entrants to all occupations; and (4) the increase in life expectancy generally, which offers more opportunities for midlife career changes. "Sometimes people retire at fifty, and they have a long productive life ahead of them," an Alabama laywoman said. "They have vitality, energy, and health, and this may be some-

---

lege graduates may explore their occupational opportunities immediately after graduation before settling on what they believe to be a final choice. Three years seemed a reasonable time for such exploration.

22. Were we to define second-career as having worked at any other occupation prior to becoming a pastor, 39 percent of Catholics, 61 percent of mainline Protestants, 77 percent of conservative Protestants, and 89 percent of historic black pastors would be considered second-career clergy.

23. The sharp median age differences need some qualification. It is likely that some who would have been ordained in the same cohort as the 31+ year clergy were older at the time they were ordained and no longer active pastors when our survey was taken; thus the median age for the cohort might have actually been slightly higher.

thing they've always wanted to do. Now they have the leisure, or at least the time, to do it." Citing her father as an example, another woman added, "He said he had felt called for a long while, but he couldn't afford to be a minister while sending us to school."

Table 3.2
Median Age at Ordination Differentiated by
Years in Ministry and Denominational Tradition

Years in Ministry	<10	10-20	21-30	31+
Catholic	38	29	27	26
Mainline Protestant	35	33	27	26
Conservative Protestant	37	30	28	26
Historic Black	39	32	27	21

There are reports that a growing number of younger students have been entering seminary in recent years, slowing if not reversing the second-career trend. It appears, however, that fewer of these younger graduates are choosing to become pastors of congregations — that number is down 19 percent in the past five years according to one estimate (Boser 2005). In the Auburn study, fewer than 30 percent of younger entering students said that congregational ministry was their first choice of post-seminary work, in contrast to 40 percent of older students. For older students, the call to ministry probably came in part through positive experiences as laity in congregations, making pastoral ministry more attractive. Nonetheless, it is worth remarking that majorities of both groups, old and young, did not pick the pastorate as their first preference. Some of this probably is a matter of seminary students "hedging their bets" prior to deciding how they will pursue their call to ministry.

Some reluctance to choose the pastorate may also reflect worries about such things as low salaries (especially in light of rising educational indebtedness), the need to be on call 24/7, congregational conflict, and other issues pertaining to the life and lifestyle of a pastor. Medical educators have noted a similar trend among senior medical students, who appear to be turning away from such specialties as general surgery and family practice and turning instead to anesthesiology and radiology, where they can enjoy both more control over their time and a relatively large paycheck (Dorsey et al. 2003). Some seminary students' preferences will likely change as a result of positive experiences of congregational ministry during seminary, often as a result of field education or internships. Yet it is still probably true that a higher percentage of older than younger students will become pastors. For these several reasons, I expect that the second-career trend is likely to continue.

Although there may be a societal trend towards older entrants into occupations, as some predict (Porter 2004), when we compare ministry, medicine, and law, it is only ministry that has been a heavy recipient of second-career entrants to date. Available information indicates that entering law students averaged age 26 in 1991; entering medical students averaged 24 years in 1996 (Wheeler 2001). Such differences are not easily explained, although the length, rigor, and specialized character of medical training and restrictions on the number of entrants to medical schools may contribute to the disparity between ministry and medicine.

From what types of careers do second-career pastors come? The majority from all traditions, especially Catholics and mainline Protestants, were in professional, managerial, or sales work prior to becoming pastors. The specific occupations, however, varied widely: teachers, professors, engineers, computer consultants, military officers, fire fighters, police officers, social workers, medical technicians, accountants, business owners, and others all became pastors. The fields from which the largest numbers of second-career pastors come appear to be teaching and the military.

Just as first- and second-career clergy differ in their career paths into ministry, they also differ to a limited degree in other demographic characteristics. Two thirds of second-career Protestant pastors in our survey grew up in small towns or on farms, whereas most first-career ones came mostly from cities or suburbs. Conversely, more second- than first-career Catholic priests were from urban areas. Second-career clergy in all groups were more likely to have come from blue-collar homes or from farm families; first-career pastors, in contrast, were significantly more likely to have had fathers who were professionals, managers, or salesmen. The majority of all clergy came from homes where the parents — especially mothers — were weekly church attendees. A majority also themselves attended church regularly as youth and took part in a church youth group, though second-career Protestants were slightly less active on both counts.

There are some differences between first- and second-career clergy in theological education across and within denominational traditions. The large majority of first-career clergy in the four traditions reported that they had a graduate theological education (a Master of Divinity or higher degree). This includes almost eight of ten historic black pastors and nine of ten clergy in the other three traditions. For second-career pastors, just over 90 percent of Catholics, 85 percent of mainline Protestants, and 56 percent of historic black pastors had graduate theological degrees. In striking contrast, only 36 percent of second-career conservative Protestants did so. Almost a fourth of this latter group reported no theological training; the rest had earned such credentials as certificates from training programs or Bible college degrees.

What are the consequences of this influx of older entrants into ordained ministry? Clearly many are able and effective pastors, and they bring to congregations considerable wisdom and maturity from prior work and life experience and congregational involvement as laity. Furthermore, given the apparent decline in young seminarians interested in parish ministry, the shortage of clergy would be considerably greater than it already is were it not for second-career clergy. There are, however, some drawbacks. One that worries church leaders quite a bit is the shorter span of active service that can be anticipated from most second-career clergy. "They definitely bring life skills and often people skills [to the pulpit]," an Austin-area layperson said, "[but], when you spend that much effort training them, getting them ready, you want them to be there for a while." On the basis of our survey, we predict that current full-time pastors who have been in ministry more than thirty years will serve an average total of forty-one years before their anticipated age of retirement. In contrast, those who have been in ministry for less than ten years can anticipate serving an average total of twenty-seven years before retiring — a substantial difference.[24] This not only raises the ratio of educational costs to years of service, but it also places a strain on denominational pension programs. Also because older entrants often have working spouses, many are not as mobile as denominational needs for filling vacant pulpits may dictate.

24. These figures are averages and hide a considerable degree of variability. The standard deviation for the older group is 15 years; for the younger group it is 16 years.

The aging of the clergy also raises a concern about why younger candidates appear not to be as interested in ordained ministry, and especially congregational ministry, as they seem to have been in the past.[25] And it leads one to wonder, along with historian Martin Marty, what the long-term impact on congregations might be: "If all the clergy are old and think old and don't last long, that does something to the spirit of the enterprise, commitment for the long haul, and maturation-in-office — all of which mean so much in many situations" (Marty 2001). In a somewhat similar vein, an Austin-area Presbyterian minister who had served on a committee overseeing the development of new pastors noted, "It's true that most of our candidates now are second-career, and a lot are women. And I praise God for it, because I think it's wonderful that they have a true call. But also, at the same time, I wish we had some young folks that we could bring up and they could make their mistakes, maybe in an associate role."

Is the second-career phenomenon a new trend? The answer is no. There have always been individuals who have worked in other occupations prior to answering a call to ordained ministry. Researchers as far back as the 1930s commented on the older age of those entering the ministry when compared with other professions (Douglass and Brunner 1935: 115-6). At that time, the average age at entry was approximately thirty — somewhat less than it is today.[26] Although not a new phenomenon, the growth in second-career clergy since the 1970s and the decline in younger persons entering pastoral ministry have been significant enough departures from the immediately preceding decades to capture widespread attention and concern.

Bivocational and Lay Pastors

The two changes in the characteristics of clergy that have been considered thus far are relatively recent — both occurring, at least in their recent guise, during and since the 1970s. A third characteristic of twenty-first-century pastoral leadership — bivocational and lay pastors — is as old as the Christian church; however, denominational use of these two types of

---

25. For a discussion of this issue, see Wheeler (2001).

26. As for clergy age, the 1920 Census reported that 53.4 percent of clergy were forty-five or older, compared with 49.4 percent of doctors, and only 27.9 of all workers (May and Shuttleworth 1934: 47).

leadership appears to be growing. The two are not the same, but they are sufficiently similar that we can treat them together.

By bivocational pastors I mean those men and women, most of whom are ordained, who combine pastoral leadership with another occupation, either another type of ministry or secular employment. These pastors earn either all or part of their compensation from their other job. Christianity has a long tradition of bivocational pastoral leadership; none other than the apostle Paul is said to have supported himself as a tentmaker (Acts 18:1-3). Indeed, most pastoral leaders in the early church were bivocational. Lay or local pastors, in contrast, are typically not ordained. Rather, most are commissioned by their denomination to provide pastoral services in a specific congregation; typically this includes celebrating the sacraments in that congregation but not others (except, of course, for Catholic lay ministers). They may be full- or part-time employees of the church. Like bivocationals, lay pastors are by no means a new phenomenon. They too have been present throughout the church's history, playing an especially prominent role in the spread of Christian churches in the United States.[27]

Strictly speaking, Catholics do not have bivocational or lay clergy. Rather, those priests who have another job while also serving as a parish pastor typically work in another church-related position — as teachers or on diocesan staffs, for example. Because of the priest shortage, the bishop may assign them parish duties in addition to their non-parish job. And among Catholics, lay parish ministers are a special category of lay ministers. Unlike Protestant lay or local pastors, Catholic lay parish ministers — who are paid and work on parish staffs at least twenty hours a week — are not permitted to celebrate the sacraments, but exercise leadership in a variety of other parish ministries. They are not our focus here, however, since our survey included only senior or solo pastors. But we can look at the experience of bivocational and lay Protestant pastors, and mention their Catholic counterparts where appropriate.

---

27. See Hatch (1989) and Finke and Stark (1992) for discussions of the success of various "upstart sects" — for example, both white and black Baptists and Methodists, Christian Churches and the Disciples of Christ, and Mormons — whose highly successful evangelistic and pastoral work on the American frontier was often done by uneducated or self-educated lay pastors. Various churches in the Pentecostal movement also have made considerable use of lay pastoral leadership. Other denominations, especially Presbyterians and Congregationalists, strongly advocated for an educated clergy, founded colleges and theological seminaries to provide that education, and opposed commissioning laity to serve as pastoral leaders.

Why single out these groups for special attention? Most importantly, they are being used more and more by denominations to provide pastoral leadership in congregations that cannot find or afford full-time or ordained pastors. Consider several examples: Although the United Methodist Church has long used lay pastors (called local pastors) to provide pastoral services in small congregations, the number has dramatically increased in recent years. In 1990, the denomination had 1,413 local pastors serving congregations; by 2000 the number had increased to 2,096, a 48 percent increase for the decade (McAnally 2001). During the same ten-year period, the number of candidates for ordination as elders (the status typical for Methodist parish clergy authorized to preach, celebrate the sacraments, and administer the life of a congregation) declined from 820 to 621, a 24 percent decline.

Similar trends are evident in other denominations. In 1976, approximately 30 percent of Southern Baptist pastors were bivocational (Price 1977); by 1999, the number had increased to 39 percent (Lawson 1999). In Alabama alone, 52 percent of the 3,200 Southern Baptist churches were led by bivocationals in 1998 (Skinner 1998).[28] In 1997, the Presbyterian Church (USA), which had long insisted on an ordained, seminary-educated clergy, authorized the use of commissioned lay pastors to meet the growing need of small rural churches as well as new immigrant congregations. A similar move to deploy lay ministers — called synodically authorized ministers — was made by the Evangelical Lutheran Church in America in 1993. Their use by the denomination is increasing.

Historic black churches have a tradition of bivocational pastoral leadership going back to pre–Civil War days when black pastors were enslaved laborers while also serving as leaders of small, often "underground" congregations (Lincoln and Mamiya 1990). Many black pastors and congregations continue that bivocational practice today, primarily to supplement the pastors' low salaries and, in many cases, because of a lack of pension and health care benefits (Mamiya 2006). Of course, clergy in historic black denominations are not the only ones who pursue another job to supplement their ministry income and benefits. A 1974 survey of clergy in

28. The Rev. Leon Wilson, President of the Southern Baptist Bivocational Ministers Association, reported in e-mail correspondence that currently (2005) there are 19,439 Southern Baptist pastors who identify as volunteer, part-time, or bivocational, all of whom, he said, are in fact bivocational.

nineteen Protestant denominations found that 22 percent of the pastors supplemented their church income with a secular job. The lower the median salary of the denomination, the more hours their clergy worked in the secular occupation (Bonn 1975).

Although Protestant lay pastors and Catholic lay parish ministers have different functions, the number of the Catholic lay parish ministers has also grown dramatically — up 35 percent between 1992 and 1997 (from 21,569 to 29,146). During the same five-year period, the number of Catholic parish priests declined by 12 percent (Murnion and DeLambo 1999: iii). The Catholic practice of using lay parish ministers for many non-sacramental tasks in parishes is not altogether different from a growing practice in large Protestant congregations, especially megachurches. Many of these churches identify, train, and commission lay members of the congregation to take on paid part- and full-time lay ministry positions in the congregation. But where Protestant megachurches tend to train their own staff, Catholic lay ministers must meet certain standardized requirements.[29]

Looking at overall use of bivocational pastors in the denominational traditions, we find that 18 percent of mainline Protestants, 29 percent of conservative Protestants, and 41 percent of clergy in historic black denominations are bivocational. While 18 percent of Catholic priests also work at a second job, they are not, as I explained above, bivocational in the same sense as Protestants.

Table 3.3 shows the percentage of bivocationals in an expanded list of denominational "families" that allows a clearer picture of their use. Like our four traditions, these families are not (except for Catholics) actual denominations. Rather, they are groups of denominations sharing historic affinities. Because the number of cases in some of these families is small, the possibility of sampling error increases. Nonetheless, the percentages within families are indicative of the varying use of bivocationals. As the table shows, independent Protestants (pastors with no denominational affiliation and often serving quite small congregations) are the most likely to be bivocational (over four of ten), followed by Pentecostal and Baptist pastors (just over one third).

---

29. Donald Miller (1997, 2003) has described these practices in what he calls "new paradigm" churches both in this country and in the developing world. The leaders of new paradigm churches often hold disparaging views of traditional forms of theological education and prefer to raise up and train their own staff.

Table 3.3
Bivocationality among Clergy

	Univocational	Bivocational
Catholic	83%	17%
Baptists	66%	34%
Methodists	85%	15%
Pentecostals	66%	34%
Lutherans	88%	12%
Presbyterian/Reformed	82%	18%
Episcopalians	90%	10%
United Church of Christ	78%	22%
Other Mainline/Liberal Protestant	69%	31%
Other Conservative Protestant	83%	17%
Independent Protestants	55%	45%

Although bivocationals in earlier years were often farmers as well as pastors — half of them farmed in the early 1930s (Douglass and Brunner 1935: 120) — the "farmer-preacher" model is, unsurprisingly, no longer typical. The majority of jobs that bivocational pastors combine with pastoral leadership are in professional or technical areas. Catholics, as noted, typically work in some type of non-parochial ministry position. A majority of all three Protestant traditions — especially mainline bivocationals — also combine a professional or technical job with ministry; however, the job may or may not be church-related. Conservative Protestant bivocationals combine ministry with being managers or administrators, service workers, craftsmen, and farmers, in that order. Historic black bivocationals are service workers, clerical workers, and managers or administrators.

What kind of theological education is characteristic of bivocational and lay pastors? The large majority of Catholic priests who work at more than one job had a Master of Divinity degree or higher: 85 percent. This compares with 70 percent of mainline Protestant bivocationals, 20 percent of conservative Protestants, and 47 percent of those in historic black churches who are bivocational. Among lay pastors, as distinct from those bivocationals who are ordained, four of ten mainline Protestants had the Master of Divinity degree; the rest had certificates from training programs or some other type of training. Only 6 percent had no theological training. In contrast, 27 percent of conservative lay pastors had no formal theological training. Six percent had a master's degree; 29 percent had a certificate from a training program; and 49 percent reported some other type of training, which they did not specify. Of the eleven black church lay pastors, nine have no theological training, and two have earned Doctor of Ministry degrees as their highest degree. There were, of course, no lay pastors serving as the primary leader of Catholic parishes.[30]

As I have already noted, a primary reason for the increased use of bivocational and lay pastors is the difficulty of finding full-time, ordained clergy to meet the leadership needs of small Protestant congregations and in Catholic parishes generally, especially in rural areas. Over eight of ten bivocational mainline and conservative Protestants serve small congregations. Similarly, between eight and nine of ten mainline and conservative Protestant lay pastors work for small congregations. Over 70 percent of historic black bivocationals are in small congregations; another 23 percent are in mid-sized churches. Over 90 percent of black lay pastors are in small churches.

What do bivocational and lay pastors bring to the churches they serve? Without them, many small, financially challenged congregations — of which there are a growing number in all Protestants denominations — would have no pastoral leadership. Like second-career clergy, many have considerable experience as lay members of congregations and often are quite similar in background to those whom they serve. As a result they are often uniquely aware of the peculiar dynamics of these churches and better able to relate to the members. This is especially true in the case of congregations made up of new immigrants, in which language and culture make it quite important that the pastor both speaks the language and knows the culture from which the members come.

At the same time, there are limitations to these patterns. The inadequate theological training of some of these pastors can be a liability, especially in churches where a growing number of their constituents are well

---

30. Had our Catholic sample been larger, it might well have included nuns or deacons serving as parish administrators in the absence of a full-time priest, though none would have been officially considered pastors.

educated and find little spiritual sustenance in the preaching and teaching of a pastor without a seminary education. Some bivocational and lay pastors do not reside in the congregation's community; they are mainly present on weekends, thus leaving members without pastoral services much of the time. Nonetheless, given current trends — the growing number of small congregations, continuing financial challenges, and the growth of immigrant congregations — I envision a continuing and increasing need for both bivocational and lay pastors. If this is the case, then denominations and seminaries must give serious attention to how they identify, train, support, and honor the contribution of these leaders.

To sum up, if current trends hold, the increasing number of clergywomen will continue to lead mainline Protestants away from a "sacredly masculine" image of ministry. This, however, will not be the case for the Catholic Church and some conservative Protestant and black denominations short of a sea change in their respective understandings of ordained ministry. Furthermore, a variety of factors, including demographic trends, suggest that a majority of both Protestant and Catholic clergy will continue to be older and in their second career. And, short of closing a large number of small congregations, especially in rural areas, and/or a substantial increase in clergy compensation in these churches, the use of bivocational or lay pastors to serve in small congregations will continue to grow.

For Catholics, absent a change from the current reality, not only will the priesthood remain the sole province of celibate males, but also pastoral ministry for Catholics will be done mostly in the absence of priests, with sisters, deacons, and lay parish ministers doing a majority of the work of parish leadership. Those priests who remain will be older and probably more conservative than the majority of their parishioners (Hoge 2002; Hoge and Wenger 2005).

The "Fit" between Pastors and Congregations

So far in this chapter we have looked at important characteristics of congregations and of the pastors who serve them. This juxtaposition raises an important and interesting question: How well do pastors and congregations fit each other? As we have seen, congregations are not all alike, and they often differ significantly with respect to how they understand their ministry and mission. Pastors also differ in age, education, gender, ethnicity, theological perspective, and so forth. They are not interchangeable parts guaranteed to fit anywhere they may be wanted or needed.[31] This is not to say that good ministry cannot take place when striking differences in backgrounds between pastors and congregations exist. But acknowledgment of these differences, a good dose of humor, and trust in the grace of God in the midst of differences are particularly important when a new pastor arrives on the scene whose background is different in significant ways from the typical backgrounds of the congregation.

In the preceding chapter, I mentioned the GoodWork Project, which asked what makes it possible for persons to do work that combines both excellence and ethics. As I noted, the researchers argued that those professionals who are most able to combine expertise with ethics in their work are those whose work is well-aligned with forces in the larger context in which they work, especially with the values and expectations of those who are primary stakeholders in their work (Gardner et al. 2001). It is also the case that some degree of alignment between parishioners — the pastor's primary stakeholders — and their pastor is critical for good ministry, but how does one assess it?

In the U.S. Congregational Life Survey, one of the questions asked was, "How strongly do you agree that the pastor is a good match for the congregation?" In general, lay members expressed satisfaction regarding the match of their pastors and congregations. The average percentage of participants in a congregation who said that they "strongly agree" that the pastor is a good match was 47 percent. Another 51 percent checked the "agree" response, leaving only 2 percent either disagreeing or strongly disagreeing. Although this would seem to suggest that there is very little disagreement over fit, given what seems to be a tendency of participants to avoid negative responses on a variety of issues, I interpret the difference between an "agree" and a "strongly agree" response to be important.

Strong agreement that there is a good match of the pastor and congregation was greatest for congregations in conservative Protestant denominations, which averaged 57 percent strongly agreeing. The lowest was

---

31. As I have noted, to meet the priest shortage, the Catholic Church has begun to recruit priests from other cultures to come to the United States to serve as parish pastors. Although some of these matches work well, many do not. Language barriers and lack of cross-cultural understanding make communication and acceptance difficult. Our data are insufficient to allow us to consider this issue, but a study is currently underway at Catholic University of America by Professor Dean R. Hoge and his colleagues.

Figure 3.3
Average Percent of Attenders Who Strongly Agree
That the Pastor Is a Good Match for the Congregation

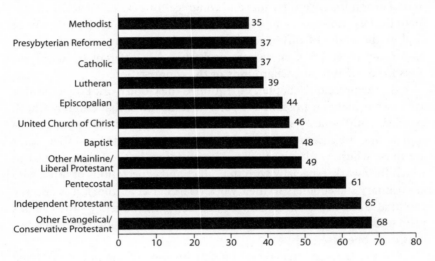

among Catholic parishes, which averaged 37 percent. A clear pattern continues to present itself when we look at fit within finer categories of denominational families, as in Figure 3.3. The highest level of perceived match was found among conservative and independent Protestant congregations; however, mainline Protestant denominations such as the United Church of Christ also had moderately high levels of match. The UCC and the Disciples of Christ, another somewhat liberal Protestant denomination, are congregational in polity, as are most conservative and independent Protestants, and, therefore, they are free to call their own pastor with little or no denominational direction. In contrast, lower levels of match are found in the mainline denominations, with the lowest being the Methodist family of congregations. It is not surprising that Catholics, Methodists, and other faith traditions that assign pastors to congregations have lower levels of perceived match than those traditions where the pastors are called directly by the congregation. Lower levels of fit are also evident in other families that we defined as having a connectional polity mixed with elements of congregationalism: Episcopal, Lutheran, and Presbyterian congregations call their own pastors; however, the denomination plays a more proactive role in the process — defining who is eligible to be considered and, in some cases, limiting the size of the candidate pool from which the congregation may choose.

What else, other than polity, determines whether a congregation perceives that its pastor is a good match? Anecdotes abound about recent seminary graduates swooping into less-educated congregations and unintentionally alienating everyone by preaching "highfalutin" sermons that fail to speak to the life experience of the members. We might guess, then, that similarity in education, age, and income would be likely candidates. Where possible, we constructed measures of similarity/dissimilarity between the pastor and lay members on several dimensions and correlated these measures with perceptions of a good match. In the correlations, education shows the strongest relationship (a correlation coefficient of .42 on a scale of -1 to +1) — that is, the more similar the pastor's level of education is to the average level of education of the congregation, the stronger the laity's perception of a good match. In contrast, whether the pastor and the congregation are of similar age makes no difference (0 correlation), and similarity of income shows a negative relationship (-.19), which in many cases probably reflects the fact that pastors receive less salary than the average income of their members, though the reverse could also be true. When we look at the perception of match in relation to the gender of the pastor, the results show that laity are significantly more likely to believe that there is a good match when the pastor is a male rather than a female — a relationship that holds regardless of denominational tradition. Although this is not surprising, it indicates the considerable distance left for many churches to travel before women clergy gain full acceptance. There are no significant differences in perception of match related to whether the pastor is bivocational or second career.[32]

In a church setting, theological perspective is another important aspect of both congregations and pastors.[33] What do they value? How would

32. In examining these three relationships, we used differences in average (mean) scores of the percentage saying that there is a good fit, and compared male and female clergy, bivocational vs. single vocation; and second- vs. first-career pastors.

33. A study by Mueller and McDuff (2004) examined the effects of theological mismatch between clergy and congregation and its effect on job satisfaction in two Protestant denominations. They found that theologically liberal clergy serving in theologically conservative congregations were most likely to experience job dissatisfaction. Clergy whose theological perspective matched their congregation's perspective and conservative clergy serving in liberal congregations did not experience job dissatisfaction to the same degree.

they like to give expression to their sense of mission and social outreach? In the two surveys, measures of theological beliefs of both pastors and laity provide some examples of these differences. We asked pastors to characterize themselves theologically using several categories, generally reflecting a conservative to liberal continuum.[34] For lay members, we used questions from the congregational survey to construct an index of theological conservatism[35] that also reflects a conservative to liberal continuum. The correlation between "good match" and the degree of similarity between the pastor and the congregation on theological conservatism is moderately strong (though not as strong as education), and it is statistically significant (.24 on a scale of -1 to 1). Consonance in the priorities of the pastor and the congregation is likely to inspire greater commitment for both pastor and laity,[36] although some level of disagreement may foster a healthy tension that avoids too narrow a focus in congregational ministries. I will return to the issue of match in Chapter 6; for now, I will simply echo the contention of the GoodWork Project that good ministry will be positively affected by a good fit between the characteristics and values of the pastor and those of his or her primary stakeholders, the congregation.

A Note on Clergy Salaries

Lastly in this chapter I turn to an issue somewhat different from the settings and changing characteristics of today's clergy, but one that is related to them and quite important for understanding how clergy are faring to-

34. We used different categories for Protestants and Catholics, since those appropriate to Protestants would not have been so for Catholic priests, but each set of categories reflected a conservative or orthodox to liberal or progressive continuum. The wording used can be found in the Appendix.

35. The index was created by averaging the percentage of worshippers who are biblical literalists and who reject a belief that all religions are equal paths to finding ultimate truth, giving us a range of scores from 1 to 100. The average score for conservative Protestant congregations was 71. For Catholic and mainline Protestant congregations, the average scores were 18 and 27 respectively. Because of the small number of congregations from historic black churches in the U.S. Congregational Life Survey, we have combined their scores with either mainline or conservative Protestants, based on their denomination.

36. Mueller and McDuff, for example, found in a recent study of two moderate/liberal denominations that theologically conservative pastors were less satisfied with their call (Mueller & McDuff 2004).

day: the complex issue of pastors' compensation. McMillan and Price (2003) considered this topic in some detail, and our much briefer discussion here draws on their research.

To accurately assess clergy compensation, we must look through multiple lenses. Using a sample of clergy from the Bureau of Labor Statistics, we find that salaries for clergy with graduate level education (exclusive of other forms of compensation) have outpaced inflation over the past twenty-five years. In 1976, the median salary for full-time clergy with graduate-level education was $25,000 in 1999 dollars, and in 1999 it was $40,000. These figures include all clergy, including military and institutional chaplains, teachers, pastoral counselors, denominational executives, and so forth. They also include assistant or associate pastors. Although the growth rate in the clergy's median salary has not kept pace with the explosive growth rate of earnings of physicians or lawyers, it has brought clergy compensation up to the median salary level for other graduate-educated, full-time professionals in comparable fields such as social work and teaching. Yet when compared with Jewish rabbis, Christian clergy still lag considerably behind. According to one report (Wertheimer 2003: 37), "Recently ordained rabbis with a few years of experience can expect wage- and housing-packages in the vicinity of $100,000. More experienced rabbis can earn anywhere from 50 to 100 percent more, and senior rabbis in prosperous synagogues command up to $300,000."[37]

One can also look at clergy salaries in the largest of our mainline Protestant denominations, the United Methodist Church. In the last decade, median clergy salaries (including housing) for full-time, fully ordained clergy in the denomination grew from $40,000 to $42,000 in 1999 dollars, a growth rate 5 percent above inflation. United Methodist pastors serving congregations in the Southeast, where much of the denomination's growth in membership has occurred, experienced a great surge, with median salaries outpacing inflation by 10 percent.

In many ways, then, clergy salaries have improved steadily over the last part of the century. Yet not all is well. Although compensation for graduate-educated, full-time, ordained, senior or solo pastors has steadily improved, the number of congregations that can afford to pay these higher

---

37. Wertheimer's estimates are for combined salary and housing, but even if one were to discount this total by 25 percent to account for housing, rabbinic salaries are still higher than those of Christian clergy.

Table 3.4
Median Salary (Including Housing Compensation) of
Senior/Solo Pastors in 2000, Differentiated by Church Size

	Catholic	Mainline Protestant	Conservative Protestant	Historic Black
Small (< 100)	$20,883 (10%)	$35,400 (55%)	$25,034 (64%)	$14,200 (61%)
Medium (101-350)	$24,063 (34%)	$49,897 (39%)	$40,700 (30%)	$34,997 (34%)
Large (351-1000)	$24,141 (35%)	$67,017 (6%)	$60,104 (5%)	$57,377 (5%)
Mega (1000+)	$26,095 (20%)	—	$85,923 (1%)	—

salaries has declined, partly because of membership decline and aging congregations and partly because of changes in the economy. These less wealthy congregations — typically with small, aging memberships — offer lower salaries and benefits more acceptable to bivocationals, lay pastors, or perhaps retired clergy who want to continue to serve part time.

The pastors' salaries reported in Table 3.4 reflect the considerable differences that exist across congregations. These figures come from our national survey of pastoral leaders. The figures include both the cash salary the pastor receives plus his or her housing allowance or an estimated value for the actual housing — parsonage, rectory, or manse — that the congregation or parish provides. Most professionals do not receive a comparable benefit as part of their compensation; therefore, it is important to include the value of housing as part of the pastor's compensation, since housing is an important component of clergy salary. Unlike the median salaries reported by the Bureau of Labor Statistics, these figures in the table include only senior and solo Christian pastors serving congregations. They include both full- and part-time clergy, both graduate-educated and otherwise, and both ordained and lay pastoral leaders. Thus, these medians represent a cross-section of the typical salary (including housing) paid to U.S. pastoral leaders at the time of the survey. Beneath the salary and housing figures, I show the percentage of pastors within denominational traditions who serve congregations in each size category — a reminder, especially for Protestants, of the difference that congregational size makes in compensation.

Salary levels for Catholic priests are typically set by the bishop of their diocese. Although there are some differences among dioceses and also by parish size, they are not dramatic. For Protestants, in contrast, variations are considerably greater. As the table shows, the median compensation for Protestants serving mid- to large-sized congregations is still modest, especially measured by the standards that apply to other professionals, but in general their compensation makes possible a comfortable standard of living. The majority of Protestant pastors, however, are not serving those mid-sized to large congregations. More than half of mainline pastors and nearly two-thirds of conservative ones serve small churches with one hundred or fewer in attendance, and these pastors' compensation is generally quite low, even when compared with that of teachers and social workers rather than the higher-paying professions. Furthermore, although the geographic location and wealth level of the congregation have some effect on a pastor's compensation package, the size of the congregation is its primary determinant.

Given the large percentage of small congregations in Protestantism, supplying pastoral leadership that these congregations can afford constitutes a significant problem, hence again the use of bivocational clergy, lay pastors, or retirees. Without taking denominational tradition into account, ordained Protestant clergy serving small congregations received a median salary and housing package of $31,234, while lay pastors in these congregations averaged $4,000 — a significant difference![38] Bivocational pastors serving small congregations averaged $20,000 in salary and housing, contrasted with $32,500 for their counterparts who have no additional occupation.

Several other forms of compensation are not reflected in these figures, in large part because they vary so widely in congregational practice that it would have been difficult to ask about them effectively in a telephone survey. These include the dollar amount of health care or retirement benefits that some clergy receive.[39] Also, some churches have unique

38. The mean salary (as compared to the median) plus housing for these clergy is $15,386.

39. Some congregations also pay the utility bills for the parsonage or rectory. Others provide continuing education and travel allowances, and some larger congregations may provide an automobile for the pastor's use. In our interview question, we asked clergy to ex-

traditions that can be factored into determining how much a pastor makes: in many historic black congregations, for example, pastors receive a significant portion of their true annual compensation as a gift given by members at the annual anniversary of the pastor's service in the congregation. And Catholic priests and many Protestant pastors typically receive cash gifts for performing weddings or funerals — Catholics refer to these as "stole fees," referring to the stole that the priest wears while performing sacerdotal duties. These various types of additional compensation are not accounted for, but should be considered as part of the total compensation that some clergy receive.

Our salary and housing figures also do not account for a significant tax benefit that some clergy receive. If a pastor lives in a church-owned house or receives a housing allowance from the congregation in addition to salary, he or she can exclude this benefit as a part of taxable income.[40] Nonetheless, clergy in the U.S. are considered self-employed and must pay the full 15 percent of their social security tax on their total income, including housing, which partially offsets the housing tax exemption. These additional sources of non-salary income and benefits, as well as added costs of such things as pastors' self-employment social security assessments, are important for gaining a fuller picture of clergy compensation.

Although clergy compensation has, for the most part, improved in recent years, other aspects of the financial realities that clergy face have changed over the years. For example, various "perks" of the ministerial office, such as free college tuition at many denominational colleges and universities for children of clergy, store discounts, free professional services, and discounts for rail travel, which at one time were common — some as recently as twenty-five years ago — are no longer part of the pastor's finan-

---

clude health care and pension benefits, but to include as compensation any other allowances that they may receive. We failed, however, to specify particular kinds of allowances. In retrospect, this was a mistake since we have no way of knowing how many clergy receive these allowances or whether they actually included them in their responses to interviewers. If the allowances were included, then the actual cash salary that clergy receive is lower than that which we report. Several years ago, Hoge, Carroll, and Scheets (1988) conducted a detailed study of clergy compensation, comparing total compensation of a sample of Catholic, Episcopal, Lutheran, and Methodist clergy. Travel and educational allowances, health care, and retirement benefits ranged from approximately $6,000 to $10,000, or an average of about $8,000 per clergy.

40. The Internal Revenue Service has threatened on several occasions to do away with these tax exemptions for housing. Thus far, Congress has prevented this from happening.

cial picture. As an example, not too many years ago, Duke University offered free tuition to any child of a North Carolina Methodist pastor that gained admission. Were that benefit offered at the present time, it would amount to over $30,000 per year! These "perks," as Matthew Price (2001) has pointed out, were important supplements to a pastor's salary, making it possible for clergy to keep their family within the boundaries of the professional middle class.

Although we did not ask clergy for dollar figures regarding their retirement and health care benefits that they receive, we did ask whether they received pension benefits from their denomination or congregation. We also asked whether they had health care coverage provided, whether by their congregation or denomination or by a second employer (in the case of bivocational clergy) or their spouse's employer. Almost all Catholic and mainline Protestant pastors are provided retirement benefits and health care coverage by their congregation or denomination. In sharp contrast, the congregations or denominations of many conservative Protestants and pastors of historic black denominations do not provide these benefits. Approximately six of ten conservative Protestants and seven in ten black pastors have no pension provided by their congregation or denomination — which, as noted previously, is one reason for the greater number of bivocational clergy in these traditions. About 30 percent of conservative Protestants and 36 percent of pastors in historic black churches have no health care benefits from either their church, a second job, or through a spouse's employer.

In their report, McMillan and Price commented that the wide disparity in compensation between those Protestant pastors serving the relatively small number of large and mega congregations and those in small and mid-sized congregations creates a two-tiered (or perhaps more accurately, pyramidal) compensation structure, and many Protestant clergy will not reach the upper tier during their career. The small number of large congregations works against them. Their report also highlights the greater financial security that is provided to pastors who serve in most of the denominations with a connectional polity. These denominations often provide compensation guidelines for their congregations, and they sometimes even provide compensating dollars (subsidies) to pastors serving financially struggling congregations, especially those congregations with a good chance of becoming self-supporting. Pastors in churches with a congregational polity do not fare as well, especially in small to mid-size congregations. When these pastors are called to large and mega congregations, their salaries outstrip pastors in comparable connectional churches. Market forces are probably the major factor pushing these congregations to pay higher salaries in order to attract and retain their pastor. The Catholic Church's compensation practice, while far from ideal, tends to provide generally consistent financial support for priests. Salaries across dioceses, while low compared with those of Protestants, are roughly the same regardless of parish size, and priests are given health and retirement benefits as well as housing and other household needs.

Income from a spouse or other family members often enables Protestant pastors' families to survive on relatively low pastoral salaries. This seems to be especially important in the case of mainline Protestant pastors. Almost eight in ten mainline pastors are married, and of those, 82 percent of their spouses work outside the home. Nearly all conservative Protestant pastors and 84 percent of black pastors are married, but only two-thirds of their spouses work in some outside job.

How pastors are compensated and how they should be compensated are complex and vexing issues — ones that need considerable further analysis and reflection. Few pastors choose ordained ministry because of the promise of a high salary. Yet it is difficult not to wonder how many promising candidates may have been discouraged from responding to a sense of call as the result of low pastoral salaries relative to other professions that require comparable educational preparation. As I will emphasize again in the concluding chapter, what is needed is thoughtful, theologically informed reflection on the question of what kind of compensation a person needs today for a well-lived life, whether he or she is a pastor or a layperson. Does one's compensation make it possible to have a lifestyle that is comfortable, if not lavish, by current standards? Is it sufficient to pay off educational debts, own a home (if one is not provided), and be able to educate one's children? Does one have adequate health care? Will one be able to enjoy a comfortable retirement?

Conclusion

This chapter has covered considerable ground in presenting a profile of God's potters. We have focused on several salient characteristics of the congregational settings in which clergy live and work, especially the size of congregations as a major influence on the pastoral work, and also ways in which denominational traditions, polity, and location influence congregations. We have also looked at three characteristics that are important for understanding today's pastors: the growth in the number of women entering the ministry, at least in mainline Protestantism; the growing number of second-career clergy; and the increased use of bivocational clergy and various types of lay pastors. We also introduced the concept of the relative match or fit between the congregations and clergy as an important contributor to good ministry; we will return to this at several points in the remainder of this book. We concluded with a brief look at clergy compensation. Next we turn to what it is that clergy do as pastors of congregations.

Chapter 4

What Do Clergy Do?
The Work of Ordained Ministry

"I went to New York immediately after the attacks and spent a few days there at Ground Zero. . . . I remember seeing people who came up to me with pictures of their loved ones. I saw them as people who were crying out to God for strength and for help and for courage and for hope. Entering into the lives of these people was humbling, and at the same time life-giving."

Fr. David McBriar, reflecting on experiences
following September 11, 2001[1]

"Being in ministry is like being 'stoned with popcorn'. . . . You know, it's just one little thing after another until you feel buried in it."

An Austin-area pastor

In *Gilead,* Marilynne Robinson's extraordinary novel, the narrator is a seventy-seven-year-old, third-generation Congregationalist minister who is dying of heart disease. The minister, John Ames, is writing an account of his life and ministry for his seven-year-old son to read after he is gone. Reading Ames's story, the reader is led to contemplate both the mundane

---

1. From an interview with Mark Constantine (2005).

and transcendent moments of ministry. He describes, for example, the un-inspiring food at church dinners: the "molded salad of orange gelatin with stuffed green olives and shredded cabbage and anchovies that has dogged my ministerial life" and a bean salad that looks "distinctly Presbyterian." He reflects on the thousands of sermons he has written over the years: "Say, fifty sermons a year for forty-five years, not counting funerals and so on, of which there have been a great many. . . . I wrote almost all of it in the deepest hope and conviction. . . . Trying to say what was true." And, telling of a time when as a child he and his siblings baptized a cat, Ames reflects on the mystery of baptism as one of the great privileges of being a minister. Baptism, he muses, is a way of conferring a blessing on another, acknowl-edging the other's sacredness. "Not that you have to be a minister to confer blessing. You are simply much more likely to find yourself in that position. It's a thing people expect of you."

Along with preaching and conferring blessings and taking part in hundreds of church suppers with their molded salads, fried chicken, and green peas, what exactly do pastors do? This is the question that we will ex-plore in this chapter.

One way is to think of the work of the pastor in terms of the purpose of the local congregation or parish. In Chapter 1, I defined this task broadly in both sociological and theological terms. Sociologically, we recall, con-gregations are significant voluntary associations that are important pro-ducers of social capital in our society: social networks where friendships and trust are developed as members share in fellowship with one another, where members' perspectives on life are shaped as they worship and study together, and where they are often engaged individually or together in ser-vice to their communities or the broader society. These elements of social capital are another way of speaking of the culture that is produced in the congregation. Theologically, a congregation is the "body of Christ," charged with continuing Christ's ministry of reconciliation in the world, inviting people to accept God's gift of salvation and be reconciled one to another. Or, to use the metaphor that gives this book its title, it is an earthen vessel or clay jar that reveals God's transcendent power in its life and practices.

When we think of the church in these ways, what do they imply con-cerning the core work of ordained ministry? Broadly put, they imply the kind of work expected of those who hold the office of pastor as I described it in Chapter 1: celebrant of the sacraments, preacher and teacher, overseer of congregational life, giver of pastoral care. In his study of urban black "storefront" congregations, Omar McRoberts observed a phenomenon similar to the one Marilynne Robinson fictionalized so poignantly in *Gilead*. Drawing from a different cultural "tool kit" than John Ames, the storefront preachers used their holiness tradition's teachings and practices to describe a life that is "in but not of this world," a life that "closely paralleled and deeply validated the existential realities of migrants [from the South to the urban North] and immigrants [from Haiti and elsewhere] struggling to navigate a strange social terrain" (McRoberts 2003: 64). Ames's small town in Iowa and the storefront preachers' urban neighborhoods are worlds apart socially and culturally; however, in each setting the pastor engages in similar core tasks — worship leadership, preaching, teaching, and congregational oversight — to draw members into the narratives of their traditions. Different denominations and pastors may hold diverse views about the meaning of the tasks and accord them differing priorities, but this way of describing pastoral work is present, one way or another, in all denominational traditions — sometimes explicit in their ordination vows or, if not, implicit in expectations for the pastoral role.

Clergy's work — however mundane some of it appears to be — is centrally defined in these core tasks. In these roles, whether in a routine Sunday service or at Ground Zero, clergy are called to be "God bearers," representing God to the people and the people to God. This is why it is not at all surprising that the core tasks of clergy change little over time.

In this chapter I will look at several aspects of the work that pastors do, informed by the results of our survey and focus groups:

- I will examine how clergy give expression to their core work by asking how much time they spend in a number of pastoral tasks in which they engage. In particular, I consider whether and how specific aspects of pastoral work have changed over time, and ask about the implications of such changes;
- I will note which tasks pastors consider to be their strong points and which, in contrast, need improvement;
- I will ask how lay members view their pastors' work and on which age groups pastors focus their ministry;
- I will also consider how pastors spend their non-work time and whether they are able to establish boundaries between work and their private lives;

- I will conclude with several important findings about the relationship of time use with several measures of clergy health and stress.

As we will see, what clergy do in their work and how they care for themselves in the process have important consequences for themselves, the congregations they lead, and the religious culture that they, together with their lay partners, produce.

How Clergy Spend Their Time in a Typical Week

How do pastors spend their time in activities related to the work of ministry? Time use by itself fails to capture the richness and depth of much of a pastor's work, but it can be a useful measuring tool. Congregational members are often unaware of what their pastors do all week and how much time they spend doing it — hence the standing joke that clergy work only one hour a week. Many lay members do, in fact, see their pastor for only one hour each week, and this makes what clergy do something of a mystery, sometimes leading to misperceptions with negative consequences. Some pastors, for example, tell of members who complain whenever they do not see the pastor's car at the church. Members have occasionally even been heard to use their ignorance regarding their pastor's work as justification for keeping her or his salary low. Clergy also have expressed concern that the lack of understanding of their work contributes to members' resistance to recognizing the need for a regular day off or time away from ministry for continuing education and renewal. Clergy time use is even something of a mystery to some pastors, who don't have a clear picture of how their colleagues use their time. When we asked about pastors' time use in our survey, a frequent request they made was, "Let me know how others spend their time!"

In the survey, we listed a variety of activities in which pastors engage, reflecting various components of the broad core tasks for which clergy are authorized in ordination. Before telephone interviews were conducted, we sent each pastor a worksheet including this list. We asked them to take time to reflect on how many hours in a typical week they devoted to each task, including preparation where applicable.[2] We hoped

---

2. In the list of tasks, we included "thinking about and promoting the congregation's vision." From the pastors' responses, we realized that this was not a discrete task apart from

that this would provide more carefully considered responses. We also asked them to look over the list and report which three tasks they did best and in which three areas they felt they most needed to improve. We then asked about the amount of time they spent in various personal and family activities apart from their pastoral work, a topic to be discussed later in this chapter.

The median number of hours spent at work each week for all clergy, regardless of denomination and whether full- or part-time, is forty-eight.[3] For those who work full-time (defined as thirty-five or more hours per week), the median is fifty-one. Part-timers average twenty-three hours a week. Looking first at how this breaks down in terms of percentage of time spent per week by all clergy (full- and part-time) in various tasks, we find that preaching and worship leadership (including preparation time for each) accounted for 22 and 8 percent respectively of a pastor's weekly work time. Thirteen percent was spent in teaching and training people for ministry. All of these are important ways that pastors engage in cultural production, especially shaping meanings and perceptions. Administration, including attending congregational meetings, took 14 percent of the week. Fifteen percent was spent in pastoral care (counseling, spiritual direction, and visitation). Evangelism, including visiting prospective members, involved 7 percent, and denominational meetings and community activities took up 3 and 2 percent respectively.

Beyond this, clergy report spending an average of seven hours each week in prayer and meditation and another four in reading that is not part of sermon preparation. Both of these activities contribute in vital ways, not only to the pastor's personal growth, but to the health of the congregation as well. Many pastors use part of their prayer and meditation time remembering particular members or congregational issues, and much of

---

several of the others. For example, one may promote a vision for the congregation in preaching, teaching, or administration; thus, we did not include it in the analysis or in determining the total hours pastors work weekly.

3. The median reflects the midpoint of all responses, with half of the responses above and half below. Unlike the mean, it is unaffected by extreme cases. For example, when we totaled the hours allocated to individual tasks for each pastor, several reported spending more hours at work than exist in a week! Obviously some of the activities we asked about overlap with one another, and as a result were counted twice. But it is also likely that some pastors tended to over-report the time spent. By using the median, we are able to correct in part for any extreme cases of over- or under-reporting.

pastors' reading other than for particular sermons is for professional growth rather than for recreation.[4]

We will look later in this chapter at the way in which various factors — clergy characteristics as well as denominational tradition and church size — affect pastors' time use. First, however, we look at how the typical workweek for pastors has changed over time.

Changes in Pastoral Work over Time

How have pastors' typical workweeks changed? We are fortunate to be able to make comparisons of time use at three points over the past seventy years. In a multi-volume study of theological education conducted in the 1930s by the Institute of Social and Religious Research, Mark May and his colleagues analyzed the work of pastors in what today we call mainline Protestant denominations (May et al. 1934; May & Shuttleworth 1934), including the time they spent in various tasks of ministry.[5] In the 1950s, Samuel Blizzard (1985) also reported on Protestant pastors' time allocation in various roles. More recently, a study of clergy in Milwaukee County, Wisconsin compared pastors' time use with Blizzard's findings from the 1950s (Brunette-Hill & Finke 1999). While I have not included the Wisconsin data in our comparisons, the findings of this study and ours are very similar.

4. For a description of clergy reading habits based on the *Pulpit & Pew* survey, see Carroll (2003).

5. May and Shuttleworth drew in part on earlier time-use studies by H. Paul Douglass, using both Douglass's data and his classification. In an unpublished study, Douglass (n.d.: 13) lists the classification scheme he used to categorize the ministers' time. We have used Douglass's list to try to make the May-Shuttleworth categories comparable to ours. In his study, Blizzard used minutes per day rather than hours; thus we had to make a conversion to hours. In interesting commentary, Douglass reflected on the time budgets prepared by the pastors he studied. He made the following observations about ministers. He found: "a. Over-insistence upon the inner significance of one's work beyond its external forms, when numerous other vocations have the right to make the same claim. b. Inability to tell when one is on duty and when off. c. Claim to longer working time than the record justifies. d. Sense of continuously living 'on the job.' e. Uneasy consciousness of always being subject to call. f. Charge that trifles are always interrupting — that values are always being interfered with by circumstances. g. Real uncertainty as to the claims of competing duties, especially as to the rightful place of certain routine requirements. h. Self-identification with an institution and a 'cause' to the point that criticism of it cannot be accepted objectively" (p. 16). We can agree with several of these observations as we have examined our data.

Table 4.1
How Mainline Protestant Clergy Spend Their Time:
Comparisons from Three Studies

Task	Average hours per week		
	1934*	1954†	2001‡
Sermon preparation and delivery	22.5	8.5	10.3
Worship leadership (including preparation and weddings, funerals, etc.)	16.6	3.3	4.9
Educational ministry (teaching, etc.)	4.2	3.4	6.8
Pastoral care			
Counseling	NA	2.2	4.3
Visiting members, sick, and shut-ins	NA	12.3	4.9
Total Pastoral care	19.5	14.5	9.2
Fellowship and recreation	NA	1.63	NA
Evangelism			
Working to convert others	NA	NA	3.7
Visiting prospective members	NA	0.8	1.6
Total Evangelism	NA	0.8	5.3
Administration			
General administration (including planning)	NA	13.3	7.4
Congregational meetings	NA	11.1	3.1
Total Administration	8.9	24.4	10.5
Civic and community involvement	4	3.5	1.8
Denominational/ecumenical involvement	NA	6.7	2
Total hours per week	75.7	66.7	50.8

*Adapted from May & Shuttleworth (1934: 180)
†Adapted from Blizzard (1985: 110, 164)
‡Pulpit & Pew Survey (2001)

Table 4.1 shows the comparisons of the 1934 and 1954 time-use findings with our own. Since each included only clergy from mainline Protestant denominations, I have restricted comparisons from our current data to mainline pastors. I have also had to try to reconcile slightly different categories of pastoral work The figures reported are the mean hours worked rather than median to make data from the three time periods comparable. Doing so gives slightly higher numbers than I will report in Table 4.2, in which I use the median.

Overall, we see a striking decline in the total hours clergy report spending at work: from 75.7 hours per week in 1934, to 66.7 hours in 1954, to 50.8 hours in 2001. In part these differences may represent differences in the way tasks were categorized and counted in the three studies;[6] however, they may also reflect a real decline in hours worked — in my judgment a healthy trend if it means that clergy are generally becoming better at establishing boundaries between their work and other aspects of their life. Establishing and strengthening boundaries between work time and personal time may be one of the positive benefits of the professionalization of ordained ministry in recent decades. Professionalization not only emphasizes competence in ministry, but it also reminds clergy that, important as their office and calling are, being a pastor is not the sum total of one's life — something that is difficult for some pastors to keep in mind. Commenting on May's 1934 data, H. Paul Douglass (n.d.: 16) observed that ministers seemed not only to claim more working hours than were justified, but they also had difficulty distinguishing when they were off or on duty. When Douglass subtracted a number of activities claimed by ministers as "work time" — for example, thinking about their sermon while shaving, relaxation, commuting to the church from home, and so forth — he reduced the minister's average workday from eleven to nine hours (Douglass and Brunner 1935: 121).

Although when compared with their forebears, clergy in 2001 seem better at establishing boundaries, some nonetheless continue to have difficulty, reporting what appear to be inordinately high workweeks. Even the workweek of the average mainline pastor — 50.8 hours — is high when compared with that of other managers and professionals, who averaged 42 hours a week in 1999. Three of ten managers and professionals averaged 49 hours or more. Only two of ten workers in all non-farm occupations worked 49 hours a week (Bureau of Labor Statistics 2000). As we will see below, Catholic priests, who average 58 hours a week, are an especially overworked segment of the clergy, one ripe for burnout.

6. May and Shuttleworth, for example, included a category called "mechanical," which we omitted from the table. By mechanical, they meant time spent repairing one's automobile for use in pastoral work as well as performing janitorial services in the church. Although we did not include this category, we acknowledge that some pastors, especially in small churches, sometimes have to serve as janitor along with their other duties.

Several comparisons in specific tasks are worth noting. Clergy civic and community involvement was low in 1934, and even slightly lower by 1954; however, in comparison with 1934, it had shrunk by more than half by 2001. When they reflected on May's 1934 report of clergy time use, Douglass and his colleague Edmund de S. Brunner observed, "The average minister actually gives very little time to extra-parochial service of any kind. While a few gifted and influential ministers are much in evidence in these fields, they stand in striking contrast with the average" (Douglass & Brunner 1935: 189).[7] Yet present-day clergy don't match even this low level of involvement! This is not to say that churches and clergy do not support community service programs, but such programs are more likely to be carried out by faith-based organizations outside the congregation, often with volunteer and financial support from congregations.[8] Apparently, however, there is little involvement outside the congregation of most solo or senior pastors. Clergy report spending just under half the time in civic involvement that they did in 1954, and two-thirds less time in denominational and ecumenical involvement.

Another notable difference is in the time allocated to sermon preparation in 1934 compared with subsequent years. It is important to note that the 22.5 hours spent in 1934 include a subcategory called "undifferentiated sermon preparation" which not only reflects pastors thinking about their sermons throughout the day but also reading that they do other than that for sermons. Both Blizzard and we excluded this category from time spent in preaching. Even so, the time difference is considerable. One probable important reason is the demise of the Sunday evening worship service, which included a second Sunday sermon, and a weekday prayer meeting at which the pastor would also typically give a short message. The Sunday

7. The Lynds in their study of "Middletown" during the 1920s also commented on limited but often frustrated efforts of the city's ministers "to share in the life of the city" (Lynd and Lynd 1929: 154).

8. In the U.S. Congregational Life Survey, an average of 28 percent of mainline Protestant lay members in each congregation reported they were involved as volunteers in community service or social justice ministries of the congregation. An average of 36 percent said that they were involved in outside (non-congregational) service organizations. Chaves (2004: 78), however, found that "most congregations engage only minimally in social services, and typically the few that do engage more deeply rely heavily on paid staff, involve relatively few congregational volunteers, and conduct their efforts in collaboration — including financial collaboration — with secular and government agencies."

evening service and weekday prayer meeting were already in decline by 1954. This decline began near the end of the Second World War and was exacerbated by the advent of television, which became widespread during the 1950s. Yet despite the effect of fewer services and the differences in the way the categories were measured, there does appear to have been an overall decline in time spent in sermon preparation, even though church members continue to attach high importance to preaching (Lummis 2003).

Similarly, the time spent in pastoral care declined sharply: from over nineteen hours in 1934, to fourteen and a half hours in 1954, to just over nine hours in 2001. Although pastors almost doubled their time counseling between 1954 and 2001, time spent in visitation dropped by over seven hours a week. This no doubt is due in part to the considerable increase of women in the workforce, making busier and more complicated family schedules for both parishioners and pastors (Brunette-Hill and Finke 1999: 53-54).

Finally, Blizzard's research found a sharp increase in time spent in administration from the 1934 survey. Clergy in 2001 do slightly more administration than those in 1934, but significantly less than in 1954. These changes are difficult to explain. Blizzard believed that the increase in administration from 1934 to 1954 corresponded with the increasing size and complexity of local church structures over the two decades. Writing about the same time, H. Richard Niebuhr (1956: 79) also maintained that the pastor's administrative load had grown and suggested that "pastoral director" was an emerging contemporary image. Ministers, he said, not only now had offices from which they directed the activities of the church, but were also adopting a "big operator" view of successful ministry — a view Niebuhr worried had great potential to distort ministry. Although that may explain the change between 1934 and 1954, it does not explain the drop in hours in 2001. The difference may be in the way the questions were asked. Blizzard asked about a number of specific types of administrative activities (board meetings, physical plant maintenance, publicity, clerical work, working with staff and lay committees, budget promotion, and planning) that we simply subsumed in a category called "administering the work of the congregation, including staff supervision." We also asked about "attending congregational board and committee meetings," while Blizzard had four subcategories of church organizational involvement (leadership, participation, fellowship and recreation, and planning). Our more general categories may have led our clergy respondents to forget some aspects of administration. Whatever the correct explanation, the drop in overall administrative time spent is quite significant. (We should recall, however, that this is far from true for Catholic priests, whose administrative load seems exceptionally heavy.)

In summary, while the several core tasks in which clergy engage in carrying out the pastoral office — preaching, worship leadership, teaching, pastoral care, and administration — are sufficiently similar for us to compare them at the three points in time, the number of hours allocated to these tasks has changed significantly. I also suspect that the substance of some of these tasks has also changed over time, although demonstrating that is beyond the scope of our data.

Clergy Workweek by Denominational Tradition

Turning from comparisons over time, we look now at how, in the 2001 survey, clergy workweeks vary by denominational tradition. Table 4.2 summarizes the typical workweek by clergy's denominational tradition. The table includes all clergy, whether full- or part-time.

From the table we see that Catholic priests and pastors in the three Protestant traditions allocate most of their time similarly, with several important exceptions. Priests (who work on average fifty-six hours a week)[9] devote somewhat less time to preaching, including preparation, but they spend more than double the time in both worship leadership and parish administration as compared to Protestants. This is no doubt because the celebration of the Eucharist is central to Catholic worship, while preaching has received less emphasis. In contrast, for many Protestants, especially in non-sacramental traditions, the sermon has greater prominence than the Eucharist. Also, given the large size of most Catholic parishes, most priests celebrate the Eucharist in multiple services both during the week and on weekends. The amount of time priests spend in administration is likewise affected by the large size of most Catholic parishes, especially if there is a

9. Research by the Center for Applied Research in the Apostolate (Perl & Froehle 2002: 24) found that priests in their study reported a median work week of 58 hours, using priests' reports of how long they worked in a typical day and the number of days per week that they worked. Twenty percent of the diocesan parish priests reported spending an average of 80 hours a week at work! Those in larger parishes worked longer hours than those in smaller.

Table 4.2
Hours Spent in Pastoral Tasks per Week Differentiated by Denominational Tradition

	Catholic	Mainline Protestant	Conservative Protestant	Historic Black
Preaching (incl. preparation)	6	10	10	10
Worship leadership (incl. preparation)	9	4	3	4
Teaching (incl. preparation)	2	4	4	5
Training people for ministry	1	1	1	2
Working to convert others	1	1	2	3
Pastoral counseling	4	3	2	3
Visiting members, sick, and shut-ins	3	4	3	4
Visiting prospective members	0	1	1	1
Administering congregation's work	10	5	3	2
Attending congregation meetings	3	2	1	2
Involvement in denominational affairs	2	2	2	2
Involvement in community affairs	2	2	2	2
Some other task	2	2	2	2
Total hours worked per week*	56	48	47	55

*The amount shown for each individual task is the median hours worked at that task. The amount shown for the total hours worked per week was derived by summing the actual hours per week for each task and then computing the median for the total hours worked; thus, the latter figure, for each tradition, is larger than the sum of the median for each individual task.

parochial school as part of the parish. Administering a parish with 5,000 participants is a markedly different task from administering a hundred-member congregation, as is so typical for many Protestants. Unlike Protestant clergy, priests did not report spending any time visiting prospective members.

The table shows that Protestants, especially in historic black congregations, spend more time than priests in teaching. Also, pastors in black churches historically have been important community leaders, and this is reflected in the slightly greater amount of time they spend in community involvement. Yet with the exception of these and a few other minor differences, the way clergy in the different traditions allocate their time is remarkably similar, indicating that there is a fairly similar understanding of the pastoral office operative across the traditions.

A final note: adding time spent in prayer and meditation and in general reading to the work week, we find that Catholics, conservative Protestants, and pastors in black denominations spend, on average, ten hours a week in prayer and meditation, while the mainline Protestants average only six hours a week — four hours fewer than clergy of the other traditions! This is a significant difference, and I have wondered about its consequences for mainline pastors' spirituality. In a set of questions about satisfaction with various aspects of their ministry (which we will discuss in Chapter 6), we included a question about pastors' satisfaction with their spiritual life. Although denominational differences are not large, mainline pastors' satisfaction with their spiritual life is the lowest of the four denominational traditions. As for reading other than for sermon preparation, Catholic and mainline and conservative Protestant clergy report a median of four hours per week. Black clergy average five hours per week.

Not only did we ask how many hours they spend in general reading, but we also asked what three authors they most often read in relation to their work as pastors.[10] The list of authors is quite large, meaning that the many authors were mentioned by a relatively small number of pastors, often only one or two. In Table 4.3, I show the top ten authors chosen by clergy in each denominational tradition. The authors are listed in descending order based on the number of pastors mentioning them. Although there were several ties in the rankings, they are not shown. What do we learn from these lists? First, there is relatively little overlap among them, although conservative Protestants and black clergy share several favorite authors. Catholic writer Henri Nouwen topped both the Catholic and mainline lists. C. S. Lewis, the Anglican novelist, lay theologian, and a late convert to Christianity, is on the mainline and conservative Protestant lists, and he was not far behind the top ten for Catholics. Among their top ten, mainline and conservative Protestant clergy share two conservative Protestant authors (Max Lucado and Philip Yancey) and

10. Using data from the NORC interviews, supplemented by a survey done in conjunction with the U.S. Congregational Life research, I have analyzed clergy reading habits in greater detail in an article in *The Christian Century* (Carroll 2003).

Table 4.3

Most-Read Authors by Denominational Tradition

Catholic	Mainline Protestant	Conservative Protestant	Historic Black
Henri J. M. Nouwen	Henri J. M. Nouwen	Max Lucado	Warren Wiersbe
John Paul II	William Willimon	John Maxwell	John MacArthur
Raymond Brown	Frederick Buechner	Charles Swindoll	Matthew Henry
William J. Bausch	Max Lucado	John MacArthur	John Maxwell
Walter J. Burghardt	Eugene Peterson	Philip Yancey	Charles Swindoll
Scott Hahn	C. S. Lewis	Rick Warren	Charles Spurgeon
Anthony de Mello	Marcus Borg	C. S. Lewis	Rick Warren
William Barclay	Lyle Schaller	Warren Wiersbe	Charles Stanley
Richard P. McBrien	Philip Yancey	Charles Spurgeon	J. Vernon McGee
Karl Rahner	Walter Brueggemann	Eugene Peterson	Max Lucado

two mainline authors (Lewis and Eugene Peterson). Lucado also made the historic black church clergy top ten. The differences in these lists add further weight to the point I made in Chapter 3 that denominational traditions reflect differing interpretive frameworks. With the exception of the similarities in the preferred authors of conservative Protestant and historic black church clergy, what is striking are the differences between these two traditions and the lists of authors favored by Catholic and mainline clergy, who themselves differ considerably in their preferences. Clearly clergy in these traditions draw from rather different "tool kits" as they lead their congregations.

It is worth noting that women authors are conspicuous by their absence. The well-known preacher and Episcopal priest Barbara Brown Taylor barely missed making the top ten for mainline Protestants, and there were also several other women on the lists of Catholic, mainline, and black Protestant clergy; however, not a single woman was mentioned by conservative Protestants. Similarly, no African American authors made the top ten lists — not even for clergy in historic black churches; however, T. D. Jakes, Martin Luther King, Jr., and the poet Maya Angelou were among several black authors receiving mention.

The lists suggest a preference for certain kinds of authors — notably those who write about ministry (including the theology of ministry), spirituality (especially pastoral spirituality), and church leadership. Biblical interpreters are also relatively popular in all four traditions. Of the four, Catholics are most likely to mention theologians among their top ten — for example, Richard McBrien and Karl Rahner. For Protestants, the lists reflect a considerable degree of pragmatism — a focus on ministry practice, especially preaching and church leadership.

Part-Time versus Full-Time Pastors

In Chapter 3 we looked at pastors who worked part time: lay pastors, bivocational pastors, and retired pastors who continue to serve congregations that need their leadership. To compare part- and full-time work hours, I broke the sample by clergy who work less than thirty-five hours per week as parish pastors and those who do so for more than thirty-five hours per week.

Just under one in five of the Catholic priests in our sample worked part-time as pastors (mostly, as noted earlier, in non-parochial ministry positions). They averaged a twenty-eight-hour parish work week, thirty hours fewer than full-time priests. In contrast, slightly more than one-fourth of the Protestant pastors (lay or ordained) were part-time by our definition; they worked twenty-six hours a week on average — half as many hours as their full-time counterparts.

As might be expected full-time Catholic priests spend more hours than part-time priests in all core tasks; however, the difference in parish administration is striking: twenty-one hours for full-time priests versus five hours for part-timers! Pastoral care responsibilities are also significantly higher for full-timers. Protestant differences between full- and part-timers are not quite as striking, but they are similar. For both, the average time spent in preaching and worship is similar, reflecting the fact that these are the tasks (along with weddings and funerals) that part-timers are primarily expected to perform in many small congregations. Otherwise, lay members carry out much of the other work of the congregation while their part-time pastor functions as a kind of chaplain to the congregational family (Rothauge 1995: 7). In the Catholic setting, the part-time priest functions mostly as celebrant of the sacraments, while a lay parish administrator (a nun, deacon, or lay pastoral minister) will carry out most of the other parish tasks.

Church Size and Workloads

His or her congregation's size also affects the pastor's workload. As I just observed, many small congregations utilize part-time or bivocational leaders. This is reflected in the fewer hours that they work per week, on average, than the full-time pastors of larger churches. But how else might size affect workload? Table 4.4 on page 112 shows both hours spent in specific tasks and in total hours worked by congregational size. I have broken the table between Catholics and Protestants, since most Catholic parishes are far larger than most Protestant congregations.

There were few small Catholic parishes in our sample, and some were served by priests who also had other responsibilities outside the parish. Judging from the hours these priests reported spending in denominational affairs, they probably work in the chancery office or some other diocesan position. Neither worship, pastoral counseling, nor administration occupies as much time in small parishes as each does in the larger ones in which the priests are much more likely to be full-time. Pastors in medium-sized and large parishes average spending the most time in parish administration, slightly more even than their peers in very large parishes. Those in medium-sized parishes have the longest work weeks, probably because they are less likely to have pastoral assistants.

Protestant pastors of megachurches report spending significantly more time in preaching (including preparation) than those in smaller congregations, probably because of the multiple services of worship at which they preach. They and their peers in large congregations also spend more time in administration than those in small and medium-sized congregations. Overall, as might be expected, a pastor's average total hours worked per week increase as congregational size increases. The total hours figure for small church pastors reflects the presence of a greater number of pastors who work part time in these congregations.

Although our data are not sensitive to substantive differences in what is required in each of the core tasks, Arlin Rothauge (1995), among others, has speculated on how the work of a pastor changes its character with increasing congregational size. The size categories that he uses differ somewhat from ours, but his insights are worth citing and some of them are reflected in Table 4.4. I have already made reference to the pastor of the very small church (fewer than fifty active members, in Rothauge's scheme) who functions as a kind of chaplain to the congregational family. As the congre-

Table 4.4
Median Hours Worked Differentiated by Church Size
for Catholics and Protestants

	(Average Weekly Attendance)			
	Small	Medium	Large	Mega
	(< 100)	(101-350)	(351-1000)	(1000+)
CATHOLIC				
Preaching	4	6	6	5
Worship	1	10	10	10
Teaching	2	2	2	3
Training people for ministry	1	2	1	1
Working to convert others	2	1	1	1
Pastoral counseling	1	5	4	5
Visiting members, sick, and shut-ins	1	3	3	3
Visiting prospective members	0	0	0	0
Administration	6	15	15	11
Congregation meetings	1	3	3	3
Denominational affairs	5	1	1	1
Community/civic affairs	0	2	1	1
Total hours per week	38	69	58	62
PROTESTANT				
Preaching	10	12	11	18
Worship	3	4	5	5
Teaching	4	4	5	5
Training people for ministry	1	2	2	3
Working to convert others	2	2	2	3
Pastoral counseling	2	4	4	5
Visiting members, sick, and shut-ins	3	4	4	3
Visiting prospective members	1	1	1	1
Administration	2	6	8	10
Congregation meetings	1	2	3	4
Denominational affairs	1	1	1	1
Community/civic affairs	1	1	1	1
Total hours per week	43	52	55	59

gation's size increases (to fifty to one hundred fifty active members), the pastor moves to the center of the congregation's life, expected to guide (and often provide) much of the congregation's program. Moving up another level (to one hundred fifty to three hundred fifty active members) adds especially to the administrative or leadership role of the pastor: helping the congregation develop a vision and direction, coordinating its various ministries, ensuring that lay leaders in the congregation have the requisite training to carry out their roles.

Rothauge's final size category (three hundred or more active members) corresponds roughly to what I called large and mega congregations: in these the head pastor functions as a corporate leader of the body, presiding over a massive family, "a symbol of unity and stability in a very complicated congregational life" (p. 31). Other professional staff and lay leaders carry out much of the congregation's programs, with the head pastor spending more time in leading worship and guiding the congregation's overall ministry. For example, in an interview, the pastor of a large conservative Presbyterian congregation described his primary role as guiding the entire congregation through teaching and preaching, while the congregation itself was divided into six "flocks" of one hundred youth and adult members under the guidance of a full-time clergy staff member and two (lay) ruling elders. Together these individuals provide additional teaching, training, and pastoral care to their respective flocks. Although these various size categories and their implications for a pastor's role are not to be taken as definitive, they suggest how congregational size affects the pastor's work.

Other Factors Affecting a Pastor's Workweek

Earlier studies of clergy time use (May et al. 1934; Blizzard 1985) reported mixed findings when they compared urban and rural clergy. May and his associates found no difference in the workweeks of the two groups of clergy; however, Blizzard found differences in what I have called pastoral care and administrative work. In each case, urban pastors spent more time in these activities than rural. Similarly, our data show statistically significant differences between rural and urban pastors. In all areas of pastoral work, urban pastors reported spending more time than their rural counterparts. This is especially true for administrative tasks, where urban pastors spend twice as many hours as rural pastors. Overall, urban pastors work longer workweeks than rural (fifty-two versus forty-three hours respectively). The two groups are roughly similar, however, in reports of the amount of time devoted to prayer and meditation and in reading other than for sermons.

Comparing male and female Protestant pastors, I found that both groups reported working approximately the same number of hours per week, but spending those hours differently. Women pastors generally allocate a slightly higher proportion of time to pastoral care and administering the work of the church and less time in preaching and preparing for worship. These differences, with only minor exceptions, were present regardless of church size.

Of course, the many figures I have presented here must be read as reflecting the pastor's *typical* week. There are without doubt many days and weeks that are far from typical. Unanticipated events regularly occur to interrupt routines: unexpected telephone calls, maintenance needs, members who drop by the church on a weekday "just to say hello" and stay for an hour or more, counselees who arrive unexpectedly with personal crises, sudden illnesses or deaths. One pastor told us of trying to leave town after his Sunday services for a five-day retreat. Late Saturday evening, a member called asking for a letter of recommendation for her son and insisting that she have the letter by Monday. So, he said, "I had to get that done. I arrived at the retreat center stressed out, hot, and sweaty." While interruptions of routine are by no means restricted to clergy, remembering them reminds us that a pastor's work rarely resembles the typical week described in the time-use tables. Clearly, however, clergy spend more than "one hour a week" on the job, and the long hours that many work make them ready candidates for burnout.

Pastors' Views about Their Performance

After pastors had reported their time allocation, we asked them to indicate the three tasks that they believe they do best and the three in which they believe they need most improvement. The overall rankings are shown in Table 4.5. Regardless of how I broke their responses — for example, by denominational tradition, congregational size, years in ministry, or gender — the top three were the same. Preaching was by far the task that all clergy

Table 4.5
Clergy Ranking of Tasks That They Do Best and Those on Which They Need Most Improvement (Ranked Highest to Lowest)

Do Best	Need Improvement
Preaching	Converting others to the faith
Teaching people about faith	Administering the congregation's work
Worship leadership	Visiting prospective members
Pastoral counseling/spiritual direction	Training people for their ministry
Visiting members, sick, and shut-ins	Visiting members, sick, and shut-ins
Administering the congregation's work	Promoting the congregation's vision
Promoting the congregation's vision	Pastoral counseling/spiritual direction
Converting others to the faith	Involvement in community affairs
Training people for their ministry	Involvement in denominational affairs
Visiting prospective members	Preaching
Involvement in denominational affairs	Teaching people about faith
Attending congregational meetings	Attending congregational meetings
Involvement in community affairs	Worship leadership

believe they do best (whether their lay members would agree is a question I can't answer!). The second and third best tasks were worship leadership and teaching,

The table also lists the tasks in which clergy reported that they need to improve their performance. Overall, the top three needing improvement are converting others to the faith, administering the congregation's work, and visiting prospective members. Training people for ministry (which I interpret to mean equipping members for their ministry as lay people) was a close fourth.

Across various groups, however, the top three lists differed somewhat. Conservative Protestants ranked converting others as the task in which they most need to improve, and it was second for mainline Protestants. For Catholic priests, visiting members, especially those who are sick or homebound, was the task most needing improvement. I suspect this to be an example of a task in which improvement means being able to give it more time rather than improve the quality of the visit, since most Catholic parishes are quite large and often understaffed. For pastors in historic black churches the number one perceived need for improvement was in preaching, probably reflecting the high level of importance attributed to preaching in African American church life.

Age-Group Focus of the Pastor's Ministry

Another way of viewing the work of pastors is to ask about the age groups on which clergy place greatest emphasis in their ministry. We asked, "In your ministry in the congregation, with which two age groups do you spend most of your time working?" In some respects their answers to this were no doubt situational. Some congregations and settings are mostly made up of one or two major age groups — for example, small rural communities where most of the members and community residents are older adults, and most younger adults and their families have moved to settings where job opportunities are more readily available. In many cases, however, there is a range of age groups present in the congregation and its surrounding community. In larger congregations, full- or part-time staff members other than the pastor often have responsibility for working with particular age groups. Even with these caveats, how pastors focus their time among particular age groups seems likely to be important for the congregation's life, especially its future. For example, a recent Hartford Seminary study of congregations reports that congregations with high levels of youth involvement are also the ones more likely to be growing (Roozen 2001). This finding does not indicate how much the pastor is involved with youth in these congregations, but it provides an example of the importance of congregational attention to particular age groups.

In Figure 4.1, I show the clergy's reports of the age groups to which they typically devote the largest amount of ministry time. Because they were asked to choose the *two* groups on which they put the greatest focus, percentages do not add to 100 percent. They show, however, where the clergy's priorities lie relative to the different groups.

There are important differences among the traditions. Mainline Protestant pastors' focus on middle-aged and older adults is the highest of the four groups. Catholic priests are not far behind in working with older adults, but they also focus on children more than do the other traditions. Among the four groups, black pastors report giving the greatest attention to married and single young adults and to youth. Conservative Protestants'

Figure 4.1
Age Groups with Whom Clergy Spend the Most Time Differentiated by Denominational Tradition

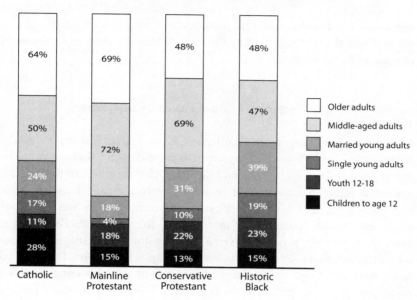

focus is greatest on middle-aged adults and lowest on older adults, but they also pay significant attention to married young adults and youth.

In part, these denominational differences reflect the average age of members of their respective congregations. In the U.S. Congregational Life Survey (which had too few black congregations for separate analysis), the median age of conservative Protestant laity is the youngest at fifty-one. The Catholic median is fifty-three, and for mainline Protestants it is fifty-seven. The question that these differences raise is whether the focus of the pastor's ministry on particular age groups is simply a response to the dominant age group(s) in the congregation, or whether focusing on particular groups tends to encourage the growth of these groups, sometimes at the expense of others. I suspect that the answer is that either or both may be the case, but, as I noted above, I also suspect that the way pastors focus their time is likely to be consequential for a congregation's future. This seems especially important when we recall the comment in Chapter 2 that young adults (single and married) currently number over 113,000,000 in the U.S. population, twice the number in the Baby Boom generation; yet, single young adults receive little attention from many pastors, especially in mainline Protestantism.

Other factors — congregational size, location, and the pastor's age — are also related to how pastors focus their ministry with particular age groups, but the patterns within the four traditions were not consistent enough to be easily interpreted.

Lay Perceptions of the Pastor's Core Work

Let's now look at things from another angle: How do lay members view the pastor's core work? What do they count as important for their pastor to be doing? In the U.S. Congregational Life Survey, lay members of the congregations completed a questionnaire about the congregation and their involvement in it. As I have said, the surveyed congregations were the congregations whose pastors we interviewed for *Pulpit & Pew*. In the questionnaire, members were given a list of pastoral roles and asked to indicate the two that they considered as the pastor's main roles. I aggregated individual responses to get an average percent of each congregation's membership choosing each of the nine roles. The results are shown in Table 4.6. Though there are some differences in the list of roles from the one given to clergy, it is sufficiently similar to allow us to see how laity view the pastor's roles and compare their views with the pastor's priorities.[11]

Several points are worth noting. All differences between the mainline and conservative Protestant rankings are statistically significant except for the role of providing vision for the congregation. The differences are especially striking for the two roles chosen most. Worship leadership (including administering the sacraments) is the top priority for mainline laity, while teaching people about faith takes first place for conservative Protestants. The differences are quite large. Why this is the case can only be a matter of speculation. It may simply be that mainline laity view the pastor's worship leadership as more important than his or her teaching role,

---

11. The U.S. Congregational Life Survey did not ask these questions of Catholics; thus they are not included in the table. As noted previously, the number of congregations of historic black denominations was too few to be broken out separately. The latter are combined with mainline or conservative responses, according to their denomination.

Table 4.6
Lay Members' Views of the Importance of the Pastor's Main Roles Differentiated by Denominational Tradition

	Mainline Protestant	Conservative Protestant
Conducting worship	66.2%	43.7%
Teaching about faith	48.2%	64.5%
Training people for ministry	7.2%	16.2%
Converting others to faith	7.0%	20.9%
Administering work of congregation	18.6%	9.9%
Visitation/counseling	42.2%	37.0%
Involvement in wider community	11.8%	4.9%
Providing vision for congregation's ministry	13.2%	12.6%
Offering prayer/serving as a spiritual guide	24.5%	35.5%

with just the opposite true for conservative laity. But it may also result from the U.S. Congregational Life questionnaire's omission of preaching from the list of pastoral roles.[12] Perhaps mainline Protestants considered worship leadership to include preaching, while conservatives may have considered preaching to be a component of teaching, which they value quite highly. When we gave a list of pastoral roles to our focus group participants, a pastor in a conservative Presbyterian church told us that he could not separate preaching from teaching. Indeed Presbyterian pastors historically have been designated as "teaching elders" in distinction from lay "ruling elders." Some senior pastors of conservative congregations in other traditions also think of themselves as "teaching pastors" and refer to their sermon in their church bulletins as "teaching." Whatever the case, mainline and conservative laity differ significantly in the importance they give to the pastor's leadership in worship and teaching.

With regard to other pastoral tasks, mainline laity give more weight to pastoral care roles (visiting members and counseling) than conservatives do, while conservative laity are more likely to look to the pastor as a

---

12. The researchers for the U.S. Congregational Life survey did not include preaching because they believed that it would not discriminate well — that everyone would choose it as one of their top two roles, thus reducing the chance for other roles also to be selected as important.

spiritual role model. Almost twice as many mainline as conservative laity consider administration a main role of the pastor, while the latter are almost three times more likely to view converting others to the faith as a main role than their mainline counterparts.

The lack of a question about preaching in the lay lists also makes it difficult to compare lay and clergy responses; but since the time that pastors report spending on worship and preaching combined is quite large for both traditions, lay priorities seem reasonably well aligned with pastors' priorities. The relative weight that each group gives to pastoral care activities (visiting, counseling, etc.) is also similar; although mainline laity give these activities more importance than conservatives, and mainline pastors spend more time in these activities than conservative clergy. Few laity give much weight to the pastor's administrative tasks, and though they are also not high in the clergy's time allocation, I suspect that they take considerably more time than laity recognize. Although neither mainline laity nor clergy give high priority to converting others to the faith, conservative laity view this to be much more important than their pastors' reported time allocation reflects. Laity and pastors are relatively similar in the low priority they assign to the pastor's community involvement. The clergy survey had no question about the pastor's role as a spiritual role model; however, this task is relatively important in the eyes of both groups of laity, especially conservatives.

What to make of these comparisons? Clergy sometimes complain that their members have little comprehension of what their work involves. These data do not bear this out. With a few exceptions, lay priorities for their pastor's core work are not substantively different from those of clergy as reflected in their time allocation. The mainline-conservative comparisons do, however, reflect the significant differences in interpretive frameworks used by the two groups to which I called attention in Chapter 3. Put another way, the two Protestant traditions operate from different theological perspectives that shape the cultures that they produce. Their congregational "clay jars" reflect these different emphases.

Time Away from the Job

Although the major concern in this chapter has been the work of pastoral leaders, especially the way that it breaks down temporally, I want here to look briefly at how they spend their non-work time. As I noted previously, taking overall hours spent on the job into account, pastors in 2001 seemed to be doing somewhat better in establishing boundaries between work and non-work time than their predecessors. Still, the issue of time-use boundaries is important, and many clergy have difficulty with it. As an Indianapolis-area pastor said,

> My predecessor was a guy who, whenever he went on vacation, if somebody died — I don't care what the family plans were — he'd always return for the funeral. I always have somebody who's going to fill in for me, and I make sure they don't know how to get in touch with me, because I'm not coming back. I need the time. . . . But I would say that many pastors cannot draw appropriate boundaries. They're on call 24/7. And, you know, they've got to make rotten spouses.
>
> The spouse can get tired of living in a fishbowl atmosphere . . . [and] clergy tend to be people pleasers, other-directed folk who don't always know their own internal wants, needs, and desires. . . . I've had my wife tell me and I've had many other wives of clergy say: "He's never around. You know, if the bell rings it's like the old fire horse: He just goes off. And if he only would put one tenth of the energy into understanding and empathizing with what's going on inside the family that he does with everybody else, we'd have a great marriage. He's there for everybody else and not there for me."

Regardless of whether we agree that pastoral boundaries should be as high as this pastor implies that they should be, clearly boundary-setting between work and non-work time is an important issue.

Our survey sheds some light on how pastors spend their non-work time and how much time they devote to family or personal time. Table 4.7 shows the median hours in each activity by denominational tradition. I have grouped pastors in the three Protestant traditions together since, with minor exceptions, they are mostly alike. Taken together they differ in important ways from Catholic priests. As was true for the categories for work-related activities, the categories in the table are rather blunt instruments. That is, they fail to capture the texture of the activities or differences in what they may mean for various pastors. Nonetheless, several important differences are evident in the table.

Obviously, many differences between Catholics and Protestants can be

Table 4.7
Median Hours per Week Spent in Non-Work Activities
by Catholic and Protestant Clergy

	Catholic	Protestant
Surfing the Web	1	1
Family life (other than meals)	0	10
Household chores	2	4
Physical exercise for health	2	2
Recreation (other than exercise)	4	2
Commuting to work	0	1
Eating out with friends	2	2
Total hours per week non-work activities	18	27

The amount shown for each individual activity is the median hours spent in that activity. The amount shown for the total hours spent in non-work activities was derived by summing the actual hours per week for each activity and then computing the median for the total hours spent. For each tradition, the latter figure is larger than the sum of the medians for the individual activities.

explained by the simple fact of marital status. Since priests are not married, they reported no time spent in family life, while married Protestant clergy, male and female, averaged ten hours a week. Even single Protestant clergy reported spending an average of three hours a week in family activities.

Priests also spend less time than Protestants in household chores — probably because many parish rectories employ a housekeeper or a cook (or both); and, because rectories are often located next door to the parish church, there is little or no commute for priests. Priests also report spending more time than Protestant pastors in recreation other than for exercise. Nevertheless, that priests spend, on average, considerably fewer hours in non-work activities is cause for concern — especially given their high overall workload (fifty-three hours per week).

Breaking down the non-work time for the three Protestant traditions, the major significant difference is that pastors in historic black denominations report spending no hours exercising for health or in recreational activities. This, too, is cause for concern, especially since, like priests, historic black church pastors also report a high number of work hours per week (a median of fifty-five).

Another finding related to non-work activities is worth noting:

When asked whether they took a regular day off, seven of ten pastors responded in the affirmative; however, just under half of historic black church pastors, whether bivocational or not, do so. This survey suggests that many of these pastors have difficulty protecting their days off. Pastors who report that they regularly take a day off spend roughly the same number of hours per week at work and in non-work activities as those who take no regular day off.

Time Use, Health, and Stress

Whether clergy take time away from the job for family and self-care, and how they manage the boundary between work and non-work, are of considerable importance for their own health, their family's health, and the overall health of the church. The bishops of the Evangelical Lutheran Church in America asked about healthy pastors and gave the following description:

> Healthy pastors [have] healthy relationships including good marriages, supportive spouses and family structures, and good relationships with their congregations. They have a passion and vision for ministry, the ability to handle stress and seek balance in life, the recognition of boundaries, both personal and professional, and the ability to manage and be accountable. They are alive spiritually with a significant prayer and devotional life. . . . Healthy pastors have mentors and collegial relationships, pursue lifelong learning, and feel valued. They take vacations and sabbaticals. Finally, they have a good sense of humor.[13]

I agree with the bishops' statement, and our survey gives an opportunity to look briefly at the relation of time use to health. In the national survey, we included several health-related items and used them to construct three additive scales:[14] one measuring physical health and its impact on the

13. Gwen Wagstrom Halaas, M.D., "Ministerial Health and Wellness, 2002: Evangelical Lutheran Church in America" (Chicago: Division of Ministry, ELCA Board of Pensions), 10. The full report is available at http://www.elca.org/dm/health/healthReport2002.pdf. Dr. Halaas has put her findings into a short but helpful book for clergy, *The Right Road: Life Choices for Clergy* (Minneapolis: Fortress, 2004).

14. They include ten items from a standard health assessment scale, "The SF-12," that

pastor's work; a second measuring emotional health and its effect on her or his work; and a third measuring the pastor's positive feelings and energy. In each case pastors were asked to rate themselves on the items for the preceding four weeks. The majority of pastors in the survey scored high on the three scales; however, Catholic priests were significantly less positive about their physical health, and mainline Protestants scored lowest on the scale measuring positive feelings and energy. I will consider these findings in more detail in Chapter 6. Here I look at their relation to time use.

Giving support to the bishops' assumption that healthy pastors have a lively spiritual life, there are significant positive correlations between time spent in prayer and meditation and the scales measuring both energy and emotional health. Time spent exercising for one's health is positively related to physical health, but not to the other two. Overall, the total time spent in non-work activities is positively related to the feelings and emotional health scales.

There is also one other important health-related measure from the pastors — their body mass index (BMI).[15] This is a standard measure used to estimate whether a person is underweight, normal, overweight, or obese. The BMI has been much in the news in recent years in connection with considerable concern about obesity in the U.S. population generally. How do clergy fare? The answer is not very well, though not much worse than the U.S. population as a whole. On the basis of standards set for

---

we used with permission. We initially had included all twelve items; however, with the need to cut items from the overall survey, we omitted two. By means of a factor analysis, I was able to construct three additive scales from the ten items. One scale measures positive feelings in the past four weeks (felt calm and peaceful, had a lot of energy, felt worn out). The reliability coefficient (Cronbach's *alpha*) for the three-item scale is .76. A second scale measures self-assessed emotional health in the past four weeks (able to do less work because of emotional health, did less careful work because of emotional health, felt downhearted and depressed). The reliability coefficient for this scale is .82. The third scale measures the pastor's physical health and its impact on her or his work (self-assessed physical health, less work because of physical health, less careful work because of physical health). The reliability coefficient for this scale is .78. I reversed the scoring on the physical and emotional health scales in order to make high scores positive, comparable to the positive feelings scale.

15. The body mass index (BMI) is a measure of body fat based on height and weight that applies to both adult men and women. Being overweight or obese is related to many significant health problems such as, for example, high blood pressure, high cholesterol, heart attacks, type 2 diabetes, and osteoarthritis. BMI standards for children and youth are calculated differently from those for adults.

adults by the National Institutes of Health, 78 percent of all clergy are either overweight (48 percent) or obese (30 percent). Correlating BMI scores with the three scales measuring health, I found a strong negative relationship between being overweight or obese and pastors' view of their physical health. There were weak negative correlations with the other two scales. Commenting on clergy health and lifestyle issues, one pastor said, ruefully, "There is something incongruous to me about a clergy person who is 50 pounds overweight and smokes like a chimney. Our bodies are the temple of the Holy Spirit" (Swicegood n.d.: 6).

In addition to the health and time-use relationships, there are also significant correlations of work and non-work time with various stress-related items: The more hours per week one works, the more likely one is to complain of stress due to congregational challenges, report that work prevents spending time with one's children, say that one's spouse expresses resentment over the time the work of ministry takes, and say that it is difficult to have a private life apart from the clergy role. The relationship between these same stress-related items is the reverse for the total time one spends in non-work activities. The more one is able to take time away from the job, the less the stress.

These are important findings that need to be taken with great seriousness by clergy, their congregations, and the denominations and other institutions that support them. It is encouraging to note that a number of denominations, in addition to the Lutherans, are beginning to take the health of their clergy with great seriousness.[16]

Conclusion

We have seen that at a general level, the core work of clergy can in large part be described under the classic rubrics used to characterize the pastoral office down through the years: celebrant of the sacraments, preacher and teacher (including providing pastoral care), and overseer of congregational life. In faithfulness to their calling, pastors work to produce congregational cultures through which God's extraordinary power is revealed. They aim not only to help their members find meaning, support, comfort,

---

16. For a review of several of these programs as well as resources that address them, see Wells (2002).

and empowerment in their personal lives, but also to lead them in practices that are faithful to God's purposes for the church. These tasks continue to be the constants, regardless of denominational tradition, church size, location, or clergy characteristics. Yet it would be an error to assume that there has been no change in the understanding of these tasks over the years, that all traditions interpret them similarly, or that the religious, social, and cultural contexts in which clergy work have not affected the meaning and importance attached to these roles by clergy and the laity with whom they minister. How effective they are in those tasks is an issue that we are unable to assess very well in a survey, although in the next chapter I try to provide some clues regarding effectiveness.

But it is not just what clergy do in their work that is important, but also how they use their time away from work and how they establish boundaries between the two. Not being consumed by one's work and the ability, within reason, to maintain boundaries have important consequences for personal and familial health. I will return to some of these issues in Chapter 6 when we consider the degree to which pastors sustain their commitment to ordained ministry and their satisfaction with various aspects of their calling.

Chapter 5

How Do Pastors Lead?
Leadership and Cultural Production

"Even if you're on the right track, you'll get run over if you just sit there."

Will Rogers

When pastors preach or teach, when they preside over the celebration of the Eucharist, when they respond to a family dealing with the death of a loved one, even when they are engaged one-on-one with members in pastoral counseling or spiritual direction, they are involved in the work of leadership. In our culture we tend to associate "leadership" with the administrative work of a pastor, and in this chapter we will focus a great deal on that kind of leadership, but there are many ways in which clergy lead as they articulate, both in words and symbols, the church's core beliefs and values in relation to the issues and challenges that the congregation or its members face. Indeed, everything that a pastor does involves (or should involve) leadership, broadly conceived, by helping both the congregation and individual members grow in faithfulness to the gospel in light of the issues they face corporately and individually in the context in which they find themselves. Recalling the cultural diamond that we discussed earlier in this book, we can see that in the act of leadership, each of its four facets — the pastor, the Bible and church tradition, lay members, and the social world of the congregation — comes into play in shaping the congregation's culture.

Elsewhere (Carroll 1998: 167) I have compared a pastoral leader's entrance into a congregation to the experience of a new lead actress or actor who enters a play that is ongoing and at least partly open-ended, a play whose script is not fixed, but rather constrained only by the story that has unfolded thus far, the set and setting, and the capacities of the other actors. The new lead's role is to interact with the others in shaping the ongoing story. In congregational terms, the cast of characters includes members — past and present — and former pastors. The congregation's story is also a part of the larger story of God's dealings with humankind and the mission of the church. The congregation's existing local story and the larger story of God's purposes set limits on how the congregation's ongoing story will unfold, but they do not determine the story or seal it off from new possibilities, new twists and turns as the new pastor and current members continue to shape the congregation's story, producing its culture as they go and sometimes taking it in a new direction altogether.[1]

This image of a play is helpful because it reminds us that leadership — more specifically the pastor's institutional leadership — is especially concerned with direction setting: helping a congregation to gain a suitable vision and direction for its ongoing drama or story and then to develop programs and practices to embody that vision. It also includes equipping lay members for their involvement in the story. In the preceding chapter, we saw that pastors spend an average of thirteen hours a week in various administrative tasks, and this is the category into which institutional leadership would typically fall.

A solid understanding of leadership is essential, given that rapid change has become characteristic of our society. Congregations, like other organizations, are regularly encountering challenges to their long-held assumptions and cherished traditions. Church leaders in today's world will need to know how to respond, for example, to differences between younger and older church members regarding how worship should be conducted. They will need to know how to respond to the impact of a declining economy in which local industries close or move their operations elsewhere. Especially in urban centers, they will need to deal with the rise

1. See R. Stephen Warner's extended case study of a Presbyterian congregation in California in which a succession of pastoral leaders brought change, but one in particular helped to redirect the formerly liberal congregation along a new evangelical path (Warner 1988: especially 156ff.). Omar McRoberts (2003: 114-115) reports a similar transformation in a United Methodist congregation.

in gang-related crime and violence by unemployed youth. They will need to know what to say to their congregations about a new Islamic Center being built down the street to serve the needs of a burgeoning Muslim population. They will need to be able to deal with the increasing encroachment on Sunday mornings of soccer leagues and other sports, and to the increase in the number of women who work outside the home and the attendant impact on volunteer time in congregations or elsewhere. And they will need to do all this in a nation still wary and on-edge following the terror attacks of 9/11.

If a congregation is to respond successfully to such changes, especially if it is to respond in ways that are faithful to the gospel, it needs good pastoral leadership. Sociologist Nancy Ammerman emphasized the importance of leadership in a study of congregational responses to their changing communities:

> What seems far more important than material resources for the survival of these voluntary organizations are the human resources that make it possible for change to be imagined and planned for. Someone has to see the connections between the congregation as it now exists and the congregation as it might someday exist. Someone has to imagine that it might remain spiritually and socially rewarding for its participants. Such human resources involve both the clergy and the laity, both those who provide leadership and those who must lend their energies to any effort for change. While lay leadership is important, pastors emerged . . . as critical players in the process of change (Ammerman 1997b: 326).

Understood this way, leadership is an activity rather than a particular position or set of characteristics that a leader might have. Both clergy and laity are typically involved in leading; nonetheless, as Ammerman emphasizes, pastors have a key role to play. Where the congregations she studied failed to adapt to their changing communities, it was often because they lacked pastoral leadership, and the pastors themselves often confessed to a lack of necessary leadership skills to face the challenges the congregations were experiencing. Some were unable and others unwilling "to undertake the difficult (and often conflictual) work of dislodging old routines" (1997: 327).

Of course, it should be acknowledged that congregations have characteristics that make leadership — even of the most skilled pastors — difficult. In contrasting congregations with denominations, R. Stephen Warner reminds us that "congregations are typically groups of amateurs spending disproportionate time on activities that are hard to define, whereas denominations will have professionals devoted to articulated goals" (Warner 1994: 61). Furthermore, church members often fear and resist change. This is hardly surprising or new; writing in 1935, sociologists H. Paul Douglass and Edmund deS. Brunner reflected on research that had asked laity about the kind of minister they wanted. Douglass and Brunner offered a notably pessimistic assessment of what the research suggested about congregational resistance to leadership: "What the churches want in a minister is essentially a successful salesman for their enterprise. A striking feature of the analysis of the ministerial qualifications desired, is the virtual absence from them of any doctrinal specifications. Still more significant is the fact that the actual demand for ministers virtually assumes the maintenance of the religious *status quo*. It is leadership in things as they are, an adaptability to conditions as they stand, rather than innovative or prophetic leadership that is demanded" (1935: 105). This being the case, it is not surprising that many pastors have a difficult time helping congregations develop a vision for their future and move toward it.

This chapter examines various facets of pastoral leadership, especially of institutional leadership, and it makes several claims about such leadership:

- First, that having a proactive leadership style that involves clergy and laity working together in developing a congregation's life and direction matters for the congregation's effectiveness;
- Second, that challenges that come from the congregation's context require that congregational leaders plan for the congregation's direction rather than simply keeping things going, as seems to be the case for a significant minority of pastors and congregations;
- Third, that it is important to give attention to theological warrants or rationales for congregational programs and practices in addition to asking what people need or desire;
- Fourth, that a changing society requires innovation on the part of leaders, though not at the expense of neglecting the wisdom of church tradition, both local and ecumenical;
- Finally, that both formal and informal bases of authority are necessary for effective pastoral leadership, but especially the latter.

The Pastor's Leadership Style

How do pastors lead? What leadership style do they use in working together with lay leaders in setting a direction for the congregation and making program decisions? Obviously, not all pastors lead in the same way, nor are the same leadership styles suitable for all congregations. Different occasions often call for different styles. As a North Carolina pastor told us, "Good leaders, lay or ordained, are capable of adapting their leadership styles to what the situation requires. Leadership when someone is dying, or with the family of someone that has just died, is different from leadership when you're at the head of the Martin Luther King Day march." Likewise, different contexts call for different leader responses. An effective leader, said an Indiana pastor, takes into account "the context in which one finds one's self, and that changes. That's a kind of floating target . . . all the way from highly urban settings to tiny rural settings."

While I strongly agree that a pastor's leadership style must vary with the needs and challenges of particular contexts, it seems likely that most pastors have a dominant style, especially when it comes to helping a congregation set its direction; thus, our survey listed several ways in which leadership might be exercised in a congregation, ranging from a "top-down" style in which the leader makes most decisions and expects the congregation to follow, to an opposite extreme in which laity set the direction and the pastor simply aids and abets the implementation of their decisions.

What do the pastors say is their preferred or dominant style? The choices are shown in Figure 5.1 on page 132. All but the first style emphasize some form of shared leadership — reflecting what, as we saw in Chapter 1, has been a dominant emphasis in Catholicism at least since Vatican II and in Protestantism's concurrent renewed emphasis on the priesthood of all believers. Shared leadership also reflects American society's generally egalitarian ethos. The pastor's leadership role in the three shared leadership styles (Styles 2 through 4) moves from a more proactive one to styles that are more reactive or, at best, modestly interactive. Given these trends in the church and in American society at large, it is not surprising that the preferred (and socially desirable) style, chosen by over seven of ten clergy, is the second: a proactive style on the part of the pastor, who inspires and encourages lay decision making but is willing to take action on his or her own when necessary. Only a small minority of pastors — just over 5 per-

Figure 5.1
Pastors' Self-Described Leadership Style

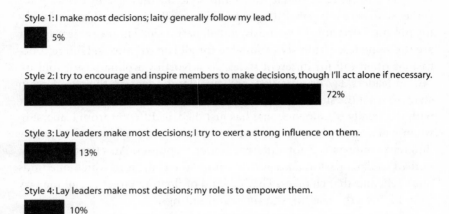

Style 1: I make most decisions; laity generally follow my lead.

5%

Style 2: I try to encourage and inspire members to make decisions, though I'll act alone if necessary.

72%

Style 3: Lay leaders make most decisions; I try to exert a strong influence on them.

13%

Style 4: Lay leaders make most decisions; my role is to empower them.

10%

cent — chose the top-down style (Style 1), making most decisions and expecting laity to follow. The third and fourth styles, which give primacy to lay initiative, were distant second and third choices.

In comparing the four style choices by denominational tradition, the preference for Style 2 remains very strong in all traditions; however, Style 1 is more favored by pastors in conservative Protestant and historic black churches than by Catholic or mainline Protestant pastors. The former groups have had a long tradition of charismatic and often autocratic leaders who make most decisions about congregational life, but for both, it has been a declining style over the years as the level of education of laity and clergy has risen and a preference for greater shared leadership has evolved. As one leader of a historic black church commented, the rising educational level of African American laity has made them increasingly insistent on having an active role in decision-making. The top-down style appears to be anathema to almost all Catholics and mainline Protestants. Other than their strong preference for the second listed style, they are more likely to choose the fourth or empowering style, no doubt reflecting the emphasis on shared ministry that I noted in Chapter 1.

Clergy in small congregations are significantly more likely than others to leave most decision-making to laity (26 percent chose one of the latter two leadership styles). This is not surprising when we recall Arlin Rothauge's view (see Chapter 4) that the pastor in a very small congregation serves essentially as a family chaplain to the one or more extended families that make up the membership. As noted earlier, these pastors are frequently part-time or bivocational, functioning mostly in leading Sunday worship, providing pastoral care to the sick or shut-in, and presiding at weddings or funerals. Lay members assume most of the rest of the congregation's leadership needs.

Do clergywomen differ from men in preferred leadership style? This has been a much-argued topic. In a study of clergy that addressed this issue, Edward Lehman (1993, 2002) described two conflicting answers to the question. Some maintain that women and men differ sharply in their approach to ministry, with men basically emphasizing a more top-down, power-over-people approach. Others, in contrast, maintain that clergy of both sexes today practice a more inclusive, empowering leadership style and that any difference between their styles is probably spurious. Lehman found some support for both perspectives: The clergywomen in his study did report preference for an empowering style more than the men, but he found that much of women's actual ministry practice in a number of pastoral tasks was not significantly different from that of men.[2] That, in effect, is what the clergy responses to our survey suggest — both for time spent in various pastoral tasks, as we saw in Chapter 4, and now in preferred style: The majority of women and men favor the second style, which, like the third and fourth styles, seeks to include laity in planning and decision-making. Yet, echoing what Lehman found, three of ten clergywomen favor the fourth style of leading and view their role primarily as one of empowering laity to implement decisions that the laity have made. In contrast, fewer than 10 percent of clergymen choose the latter style. These differences hold regardless of church size.

Thus, despite the differences among clergy, their overwhelming choice is the second style, with smaller groups preferring the third and fourth styles — all three emphasizing some form of shared decision-making and leadership. Not surprisingly, our focus groups also confirmed this dominant emphasis: Over and over clergy told us that good pastoral leadership involves a willingness to share ministry with laity. In one exercise

2. See also Zikmund et al. (1998: 50-69) for a discussion of these issues. This study found less difference in male and female styles than we found.

we asked participants to draw a picture of their conception of good ministry; their drawings almost invariably reflected a shared ministry perspective. A comment by a pastor in southern California can stand for the many that were similar: "I play the role of pastor as a player-coach. I see myself in ministry alongside the people, and yet empowering them to be better and do what they can, and figure out what God has empowered them to do, and how they can do it. I'm on the team with them. I'm not removed from it. . . . However, I'm gifted and have certain talents to be able to help harness them and liberate them . . . , so they are expanding their sphere of influence in terms of reaching other people, and teaching, and living out Christ [in their lives], and allowing others to see Christ, and bringing them to Christ." His comment recognizes the important contribution that clergy bring to congregational leadership — their distinctive gifts and competence — along with a concern to involve and empower laity to share in the task.

Lay Views of Pastoral Leadership Styles

Do lay members in the pastors' congregations also share this egalitarian view? Figure 5.2 uses data from the U.S. Congregational Life Survey to show lay members' views of their pastor's leadership style compared with the pastor's preferred style.[3] The wording of the question for the laity was slightly different from that for the pastors, but the meanings are essentially similar.[4] Like the findings for clergy, the typical lay view was that their pastor's style is one of inspiring members to action — the second style. But in spite of their relative agreement, significantly fewer laity than clergy said that this is the pastor's dominant style — 49 percent for laity compared with 75 percent for pastors. In contrast, considerably more laity than clergy believed that their pastor uses a "take charge" style. Almost 20 percent of

3. The percentages for pastors in Figure 5.2 do not exactly reflect those reported in Figure 5.1. Figure 5.2 reports only those pastors for whom we also have comparable data from lay members of their congregations. The laity percentages are the average percent of laity in each congregation responding.

4. The U.S. Congregational Life Survey's four leadership categories were: (1) Leadership that tends to take charge; (2) Leadership that inspires people to take action; (3) Leadership that acts on goals that people have been involved in setting, and (4) Leadership where the people start most things. Attenders were asked to choose the one that best described the style of leadership of their pastor, minister, or priest.

Figure 5.2
Comparison of Clergy's Preferred Style with Lay Views of Their Pastor's Style

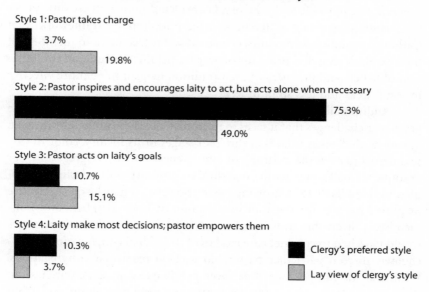

Style 1: Pastor takes charge

3.7%

19.8%

Style 2: Pastor inspires and encourages laity to act, but acts alone when necessary

75.3%

49.0%

Style 3: Pastor acts on laity's goals

10.7%

15.1%

Style 4: Laity make most decisions; pastor empowers them

10.3%

3.7%

◼ Clergy's preferred style

◻ Lay view of clergy's style

laity said this is their pastor's preferred style, compared with only 4 percent of the clergy! Clearly a significant number of clergy come across to their lay members as top-down leaders whatever their intentions to the contrary. It is likely that the emphasis in recent years on shared ministry has been so strong that some pastors find it difficult to believe, much less to acknowledge, that they come across to their lay members as practicing a top-down leadership style. Correctly or incorrectly, however, a significant number of laity perceive that the pastor is the one who makes most decisions about the congregation's life and ministry. As we shall see in the next section, this is not always negative.

Leadership Style and Congregational Effectiveness

Does the pastor's leadership style matter? Does it make a difference in a congregation's effectiveness? Congregational effectiveness, as I use the term here, is a both a theological and contextual matter. People with different theological perspectives about what God is calling their congregation to be and do will likely also hold different views of what makes a congregation effective in its life and ministry. I considered some of these differences in Chapter 3, especially differences in the interpretative frameworks that Catholics, mainline Protestants, conservative Protestants, and members of historic black churches bring to congregational life. The unique combination of beliefs and practices of each tradition helps it to be more effective in some areas and less so in others.

Additionally, as previously emphasized, a congregation's size, the particular challenges that it faces in its immediate environment or context, as well as challenges it faces at different stages of its history, color the assessment and even the meaning of effectiveness for the congregation. For example, a small congregation in a rural community with a declining population is not likely to be growing in size; however, it may be quite effective in providing care for those in its community, both members and non-members. Given the diversity of congregations and their challenges, we would have had to conduct case studies of individual congregations to adequately discern particular pastors' impact on particular congregations. While this was not possible, it has been possible to gain some purchase on the question from survey data by comparing responses about leadership style with various measures of congregational performance available in the U.S. Congregational Life Survey. The effectiveness measures used are, of course, not the only ones that might have been considered. They are, however, a representative set of factors that have to do with both internal and external congregational functioning. Each, too, may be thought of as an element of the congregational culture that clergy and laity together produce.

Table 5.1 shows correlations between lay perceptions of pastoral leadership style and congregational performance. The correlation coefficients[5] show how one measure varies either positively (ranging from 0 to +1) or negatively (ranging from 0 to -1) when considered in relation to another measure. In this case, our measures are congregational effectiveness and pastoral leadership style. All correlations shown in the table are statistically

5. The correlations shown here and elsewhere in the book are Spearman's Rank Order coefficients. This is a nonparametric version of the Pearson correlation coefficient. It is based on the ranks of the data rather than the actual values. It is appropriate for ordinal data. As with Pearson coefficients, values range from -1 to +1.

Table 5.1
Correlations between Lay Members' Perceptions
of Pastoral Leadership Style and Selected Measures
of Congregational Effectiveness

Pastor's Leadership Style as Lay Members View It:	1	2	3	4
% Church growth in last two years	ns*	.16	-.26	ns
% Who are at least weekly attenders	.13	.24	-.41	-.41
% Who are involved in Sunday school or Bible study	.14	.30	-.45	-.29
% Who are involved in fellowship, clubs, or small groups at church	-.14	.17	.21	.23
% Who are involved in evangelism or outreach activities	.18	.28	-.37	-.31
% Who are involved in church-related social justice and community service	-.30	.15	.11	.19
% Who sense God's presence in worship	-.12	.36	-.31	-.34
% Who have a strong and growing sense of belonging	ns	.37	-.23	-.33
% Helped in daily life by congregational participation	ns	.43	-.55	-.49
% Who strongly believe the church serves its community	.19	.33	-.27	-.32
% Who value congregation's openness to social diversity	-.15	ns	.38	.18
% Whose spiritual needs are strongly being met	ns	.55	-.54	-.48
% Who believe there is clear vision and are committed to it	ns	.45	-.43	-.56
% Who are very excited about the congregation's future	ns	.42	-.38	-.38
% Who feel strongly encouraged to use their gifts	ns	.35	-.27	-.51
% Who give 5% or more to church	.29	ns	-.31	-.34
% Who are aware of major conflict	.22	-.20	ns	.13
% Who say there's good match between pastor and congregation	ns	.67	-.41	-.51

ns = not statistically significant

significant; that is, they would not be likely to have happened by chance at least 95 percent of the time. Of course, it is important to emphasize that *correlation does not imply causation.* It simply indicates a positive or negative relationship between two variables: that is, how they vary together. The strength of the relationship is reflected in the size of the coefficient. I chose to use the laity's view of the pastor's leadership style rather than the pastor' own assessment of her or his style, since the way that laity perceive the pastor's style should be strongly related to their views of other aspects of congregational life.[6]

The table shows mostly strong positive correlations between the majority of the performance measures and the second leadership style: one in which laity believe that the pastor encourages and inspires them to take action. The belief that there is a good match between the pastor and the congregation is especially strong. While not necessarily an indicator of congregational effectiveness, members' belief that there is a good match seems to be an important correlate of other measures of effectiveness. The negative correlation between the second style and awareness of major conflict in the congregation implies the relative absence of such conflict. The other three leadership styles show mixed relationships to effectiveness. There are weak to moderate correlations (some positive, others negative) between several effectiveness measures and the Type 1 leadership style. The strongest include the percent who are involved in the congregation's social justice and community service ministries (negative), percent giving 5 percent or more to the church (positive), and the percentage of members aware of major conflict (a positive correlation indicating a high-conflict congregation). Ironically, a fourth moderate-sized correlation shows a positive relationship of this first style with a belief that the congregation serves its community. Evidently, most members in these churches believe the congregation serves its community but leave involvement to others — perhaps to paid staff members.

Most of the correlations of effectiveness with Styles 3 and 4 are negative except for involvement in fellowship activities and small groups at church, involvement in congregational social justice and community ser-

6. Because of the wording with regard to the clergy's self-assessed leadership style, it was not possible to compute meaningful correlations between the four styles and the effectiveness measures as was done with lay perceptions. When mean scores were computed for the effectiveness measures for each of the clergy leadership styles, there were several statistically significant relationships though not always the same as those with lay perceptions of the pastor's style. This is likely partly due to the differences in wording and partly due, we assume, to differences in how pastors and laity assess the styles. Scatter plots for various effectiveness variables and lay-perceived leadership styles visually confirmed the correlations between the sets of variables. Further research is needed to untangle the differences between lay and clergy perceptions of leadership styles and their relation to effectiveness.

vice activities, and valuing social diversity in the congregation (see note 7). This latter style is also positively correlated with awareness of major conflict — suggesting that the congregation's members are not always in agreement over the goals they have set for themselves.

What to make of these differences? They strongly suggest that where lay members believe that the pastor is exercising proactive leadership, especially by inspiring and encouraging people to take action themselves, congregational effectiveness (as I have measured it) is also generally positive. This is also true to a lesser extent for the "take charge" style of leadership. With either style, lay members seem to sense that the congregation is being led rather than allowed to drift; however, the strong relation of effectiveness with the second style indicates the importance of lay participation in setting the congregation's direction. In contrast, when laity believe that they are the primary initiators and actors, with the clergy playing a supporting role, congregational performance, for the most part, flags.

As I have said, many factors other than pastoral leadership contribute to congregational effectiveness: demographics, available resources, and so forth. In additional analyses, I controlled for these and other factors, but the analyses continued to show the importance of strong, proactive pastoral leadership, especially of the kind that also values shared ministry.[7] To repeat Ammerman's important point about pastoral leadership, "Someone has to see the connections between the congregation as it now exists and

7. I used the statistical technique of multiple regression analysis to consider the effects of several of these factors on our measures of effectiveness. In several instances when other variables were controlled, the relationship between one or the other of the leadership styles and effectiveness was not statistically significant. In every case, however, one or more styles continued to be significantly related to each of the effectiveness measures. The impact of Style 2 was especially strong in every regression analysis. The correlations of Styles 2, 3 and 4 with social justice and community service and with valuing social diversity are especially interesting, since they are among the few measures of effectiveness included in the table that are positively correlated with the third and fourth styles. It is important to say that there were not large numbers of congregations scoring high on either measure, especially the latter. Nevertheless, regression analysis revealed that congregations where members reported involvement in social justice and community service were more likely to be mainline Protestant, located in an urban area, and served by either a woman or African American pastor. Having a pastor with a graduate theological degree was also somewhat important. Catholics and mainline Protestant congregations, especially in urban areas, were more likely to value social diversity as were also congregations served by African American and women pastors (the latter obviously Protestant rather than Catholic). Having a pastor with a graduate theological degree also was predictive.

the congregation as it might someday exist. Someone has to imagine that it might remain spiritually and socially rewarding for its participants" (1997b: 326). And that someone is most often the pastor, whose proactive but shared leadership is critical for faithful and effective congregational ministry in a rapidly changing world.

Leadership Style and Congregational Conflict

As we have just seen, some leadership styles are related to lay reports of major conflict in the congregations. We also asked pastors to report on the presence or absence of conflict, and we asked further about reasons for the conflicts that were reported. The level of clergy-reported conflict is higher in relation to the more proactive Styles 1 and 2. Almost two-thirds (64 percent) of the Style 1 pastors reported some minor conflicts in the past two years, and another 23 percent said that there had been significant or major conflicts that involved members leaving the congregation. Just under half (47 percent) of those who said they practiced Style 2 also reported minor conflicts, with another 21 percent saying that their congregations had experienced significant or major conflict. Just over a third of the Style 3 pastors reported minor conflicts with another 21 percent reporting significant or major conflict. A third of the Style 4 pastors also reported minor conflict; another third reported significant or major conflict.

When pastors were asked about the reasons for the conflicts they reported, the results were especially telling. Regardless of the pastor's style, by far the largest percentage of conflicts (23 percent) had to do with pastoral leadership. The next most frequent was conflict over lay leadership (10 percent). Considering the reasons for conflict in light of the pastor's self-reported style, we found that 36 percent of pastors with the top-down style (Style 1) gave pastoral leadership as the primary reason for the conflict. The style with the second highest percentage of conflicts over pastoral leadership was Style 4, where lay leaders take most initiative (30 percent). In these congregations, lay leadership conflicts were also prevalent (18 percent). The pastor's leadership was the major reason for conflict for approximately 20 percent of the cases for each of the other two styles.

All of this is to further emphasize the importance of leadership and pastoral style. Leadership is critical for congregational effectiveness, but it is not without its costs. Of course, we need to remember that conflict need not be negative for either the pastor or the congregation. A congregation often requires debate and disagreement to clarify its priorities and move forward. Speaking of his present congregation's debates over whether to officially identify itself as welcoming to gay and lesbian persons, an Indiana pastor commented, "A church can be proud of what it is but it can never be complacent. It has to take risks and be open to conflict and stretch itself. My previous congregation was, I felt, too proud of what it was. It never stretched itself. And I just think that's real important, that the leaders have to continually be bringing up issues: what do we need to talk about? Where else do we need to go?" This echoes the philosopher Alasdair MacIntyre's point that any tradition that is truly living will experience conflict from time to time (1984: 221-22), and leadership, whether by the pastor or laity, is essential for such arguments to be productive. To be sure, unresolved conflicts can be destructive, both of congregational life and of pastoral health and commitment, but that is a topic to which we will return later.

Leadership and the Congregation's Direction

Helping a congregation shift directions in the face of change has never been easy. Nonetheless, in recent years denominations and organizational consultants have stressed the importance of congregational planning in response to the rapidity and scope of changes that congregations are experiencing in the world around them. And they have an eager audience: authors who write about pastoral leadership and planning are among the ones that pastors in our survey most often cited as authors whose books they have recently read and who have influenced their ministry.[8]

Given this emphasis on planning as a part of leadership, it was somewhat surprising to find that a significant minority, just over four of ten pastors (44 percent), said that the time that they and their lay leaders spend together is mostly taken up with keeping things going, keeping the congregation functioning. A slight majority, the remaining 56 percent, said that they take time to discuss and define future needs and directions of the congregation. Although the latter received the majority of responses,

8. Mainline and conservative Protestants most often cited Lyle Schaller, a mainline Protestant, and John Maxwell and Rick Warren, both conservative Protestants. Catholics did not list any church planners in their top list (Carroll 2003).

which I find encouraging, the large percentage who say they mainly focus on keeping things going is significant. Like the Alabama pastor who said that although Birmingham is still in the same place, the way to get there has changed, I believe that congregations must give attention to how a changing context requires planning and adaptability if they are to fulfill their calling to be the Body of Christ. What are some of the correlates of congregations that plan for their future or, conversely, focus more on keeping things going?

The congregation's denominational tradition makes a difference. Catholics and mainline Protestant clergy reported in much higher numbers that they regularly discuss their congregation's future direction. Conservative Protestants and those in historic black denominations were roughly evenly split between planning and focusing on keeping things going — conservatives with a slight edge for planning and black clergy giving a slight edge to focusing on keeping things going. Surprisingly, congregational size made no statistically significant difference in whether congregations emphasize planning, although clergy in small rural congregations were almost evenly divided on the matter. Leaders in large congregations were the most likely to report that they regularly discuss the congregation's future needs and directions.

The pastor's self-described leadership style, like his or her denominational tradition, makes a difference in whether or not the congregation stresses planning for its future: Style 1 and Style 3 pastors were more likely to focus on keeping things going. In contrast, Style 2 and Style 4 pastors were considerably more likely to discuss the congregation's future. These relationships are shown in Figure 5.3.

Does it matter whether the congregation plans for its direction or not? We found that in congregations where pastors report planning for the congregation's future, laity are more likely to believe that their congregation has a clear vision for its future, are excited about its future, and believe that the congregation is serving its wider community. In congregations that primarily emphasize keeping things functioning, lay members are significantly more likely to report having a strong sense of belonging; however, at the same time, they also are more likely to report congregational conflict. Again, I must emphasize that other factors than whether a congregation plans for its future also influence these measures of effectiveness, but the relationships that I found make a strong case for lay and clergy leaders regularly discussing and defining their congregation's future needs and direction.

Figure 5.3
Relation of Leadership Styles and the Congregation's Direction

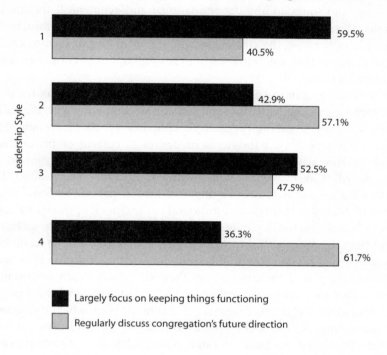

Largely focus on keeping things functioning

Regularly discuss congregation's future direction

Bases for Making Decisions

To what ends do leaders plan? What purposes drive their discussion about directions and future needs? Businesses may be driven in large part by the "bottom line"; political organizations are motivated by the desire to win votes for particular candidates and policies. Churches, on the other hand, must have a different rationale for what they do: they must try at all times to be faithful to the Christian gospel. Put simply, then, the question for churches is, "How does this or that program or congregational practice give expression to our calling to be the Body of Christ?"

One way of trying to answer this question is to reflect theologically about whether and how a particular program or practice seems to mirror the character of Jesus' ministry and teaching or the practices of the early church as we know them from the New Testament. Some churches also consider whether any proposed program or practice is compatible with the traditions of the church — that is, not just the traditions of their own congregation, but longstanding denominational and ecumenical traditions, practices developed by the church in the past as it tried to be faithful to its calling. In either case, the answers sought are normative or theological in character rather than solely pragmatic. They attempt to be consistent with the church's story.

Of course, as in any organization, other rationales also enter the picture, sometimes complementing and sometimes competing with the basic calling of the congregation. For example, churches will ask of any new program, "How will it meet the needs or desires of current or prospective members? How will it affect membership? Will it help the congregation to grow, or will it likely alienate some members? And how will it affect the 'bottom line' — that is, how will it impact the congregation's budget?" Such questions are not in themselves antithetical to the church's primary calling, nor are they always theologically suspect. In his image of clay jars, no less a leader than the Apostle Paul recognized that the church, despite its divine calling, is a very human community. And because their purpose is to bear witness to the gospel, the condition of these clay jars is clearly important: whether they are cracked and leaking or whole and functional matters.

In sociological terms, churches are communities in which the *voluntary* commitment of members — their time, talents, and treasures — must regularly be elicited, nurtured, and strengthened. It is also important to attract new members who bring new human and material resources to the congregation and its mission. Thus, a congregation's human character must be taken seriously, tended, and maintained if it is to be effective. And so a number of other questions arise: How do churches' programs and practices meet the needs and sustain and enrich the lives of members whose participation is voluntary? How do they lead members to a deeper experience of discipleship and empower them to live out their vocations in their daily life? How do they affect the congregation's engagement in ministry and mission? Paying attention to the "earthen" characteristics of the church by clergy and lay leaders is therefore highly important as they make decisions about their congregation's direction and its programs and practices.

Yet an uncritical focus on these kinds of questions can subvert a congregation's calling. Given the increasingly consumer-oriented approach to religious life characteristic of our culture, we must ask, To what extent are a congregation's leaders tempted to focus primarily on what religious "consumers" will buy, with little or no attention to theological criteria? To what extent do leaders become so concerned to attract spiritual seekers that they are willing to play down their congregation's distinctive calling as Christ's body — a charge that has been leveled with some justification at some recent expressions of congregational life and practices such as seeker or mall churches, for example?[9]

Thus the question of rationales for making decisions about programs and practices is an important one in our effort to understand how clergy exercise leadership. We attempted to get at this issue by asking pastors two questions, each of which we will consider in turn.

Theological Warrants vs. Members' Needs and Desires

The first question asked pastors to choose between the following two statements:

- "When deciding on a new program or ministry, we discuss the theological rationale for what we are considering"; or

- "When deciding on a new program or ministry, we primarily take into consideration how well it meets the desires and needs of members or prospective members."

By the way we asked the question, pastors were deliberately forced to choose between the two responses rather than allowed to take a middle position. The two responses are a rough reflection of James MacGregor Burns's distinction between "transformational" and "transactional" leadership. Transactional leaders focus primarily on a *quid pro quo* exchange with their followers, meeting followers' needs in exchange for their participation and support. Transformational leaders, in contrast, exhibit a kind of moral leadership that focuses on "the fundamental wants and needs, aspirations, and values, of the followers" (Burns 1978: 4). Although our forced-choice question obviously oversimplifies matters and obscures

---

9. Elsewhere, I have described and assessed new congregational forms that I have called "post-traditional." I believe they have arisen in part in response to a consumerist approach to religion. They offer "seeker services" that are devoid of traditional Christian symbols and practices and that make few demands on participants. I have considered both their positive attributes and what I believe to be their failings (Carroll 2000).

middle positions between the two types of leadership, we were concerned to discover which takes priority — theological criteria or an effort to address the essentially voluntary character of church participation, perhaps even responding to religious consumerism. What did we learn?

Only 27 percent of the clergy overall said that they give priority to the theological rationale for establishing new programs or ministries. In contrast, 73 percent primarily consider how well the program or ministry will meet the desires and needs of members or prospective members. Differences by denominational traditions were not statistically significant, although mainline Protestant clergy were somewhat less likely than others to consider the theological rationale for new programs or ministries. There was also no significant difference by church size, or by the pastor's educational level or leadership style. Only in two groups did we find statistically significant differences: younger clergy were more likely than older to engage in theological discernment when considering new programs or ministries, although the majority of them still gave priority to member needs or desires; and bivocational pastors, especially those employed by their churches for fewer than 35 hours a week, were less likely to consider theological criteria than full-time clergy.

Had respondents been permitted to choose a middle category (saying that they consider both the needs of members and theological criteria), there would likely have been a majority opting for it. Indeed, Burns's understanding of transformational leadership involves a leader's efforts to recognize and satisfy the higher needs of followers, ones that reflect their deepest aspiration and values. Clearly, meeting followers' deep needs — whether understood as salvation or the need for meaning in life and participation in a sustaining community — is important and not antithetical to a theological understanding of congregational life and mission. Nevertheless, forcing the choice as we did in the survey helps to sharpen the distinction and serves as a reminder that the church has a transformational purpose that is greater than meeting the needs of its individual members.

Innovation or Tradition?

The second question that attempted to get at rationales for decisions about the congregation's direction also required pastors to make a choice between alternatives:

— "It is essential in a rapidly changing world that congregational leaders should seek to be innovative in such things as worship and music
style"; or

— "In a rapidly changing world, it is essential that leaders keep their
congregation focused on the inherited traditions and practices of the
church."

Of course, worship and music styles are not the only areas that have under-
gone change in recent years; but they are among the most prevalent and
controversial.[10] And the second choice does not specify whether inherited
traditions and practices refer mainly to a local congregation's traditions
and stories or whether they refer to broader denominational or ecumenical traditions and practices.

Six in ten pastors affirmed their belief in innovation; however, when
I broke the responses by denominational traditions, I found the Catholic
priests to be a mirror opposite of the total sample: Six in ten priests said
that rapid change requires a focus on church tradition — by which I suspect they mean primarily the Catholic Church's tradition rather than their
local parish tradition. This is not surprising. The Catholic Church historically has had a much deeper respect for tradition in its decision making
than has been true for most Protestant denominations. Pastors in historic
black denominations were almost evenly split between the choices, with a
very slight majority giving priority to innovation over tradition. Mainline
and conservative Protestants are similar in their preference for innovation
over tradition. Conservatives are especially leery of church tradition, as we
found in our focus groups. They argue that Scripture — especially what
they understand to be the practice of the New Testament churches — is a
sufficient guide for the church today, and even when they engage in innovation, they frequently will justify the innovation by saying that the new
practice more accurately reflects the spirit of the early church.

As Figure 5.4 on page 148 shows, church size also makes a difference

10. In addition to worship and music styles, other innovations include architecture,
especially in worship space; multiple small groups — some patterned after twelve-step
groups — in place of more traditional Sunday school classes for adults; a renewed emphasis
on spirituality and healing that often draws from the Pentecostal tradition; and raising up
and training staff from within the congregation while bypassing traditional educational institutions such as theological seminaries. Donald Miller (1997) and I (2000) describe many
of these innovations and consider their implications for more traditional congregations.

Figure 5.4
Innovation versus Tradition Differentiated by Church Size
(as Measured by Average Weekly Attendance)

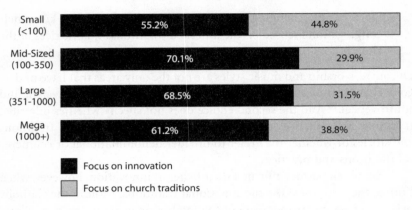

Focus on innovation

Focus on church traditions

in how clergy view the matter. Clergy in small congregations, which are in majority Protestant, are significantly more likely to turn to tradition as they face change. I suspect that pastors in these small congregations turn mostly to practices that the congregation, rather than the denomination, has followed in the past, "the way we have always done it." This is no doubt in part due to their small size, which gives their leaders and members a sense of precariousness, especially if the membership is aging and not being replaced. Congregations are also more likely to favor tradition if their pastor is bivocational or part time. We found that almost two thirds of bivocational clergy in small congregations say that they and their lay leaders face change by following the well-worn paths of tradition rather than attempting innovation, almost exactly opposite the response given by full-time pastors serving in similarly small congregations! When pastors work full time, whether in small or large congregations, it clearly makes a difference in how they and their lay leaders think about change. That which is new does not seem quite so threatening.

Considering the responses to our two questions about the bases or rationales for decision-making, we can conclude that a considerable minority of clergy report that they and their lay leaders give priority to discerning the theological warrants for decisions about new programs or ministries. Likewise a minority turns to inherited traditions, either those of the congregation or of the broader Christian tradition for guidance. Catholic priests are the exception in both cases, though they are still somewhat more likely to give priority to the needs and desires of members than to theological reflection.

How are clergy's responses to each of our two sets of methods of decision-making related to our measures of congregational effectiveness? Although the differences in most instances are not large, several of them would be unlikely to have occurred by chance. In each case, giving priority to member needs and desires resulted in a positive relationship with the percentage of members attending at least weekly, reporting a strong and growing sense of belonging, giving five percent of their income or more, and belief that there is a good match between the pastor and the congregation. For the second comparison — innovation versus tradition — looking to tradition is positively related to involvement in fellowship activities and small groups, finding help for daily living, and sensing God's presence. Emphasis on innovation is associated with a greater sense of excitement about the congregation's future and is positively related to membership growth over the past two years; however, it is also positively related to major conflict in the congregation. Although these various measures may be blunt instruments for grasping what are complex and subtle issues, and while the limited number of significant relationships are not large and could be the result of factors other than the two sets of warrants, they suggest that leaders' focus on member needs and desires is more positive for measures of effectiveness than giving priority to the theological warrants for programs. Giving priority to theological warrants is not significantly related (at least statistically) to any of the effectiveness measures.

Overall, responses to the two questions are not overly surprising, but they are somewhat disappointing. While it is clear that congregations cannot ignore member needs and desires — nor should they, I had expected (or perhaps hoped) that a larger percentage of clergy would report that they and their lay leaders give priority to theological reflection in deciding on new programs and ministries. The forced-choice question format without doubt obscured some combination of the two rationales, but it was nevertheless troubling to find the overwhelming attention given to members' needs and desires, especially if this indicates an accommodation to religious consumerism or a kind of therapeutic ideal at the expense of theological integrity in congregational life. As one pastor expressed it,

"[Some congregations] are so busy meeting people's needs and attracting people in, that they don't have any sense of what it means to be a church. . . . A lot of pieces of faith have been sacrificed." Since it is not possible to know how much the pastors' tilt in their response is a capitulation to consumerism as opposed to an effort to balance a theological rationale with the voluntary character of the church, I can do no more than pose the matter as one begging for further reflection and discussion and encourage readers to ask how they would answer the question and why.

As for the second question, it is not overly disappointing that the majority of clergy said that the need for innovation takes precedence over a primary focus on tradition. Given the rapidity of change, no organization, much less the church, can afford to ignore the constant pressure to adapt to new challenges that arise. In the words of the familiar hymn, "New occasions teach new duties; time makes ancient goods uncouth." At the same time, congregations ignore their traditions at a cost. There is much wisdom to be gained from past practices of Christians, both local and ecumenical, as they have sought to be faithful in their own time and place, and churches are much the poorer if they ignore tradition as an important means of grace. All too often a new pastor assumes leadership in a congregation and proposes new directions without making an effort to learn the existing culture of the congregation, its stories and traditions, that might serve as warrants for needed innovations. How has this congregation faced change in the past? Are there stories of previous innovations that helped it face past challenges? Is there a usable future in the congregation's past? It is not surprising that there is a strong relationship between conflict and innovation — especially if questions like these are not asked and taken seriously.

It does not seem entirely contradictory to be disappointed at the first response and moderately encouraged by the second. Yet it would have been more encouraging had clergy favored both theological reflection and innovation, without neglecting either the needs and desires of members or the wisdom of the tradition. Holding these polarities together is central to the kind of agility or reflective leadership that is required of clergy and laity in leading their congregations in a changing world — characteristics to be considered further in Chapter 7. When such balance is achieved, meetings of congregational leaders and, indeed, congregational gatherings generally, become learning communities where together clergy and laity explore the implications of Scripture and church traditions, their own and those of the larger church, for their life together and their ministry in the world about them.[11]

Authority to Lead

Now a final question about leadership: What gives clergy authority to lead? The church has answered this question in several ways over the years, roughly corresponding to distinctions I made in Chapter 1 between office, profession, and calling. Although these three ways of thinking about pastoral ministry are not mutually exclusive, ordination is especially related to the *office* of ministry. That is, when a denomination or a congregation ordains a pastor to lead, it grants her or him authority or the right to preach the Word, administer the sacraments, and order the life of the church, as the rubrics used in many ordination liturgies emphasize. But they also ordain the person for at least two other reasons: a belief that this person has been specially called by God to this ministry (ordained ministry as a *calling*) and that she or he has the requisite knowledge or practical wisdom to lead, usually, though not always, based on specialized education (ordained ministry as a *profession*). Some churches have downplayed one or the other of these bases, and each has waxed and waned over time; yet overall they have been important for giving clergy the right to lead in their congregations, both in a broader and a more narrow sense.

Elsewhere, I have applied the distinction between formal or official authority and informal or personal authority to clergy leadership (Carroll 1991: 54-60).[12] Formal authority or authority of office is that which the church grants as it officially recognizes, usually in ordination, that the candidate has a call from God, meets the required educational standards, and

11. For an important and helpful look at how theology comes alive in practice, see Volf and Bass (2002). Several of the essays provide good examples of congregations engaging in theological reflection about their programs and practices. See also the Winter 2004 issue of *Congregations* from the Alban Institute, which has as its theme, "Theology Matters: How Congregations Reach for God." This issue has several helpful articles about theological reflection in the midst of congregational life.

12. See also Heifetz (1994), who provides a number of helpful examples of how informal or personal authority makes leadership possible in difficult situations where there are no easy answers. He also considers how some have exercised leadership when they had no official authority.

is considered to have the requisite gifts and graces to serve in the pastoral office. Ordination confers a kind of "seal of approval" on the pastor. Informal or personal authority, in contrast, is that granted a leader by constituents, based on a belief that the pastor's personal qualities — demonstrated competence, ability to relate to people, and especially spiritual and moral integrity — warrant a congregation's or individual's trust.

Both kinds of authority are important and necessary for effective leadership. Formal authority provides the stamp of approval that gives a pastor initial entrée or legitimacy. It also gives the pastor legitimacy to lead when he or she speaks or acts on controversial issues, even when such speech or action is contrary to the views of many in his or her congregation. Being ordained to preach the gospel gives a pastor not only an obligation but also the freedom to speak and act as she or he best understands the gospel's claims. While speaking or acting prophetically or counterculturally is never easy, clergy whose formal authority or ordination is granted by their denomination are somewhat less vulnerable than those whose ordination comes from the local congregation (Wood 1981). In churches whose polity is congregational, clergy are more dependent on the support of the congregation and have a greater risk of being fired for saying or doing unpopular things.

As important as formal authority is, whether in exercising prophetic leadership or in leading generally, clergy are on much firmer ground when personal authority augments formal authority, especially by being trusted by one's congregation. Trust is at the heart of personal authority, and it is not automatically achieved. As an Alabama pastor told us, "You know, . . . shepherds lead sheep, and we as pastors lead people. If you can't relate to people, then maybe you need to really examine yourself to see whether or not you need to be pastoring." Personal authority to lead is gained in a kind of "second ordination," an acceptance of the pastor that comes after she or he has had time to earn members' trust.

The first ordination — the official one — grants a pastor entrée into a congregation and certifies his or her fitness to lead, at times against the congregation's grain. But the second ordination — the unofficial one that takes time to earn — makes it much more likely that members will share in the direction that the pastor is leading or at least trust him or her to lead them on new paths that they had not considered. In an article in *Leadership*, Gordon MacDonald draws on his pastoral experience to describe the contrast between the two types: "I was tempted to think that just because I had a seminary degree, because I was ordained, and because I was more knowledgeable about biblical ideas, people should have unlimited faith in me. That stuff works for a while, but in crunch time deeper questions began to emerge. Did I have integrity and wisdom, or was it all froth? Was I reliable? Could I take people into unknown territory spiritually? Organizationally? Charm and charisma are like a glider; they fly, but not indefinitely. And they don't do well in turbulent times" (2003: 56). MacDonald calls attention to several factors that contribute to what I am calling the second ordination: consistency, dependability, openness, hard work, impartiality, and an ever-deepening spirituality.

The importance of time or length of tenure for nurturing one's second ordination is also reflected in the following conversation among pastors in a focus group:

Pastor 1: I wonder about the length of clergy tenure in denominations that tend to move people every four years. Studies have shown that a pastor needs to take at least four to five years to get to the point where you have developed the stability and the trust so that you can do outrageous things and get away with them because they know that you love them and they trust you. [But too often, by that time] the pastor is moving on to some place else. I know a lot of colleagues who have done that because the grass seems greener, or because they have itchy feet. I think that is a great detriment to the church.

Pastor 2: When I've moved, I've been primarily "manager" and a little bit "leader" for at least the first five, six or seven years, depending on the size of the congregation. It's not until you've been there awhile that you really move a little way from being the manager toward being a leader. . . .

Pastor 3: This may sound defensive, since I've been in my church for twenty-three years, and perhaps it is defensive, but every church has someone in it with longevity capital, with a bank account. Usually it is a layperson, sometimes, as in my case, it is also the pastor. But whoever has that treasury of capital, whether pastor or lay leader, how they use that capital is critical for the ministry of the church. If they use it by jumping in to support someone who is not so popular in the church but is doing a good ministry so that they are not left alone, that is an appropriate use of capital. But you have to know that you have it, and if you have it, it's like the parable of the talents. You'd better use it. Somebody's got it, either the pastor or someone else.

This last pastor's concept of "longevity capital" is a helpful way of describing the trust that a pastor wins over time. It is a resource of personal authority, a form of capital that is there to be spent in leadership.

A word of caution is in order. Both kinds of authority can be abused; we need only think of the highly publicized cases of priestly pedophilia or of reports of high-profile ministers skimming funds from their churches' budgets to support their lavish lifestyles to know that clergy are not immune to moral failures. Such failures breach the trust that people have placed in a pastor because he or she has both been authorized by the church's official ordination and also, in many cases, earned the congregation's "second ordination." It is always painful when someone breaches another's trust; it is tragically so when that person is one who is trusted to be God's representative.

Although a survey is not the most effective way to get at these important yet subtle authority issues, we nonetheless attempted to do so by listing several bases for a congregation's acceptance of a pastor's leadership. Among them were being ordained, having a seminary degree or certificate, having a call from God, competence in the work of ministry, and trust. We asked, "How important is each in your current congregation for their acceptance of your leadership?"[13]

Overall, 56 percent of the clergy believed ordination to be of great importance for the acceptance of their leadership; 44 percent also said that a seminary degree or certificate is of great importance; but almost 90 percent considered a call from God, competence, and trust to be of great importance! In other words, two bases most directly related to official authority — ordination and a seminary education — are not considered to be of great importance by a significant number of clergy; however, almost all emphasize the great importance of having a call from God, being competent in ministry, and gaining member trust. Although God's call is an important part of both official and personal authority, competence and trust are especially important for personal authority.

13. Although the list included physical appearance, gender, and race or ethnicity, we have not included these in our analysis because of ambiguity in interpreting the responses.

As might be expected, the pastor's denominational tradition makes a significant difference in what pastors believe important for gaining authority to lead, since, as I emphasized earlier, denominations differ in their understanding of what is particularly important in the pastoral role. Figure 5.5 shows the mean or average score that clergy give to each of the five bases, grouped according to their denominational tradition, on a scale of one ("of little importance") to four ("of great importance"). Although the differences among the traditions appear to be small for several of the bases, all are statistically significant.

Catholics, who emphasize a sacramental view of ordination, value ordination highest among the four traditions. As I noted earlier, Episcopalians and Orthodox clergy also hold a similar sacramental view of ordination, and they would probably rate ordination highly. As we see in the figure, mainline Protestants generally and, to a lesser degree, pastors in historic black traditions also value ordination, believing that the pastor has a special function in preaching and teaching the Word. This also leads mainline Protestants to give an especially prominent place to seminary-educated clergy, reflecting their conviction that such education is foundational for the preaching and teaching task. Conservative Protestants are lowest among the traditions in the importance that they attribute both to ordination and a seminary degree. Further analysis shows this to be especially true for Pentecostal pastors and those in independent congregations. Most conservative Protestants are more concerned with the pastor's inward call from God and with his or her competence, which, it would seem, they do not necessarily associate with a seminary degree. Indeed there continues in some conservative Protestant churches a profound suspicion of an educated clergy.[14] All traditions value a pastor's inward call from God, which they hold to be a sign of the pastor's spiritual authenticity, and all believe that competence and trust are essential for giving clergy the authority to lead. Although their average score for the importance of trust is

---

14. As has been emphasized previously, the distrust of education may be changing. A colleague shared an article from the *Louisville Courier Journal* (September 14, 2003) describing the experience of a 37-year-old man with a limited educational background who felt called to ministry. Although some friends discouraged him from seeking further education, saying that it showed a lack of faith in God's ability to equip ministers for service, others encouraged him to do so. An administrator at the Bible college he chose to attend responded to those who discouraged education for pastors by asking, "Would you go to a doctor who has not been educated and expect he'll just know where to cut you open?"

Figure 5.5
Bases of Pastoral Authority
Differentiated by Denominational Tradition

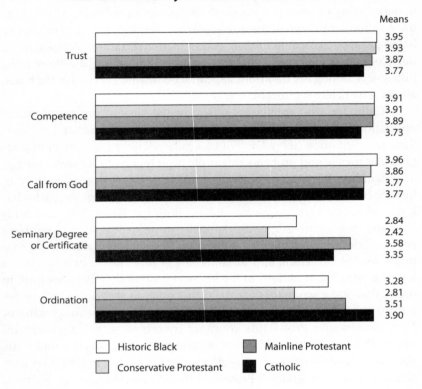

Means

Trust	3.95
	3.93
	3.87
	3.77
Competence	3.91
	3.91
	3.89
	3.73
Call from God	3.96
	3.86
	3.77
	3.77
Seminary Degree or Certificate	2.84
	2.42
	3.58
	3.35
Ordination	3.28
	2.81
	3.51
	3.90

☐ Historic Black ■ Mainline Protestant
☐ Conservative Protestant ■ Catholic

high, it is nonetheless noteworthy that Catholic priests give it the lowest average importance score of the four traditions.

Other factors also affect what is considered important for authority to lead. Female clergy were significantly more likely than male clergy to value the importance of ordination and a seminary education as important for their authority to lead — factors that are especially important symbols of office or formal authority. Women did not differ from men in the importance they attribute to having a call from God or winning members' trust. Their rating of the importance of competence, however, was significantly lower than that of clergymen. Given the resistance to their leadership that clergywomen have often encountered, it is not surprising that they believe it important that they have the marks of formal authority — ordination and education — to give them time to establish their personal authority to lead.

In contrast to clergywomen, part-time and bivocational pastors are less likely to believe that either ordination or a seminary degree is of high importance for their authority to lead. Many are commissioned rather than ordained and do not have a seminary degree. Since many of these pastors serve in small congregations, it was not surprising to find that congregational size and location also make a difference. Having a clear call from God, competence, and trust — factors especially important for personal authority — are the factors that count the most for pastors who lead small congregations, especially in rural areas.

Unfortunately, we do not have measures from lay members of the pastors' congregations regarding what is important for their acceptance of their pastor's leadership. This would have helped to round out the picture in an important and helpful way. We did, however, see previously (Table 5.1) the importance of a pastor's leadership style for lay members' perception that there is a good match between pastor and congregation. Although we do not have more direct measures, being attentive to the factors that help to "authorize" clergy leadership in the eyes of lay members and the differences among them are important ingredients of pastoral self-awareness.

Conclusion

To sum up these various probes into pastoral leadership, I have used leadership as a way of speaking inclusively of the clergy's core work in articulating the church's essential beliefs and values as they relate to the issues and challenges that a congregation or its individual members face. Pastoral leadership also has a more specifically institutional meaning as guiding the life of a congregation, working along with lay leaders to set a direction for the congregation's life and move toward it. This chapter has focused especially on the latter, though much of what we have considered has implications for leadership's broader meaning. Indeed, a pastor's preaching and teaching may be the most effective means by which she or he leads a congregation to reflect theologically and draw on the wisdom of the tradition, thus influencing and guiding action both collectively and individually. I have emphasized that without leadership that helps a congregation understand how its unique resources and capacities can be used to respond to God's call in its particular time and place, the congregation is likely to circle the wagons and try to avoid dealing with the challenges and opportunities that it faces. We have seen that leadership that is proactive, especially when clergy attempt to inspire and empower laity to act, is positively associated with a number of measures of congregational effectiveness. In contrast, congregations whose clergy leaders leave most initiatives to laity are less likely to be effective, at least as I have measured it. Although I cannot claim that proactive, shared leadership *causes* congregations to be effective, I can say that such leadership and effectiveness are significantly related.

I have also emphasized how important it is for a congregation's leadership to pay attention to the direction in which it is heading rather than simply drifting or seeking to maintain the status quo. Further, I have argued for theological reflection and discernment in addition to attention to member needs and desires when developing new programs and practices — transformational rather than transactional leadership, in other words — and for innovation that does not ignore the wisdom of the church's traditions, both local and ecumenical. Finally, I have considered the importance of both formal and personal authority in giving pastor's legitimacy to lead.

All of this is to emphasize the critical importance of pastoral leadership for congregational effectiveness, both in the inclusive sense that I described at the beginning of this chapter and in the institutional sense of giving direction to the programs and practices of a congregation. The two are not ultimately separate; rather each complements and feeds the other.

In addition to all that has been said, however, it is essential, finally, that leaders move beyond *talking* about the direction of the congregation to *acting* on it. As Will Rogers rightly observed: "Even if you're on the right track, you'll get run over if you just sit there."

Chapter 6

Potters' Problems:
Commitment, Satisfaction, and Health

"The greatest crisis the institutional church faces at the beginning of the third millennium is [one] marked by clergy burnout, drop-out and kicked out."

Terry Swicegood

"I've loved being a pastor, almost every minute of it. It's a difficult life because it's a demanding life. But the rewards are enormous — the rewards of being on the front line of seeing the gospel worked out in people's lives. I remain convinced that if you are called to it, being a pastor is the best life there is. But any life can be the best life if you're called to it."

Eugene Peterson

Thus far, we have looked at the broader context in which American pastoral leaders work, who they are, what their core work is, and how they practice leadership as pastors. In doing so I have hoped to shed some light on how pastors, as God's potters, produce and shape the culture of their congregational clay jars. The focus of this chapter is on how clergy are faring in their work. How committed are they to staying the course in their calling to ordained ministry generally and to congregational leadership in particular? To what degree are they satisfied with various aspects of their work life? And what about their emotional and physical health, an issue that we looked at briefly in Chapter 4? Finally, returning briefly to the question of the match or fit between pastor and congregation, how does the laity's perception of the match affect clergy commitment, satisfaction, and health? The issues that the chapter addresses are not easy matters to sort out, and there are clearly opposing points of view about them.

On one side are those who claim that being a pastor has become such a difficult and unappealing occupation that many clergy are considering "bailing out" because of lack of support, continual conflict in their churches, and stress and burnout. The first of the epigraphs at the beginning of this chapter expresses this view. It comes from Terry Swicegood, a veteran Presbyterian pastor, in a lecture with the provocative title, "Mammas, Don't Let Your Babies Grow Up to Be Preachers!" Here is more of what he had to say:

> The facts are indisputable. There is a growing crisis in church life, which robs our churches of good pastoral leadership and brings pain and hurt upon pastors and pastors' families. A growing number of ministers, priests, and rabbis are experiencing depression, loss of vocation, and dissatisfaction in their work. Conflicts in congregations between parishioners and clergy are increasing because of the changing nature of the church and because the church and synagogue are embracing cultural values rather than Biblical ones. Pastoring has become a profession that extracts so much that it is nearly inhumane to expect the person to consistently manage all the multiple and conflicting expectations (2).

In one of our focus groups, a denominational executive made a similar assessment about the difficulties that pastors face today. He spoke of "a frightening number of clergy who are unhappy in ministry. They are doing [the job] because they feel stuck in it. The only thing that keeps them there is their pension. They would love to be doing something else and don't see a way to get out." In a similar vein, recall the previous reference to the study of pastors in the Lutheran Church — Missouri Synod. As I noted, the authors of the research concluded that "about 20 percent of LCMS pastors are severely depressed, highly distressed, and experiencing advanced stages of burnout . . . [and] that an additional 20 percent are moderately distressed and are approaching burnout." The authors list a number of problems that they heard in their interviews that contribute to dissatisfaction and low morale: people beating up on each other in congregations; mismatch of pastors and congregations; the difficulty of getting help to pastors; poor support for clergy spouses and children; low clergy income; grossly unreasonable expectations of pastors; fighting and sick congregations; and congregations where a few members dominate the majority (Klaas and Klaas 1999).

Others have pointed to the declining percentage of entering seminarians who say that they plan to enter parish ministry and to declines in the academic ability of entering seminarians generally as signs of the growing lack of appeal of ordained ministry, especially of the pastorate (Wheeler 2001; Chaves 2004). I too have expressed concerns about the health of the profession. In the initial proposal for *Pulpit & Pew* to the Lilly Endowment, I referred to ordained ministry as a "troubled profession." In part my assessment was based on the various changes that have affected clergy and the challenges of the present social context that we looked at in the first two chapters of this book. But it also reflected what my colleagues and I have regularly heard as we have listened to clergy and to the denominational officials who work directly with them. Laypeople can get a sense of this simply by looking at their local bookstore or on the Internet at the cottage industry of books, seminars, retreat centers, and so forth that has developed to aid pastors who are dealing with stress, conflict, and burnout.

With so many agreeing that there is "trouble in Zion" when it comes to God's potters, how could there possibly be a countervailing view? Yet the second epigraph to this chapter, the quotation from Eugene Peterson, presents a very different take on the matter: being a pastor is "the best life there is." Also, consider the following: A 1981 study of pastors from seven Protestant denominations concluded that clergy were not only highly committed to their present pastorates, but even more strongly committed to ministry as a vocation (Hoge, Dyble, and Polk 1981). Much more recently, two surveys, one of Protestant clergy and one of Catholic priests, also found a generally committed and satisfied clergy. The Protestant survey, conducted in 2001 by the evangelical journal *Leadership*, reported that 91 percent of the clergy responding were "very satisfied" or "satisfied" with their ministry, and 71 percent "definitely" want to stay in ministry (Miller 2001). The Catholic research, undertaken by the Center for Applied Research in the Apostolate (Perl & Froehle 2002), found that 88 percent of all non-retired priests strongly agreed that they were satisfied with their lives as priests, and 87 percent said they were happy in ministry. Seventy-two percent strongly disagreed that they had ever considered leaving the priesthood in the past five years. Only 10 percent said that they had seriously considered leaving. Even in the Netherlands, where in 1996, regular churchgoers comprised only 21 percent of the population and where clergy reported high levels of conflict with parishioners and limited support from fellow clergy, a survey of Catholic and Protestant clergy found that 87 percent said that they are generally satisfied with their profession (Zondag 2004).

These sharply contrasting perspectives on clergy commitment and satisfaction frame the focus of this chapter. Which is right? What can we learn from our survey and focus groups?

Commitment to the Call

We look first at pastors' commitment to their call, as well as whether they have considered leaving parish ministry for some other occupation, church-related or not. In our earlier discussion of ordained ministry as a calling, I noted that believing that one is called by God to ordained ministry is an important aspect of a pastor's personal spirituality and provides a kind of moral compass for his or her work in ministry. Thus, whether pastors entertain serious doubts about their call is of considerable importance. Figure 6.1 shows how pastors in our survey answered three questions about commitment: whether, in the past five years, they have

- Doubted their call to ministry;
- Considered leaving pastoral ministry for another church-related position; or
- Considered leaving ordained ministry altogether to take up some secular occupation.

The results make it clear that the clergy's commitment to their call is strong. Six of ten pastors told us that they have never doubted their call in the last five years. Only slightly fewer have not considered leaving the pastorate for another church-related position; and seven of ten have never considered leaving ordained ministry for a secular job. Overall, then, pastors exhibit a quite strong commitment to their call to be in ordained min-

Figure 6.1
Commitment to Ordained Ministry

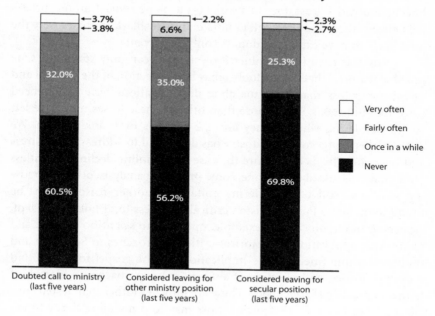

	Very often
	Fairly often
	Once in a while
	Never

istry generally and pastoral ministry in particular. These findings generally agree with the other surveys cited above that also found most clergy to be deeply committed vocationally.

At the same time, it is not inconsequential that almost one-third of the pastors say that they have doubted their call once in a while during the past five years, and the remaining 7 percent say they have done so often. Although these doubters are not an especially large number and their doubts are not at all surprising given the various demands that clergy experience day-to-day in their work, we can nonetheless gain some insight into commitment by considering who the more likely doubters are and what aspects of their current pastoral setting seem especially related to questioning their call, even if they do so only occasionally.[1]

First, what are the characteristics of those who are regular or occa-

---

1. In the comparisons that follow, we have used various statistical methods to draw our conclusions: cross-tabulations, correlations, and multiple regression analysis. The latter allows us to consider the effects of a number of factors at the same time.

sional doubters of their call? Among the four denominational traditions, mainline Protestants were twice as likely as conservative ones to report having doubted at least once in a while (55 to 28 percent). Catholic priests fell between them at 43 percent. Pastors in historic black churches were the least likely to have expressed doubts (only 23 percent).

Why this is so for mainline Protestants, I can only speculate. One possible reason is that clergy doubts may be a reflection of the turmoil and membership loss that most mainline denominations have experienced since the mid-1960s, some more than others. These losses may have left clergy wondering whether they are like captains of a sinking ship. We noted earlier that a cottage industry has developed to address clergy stress and burnout. This is even more the case for mainline decline. Countless books have discussed the decline, some providing analysis, others proposing solutions, still others offering epitaphs. Another reason might be found in mainline Protestantism's critical openness to, if not embrace of, aspects of modernity — for example, openness to scientific method and discoveries, application of historical-critical approaches to Scripture and tradition, commitment to the implications of the gospel for social and economic justice, and rejection of authoritarian approaches to matters of faith and practice (Farley 1990). These are hunches rather than tested conclusions, but I suspect that such factors may lead mainline clergy to express more doubt about some matters of faith than their conservative counterparts, and their doubts may extend to their call to ordained ministry. Such doubts can make life difficult for pastors, especially when some in their congregations look for more certainty than clergy are able to provide.

Catholics, too, given the changes wrought by the Second Vatican Council, by declining recruits to the priesthood, and, more recently, by the pedophilia crisis, have experienced considerable upheaval that could account for their somewhat greater propensity to express doubt about their call.

Younger pastors of all traditions (and correlatively those who have been fewer years in ministry) were significantly more likely to express doubt. Although almost five in ten pastors under age forty-five reported doubting their call once in a while, only two in ten of those over sixty reported doing so. It makes sense that older, longer-serving pastors will have come to terms with the issues that may lead younger or more recently ordained clergy to express doubts. Older pastors also have fewer years left to pursue another type of work should they consider leaving ordained ministry.

Table 6.1
Factors Related to Pastors Expressing
Doubts about Their Call to Ministry

	Correlations
Perceiving that people relate to me differently because I'm a pastor	.30
Lack of agreement over what the role of a pastor is	.22
Personal and/or professional criticism from the congregation	.22
Spouse voicing resentment over family's financial situation	.21
Difficulty of having a private life apart from the clergy role	.18
Excessive demands from congregation	.16
Spouse voicing resentment over amount of time ministry takes up	.15
Ministry having a negative effect on family	.15
Experiencing stress as a result of congregational criticism	.14
Difficulty finding time for recreation, relaxation, and personal reflection	.13
Feeling lonely and isolated	.12

Neither congregation size nor gender is related to pastors' doubts about the call. We saw earlier, in Chapter 3, that clergywomen are more likely to leave pastoral ministry than men, but, in many cases, they leave in order to start or raise families, not because of a loss of commitment to their calling. Also, many clergywomen who no longer pastor churches remain active in ministry, functioning in their local churches and judicatories, and have kept open the door to return to pastoral ministry as circumstances permit.

Patterns among denominational traditions for the other two measures — considering leaving for another ministry position or dropping out of ministry altogether — are similar to patterns for doubting the call, although the percentages of clergy considering dropping out altogether are lower in all four traditions. Clergy may doubt their call on occasion; they may consider leaving the pastorate for some other form of ministry; but they are not likely to consider leaving altogether.

What leads pastors to doubt their call? Table 6.1 lists a number of family and congregational factors that I found to be significantly correlated with such doubts. Since the figures reported are correlations, it is not possible to say that the factors *cause* a pastor to doubt his or her call; rather, one can only say that they are significantly related to expressing doubt. They are listed in order of strength of relationship. None of the co-efficients is large; however, all are statistically significant.

Some of these factors are more important for Protestants than for Catholics. For example, Catholics do not report experiencing much lack of agreement with laity over the role of the pastor, a significant problem for Protestants. The priest's sacramental role is firmly established in the theology and practice of the Catholic Church, and, despite the changes wrought by Vatican II, it is probably much less contested than it is in any Protestant denomination. Likewise, given the rule of celibacy, it is obvious that the priest has no spouse to voice resentment over the time ministry takes or over the family's financial situation. But for both Protestant and Catholic clergy, doubt about their call is significantly related to having people respond to them differently because they are pastors; it is this contextual factor that has the strongest relationship overall to doubt. Many pastors, Protestant and Catholic, resent being treated differently or being held to different standards because of their ordination. In Marilynne Robinson's novel *Gilead*, which we mentioned earlier, the Congregational minister John Ames tells of watching two young men, neither of whom was church-going, laughing about something that they found amusing.

> When they saw me coming . . . the joking stopped, but I could see they were still laughing to themselves, thinking what the old preacher almost heard them say.
>
> I felt like telling them, I appreciate a joke as much as anybody. . . . But it's not a thing people are willing to accept. They want you to be a little bit apart. . . .
>
> That's the strangest thing about being in the ministry. People change the subject when they see you coming. And then sometimes those very same people come into your study and tell you the most remarkable things (5-6).

One reviewer of *Gilead*, apparently a "P.K." (preacher's kid) himself, wrote, "As anyone who grows up in a clergyman's home can attest, most laymen . . . shy away from men and women of the cloth. A minister or a priest or rabbi may be important in a community's life and still live in a kind of exile" (Jones 2004: 87). It is this sense of "exile," of being treated differently for being a clergyperson, that is a major correlate of expressing doubt about one's call.

Congregational criticism and the stress that it causes are also significantly related to doubt of one's call for both Catholics and Protestants. For mainline Protestants and especially for Catholics, feelings of isolation are strongly associated with doubt as well as with considering leaving parish ministry altogether or for another church position. The priest shortage has left many priests living alone, where in earlier days they would have shared living space with several other priests in a parish rectory. Without question, this has contributed to their sense of isolation.

When we asked pastors in an open-ended question if there were other factors that helped to sustain their sense of call, quite a few said that having a conviction that their call was from God and not simply from a denomination or congregation was very important. Believing that God had called them, despite the difficulties they faced, sustained them — echoing Eugene Peterson's comment that "any life [including pastoral ministry] can be the best life if you're called to it." Several other pastors mentioned support from their denominational officials and the friendship and support of fellow clergy. Positive feedback from both parishioners and denominational supervisors was also important to them. Another pastor cited the opportunity to lead people to a relationship with Jesus as essential for keeping him going.[2]

Conflict and Commitment

I noted earlier that conflict in congregations appears to be on the rise, speculating that this is due in large part to factors like a consumeristic mentality and the prevalence of what we have called de facto congregationalism. It is not possible from our survey to confirm or disconfirm whether conflict has increased in recent years; we can, however, look once again at the pastors' reports of conflict in their congregations to see what its effect is on pastoral commitment. That it negatively affects commitment is the clear assumption made by those who believe that there is a crisis of morale among today's clergy. Furthermore, many observers attribute

2. This pastor's comment recalls another reflection of *Gilead's* John Ames. After the young man who was both Ames's namesake and nemesis comes to ask for Ames's blessing, Ames says, "[I]t was an honor to bless him. And this was absolutely true. I'd have gone through seminary and ordination and all the years intervening for that one moment" (Robinson 2004: 242).

Figure 6.2
Relation of Congregational Conflict to Doubting Call to Ministry

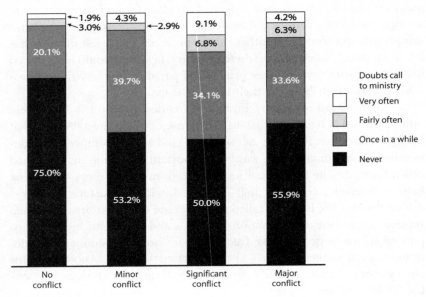

the growing shortage of clergy willing to serve as pastors of congregations to an increase in congregational conflict. In this view, conflict leads clergy to look for some other avenue for pursuing their call than the pastorate, or, worse, compels them to drop out of ordained ministry altogether. Why remain in an occupation in which one experiences hurtful conflict? Similar reasoning may also be a factor that deters young people from considering a call to ordained ministry.

Figure 6.2 makes it clear that congregational conflict — whether the conflict involves the pastor or not — is significantly related to doubting one's call. The presence of even minor conflict reduces the number that said that they never have doubted their call by almost 25 percent. Pastors who describe the conflict as significant were more likely to report doubting their call fairly or very often. The types of conflict most likely to cause clergy to doubt their call are, in order of importance, disputes over pastoral leadership, building matters, sexual misconduct (either on the part of the pastor or lay members), worship or programming, and finances.

Further analysis shows, however, that as important as congregational conflict is in leading a pastor to doubt his or her call, it is more likely to lead to considering leaving the pastorate for another church-related position rather than to dropping out altogether. This is an important finding, suggesting that pastors' call to ordained ministry is stronger than their commitment to pastoral ministry per se. It also provides support for the hypothesis that conflict is one of the important factors contributing to the shortage of clergy interested in serving as pastors of congregations. It is important, nonetheless, to reiterate that congregational conflict need not be negative. Indeed, it can be healthy if it is worked through constructively. Needed changes in congregational life — especially if they are important for the health and future of the congregation — rarely come without struggle.

All of this may seem like grim news — that there are many reasons for pastors to consider getting out of the ministry. But this is not the main message of the data. Overall, America's clergy express a high degree of commitment to their calling. Our data simply do not show the high degree of morale problems and despair that some observers have described. Of course, it would be wrong not to acknowledge that many clergy are in crisis, and I have tried to indicate some of the personal and situational factors that contribute to this. Nonetheless, crisis is not the experience of the majority. I will come back to commitment issues later in this chapter in relation to work satisfaction and health.

How Satisfied Are Pastors with Their Jobs?

Although clergy's commitment to their call is relatively strong, what about their work satisfaction? In our national survey, we listed several factors about which we have heard clergy express varying degrees of satisfaction or dissatisfaction. The factors and responses to them are shown in Table 6.2 on page 170.

As we can see, clergy satisfaction is mixed. Although in most cases, clergy told us that they are at least "somewhat satisfied" or "very satisfied," the "somewhat satisfied" responses on several items are relatively high; and, in spite of the overall positive tone of the table, we should remember that responses other than "very satisfied" reflect at least some dissatisfaction with the attribute being measured. Thus, we might learn about what leads to dissatisfaction by probing these responses further.

Table 6.2
Clergy Satisfaction with Selected Aspects of Their Ministry

	Very Dissatisfied	Somewhat Dissatisfied	Somewhat Satisfied	Very Satisfied
Overall effectiveness in this congregation	1	4	59	36
Current position	0	2	24	74
Housing	1	6	19	74
Spiritual Life	0	5	53	42
Continuing education opportunities	1	12	38	50
Support of denominational officials	3	10	35	52
Relationships with fellow clergy	2	10	36	52
Relationships with lay leaders	0	1	28	71
Relationships with other staff	0	2	25	73
Salary and benefits	2	6	41	51
Family life	0	4	23	73

As a way of characterizing the eleven items in this table, I have grouped them into four "themes" or "dimensions" of satisfaction derived from a factor analysis of the items.[3] I will use these four later as scales when considering their correlates of satisfaction or dissatisfaction. For now, however, grouping the items according to the four dimensions is useful in seeing how the different areas of satisfaction in Table 6.2 are related.

First, there is satisfaction with aspects of the pastors' current congregation: their relationships with lay leaders and with other staff, where applicable, and their sense of their overall effectiveness in the congregation. Clergy express considerable satisfaction with the two relationship items. They do not, however, voice high satisfaction with their own sense of effectiveness in the congregation. Of the eleven satisfaction measures,

3. The four areas of satisfaction are based on a principal components factor analysis of the items that yielded four clear factors with high factor loads and discernible meanings: (1) *satisfaction with one's current congregation* — relationships with lay leaders, relationships with other staff (where applicable); sense of one's overall effectiveness in this congregation; (2) *satisfaction with aspects of the position* — the position itself, housing, salary and benefits; (3) *satisfaction with external support* — support of one's denominational officials, relationships with fellow clergy, opportunities for continuing education; and (4) *personal-spiritual satisfaction* — satisfaction with one's spiritual life, satisfaction with one's family life.

this is the one that received the lowest percentage of "very satisfied" responses.

A second dimension has to do with satisfaction with one's present position, which also includes housing arrangements and salary and benefits. Of all the measures, clergy expressed greatest satisfaction with the first two: the position itself and their housing. In contrast, they are not nearly as satisfied with the salary and benefits that they receive from their congregations; just 50 percent were very satisfied. Given the relatively low level of compensation that we discussed in Chapter 3, this is hardly surprising.

It is interesting that the factor analysis distinguished clearly between satisfaction with one's congregation and aspects of the position. It suggests that a pastor can be satisfied or dissatisfied with one and not with the other, or with both. A congregation can be quite fulfilling in what it offers — for example, in relationships with lay members and other staff — while the position itself and its benefits (housing and salary) may be unsatisfactory. Or the reverse may be true.

A third dimension involves aspects of external support. Pastors expressed moderate levels of satisfaction (about 50 percent said they are very satisfied) with the support of their denominational officials, relationships with fellow clergy, and opportunities for continuing education. These three categories, which form the kind of infrastructure that supports clergy work, also had the largest percentages responding that they are "somewhat dissatisfied."

A final theme includes two measures of personal satisfaction: satisfaction with one's own spiritual life and, for those with families, with one's family life. Only about 40 percent expressed great satisfaction with their spiritual life. In contrast, over 70 percent were highly satisfied with their family life.

It may be instructive to take note of the two measures of satisfaction about which clergy expressed least high satisfaction: their overall effectiveness as leaders in the congregation and their personal spiritual life. I suspect that these are honest expressions of dissatisfaction. Many pastors often feel inadequate to face the demands of their work. So much of it, as some pastors told us, is "ephemeral" and "difficult to evaluate or to see results." "It can only be judged," as one said, "in the long, long run." The Dutch study of pastoral satisfaction cited previously found that "almost two-thirds of the pastors are not entirely sure that their pastoral work is having any effect" (Zondag 2004: 261). Pastors also know that their spiritual life could be strengthened, that there are times of spiritual drought when they are stressed out and feel as if they're "running on empty," as one pastor put it. So it is not surprising to find the dissatisfaction with one's spiritual life. But I suspect that clergy's relative dissatisfaction may also reflect a kind of humility, a reticence about claiming too much about their own effectiveness or their spiritual life.

Are there any clues in our survey data about what contributes to greater satisfaction about these two areas of ministry? As for leadership effectiveness, those clergy who report that they have regular performance evaluations, those who take part regularly in continuing education, and those whose congregations have allowed them to take a sabbatical leave (a relatively new practice for most clergy and congregations) expressed greater satisfaction with their effectiveness as leaders. Although the increase in satisfaction for each relationship is not large, each is statistically significant. Similarly, and perhaps not surprising, satisfaction with one's spiritual life is positively correlated with the number of hours that a pastor reports spending in prayer and meditation in an average week.

These various findings suggest several important ways that pastors can themselves take initiative to increase satisfaction with their effectiveness as leaders and with their spiritual life — especially through regular disciplines of prayer and meditation and taking advantage of opportunities for continuing education and ongoing renewal. But it also helps greatly if lay members of their congregations support them by giving regular and honest feedback about their performance, encourage and permit their pastor's participation in continuing theological education, and provide sabbatical leave time. Having clear policies, especially regarding continuing education and sabbatical leaves, can both strengthen the pastor's ministry in the congregation and avoid conflict and misunderstanding about the time away from the congregation that these experiences require. I will say more about this in the final chapter.

Satisfaction and Commitment

What does the survey tell us about how satisfaction and commitment to the call and to pastoral ministry are related? We would clearly expect that the greater a pastor's satisfaction with his or her own ministry and congregation, the less he or she would express doubts or consider leaving pastoral

Table 6.3
Relationship of Commitment Measures to
Dissatisfaction with Selected Aspects of Ministry

Doubted Call to Ministry	Considered Leaving for Church-Related Job	Considered Leaving for Secular Job
Dissatisfaction with:	*Dissatisfaction with:*	*Dissatisfaction with:*
Salary & benefits (.16)	Salary & benefits (.25)	Salary & benefits (.24)
Family life (.15)	Family life (.22)	Relationships with lay leaders (.18)
Spiritual Life (.14)	Relationships with lay leaders (.20)	Housing (.17)
Relationships with fellow clergy (.13)	Housing (.19)	Family life (.17)
Overall effectiveness in this congregation (.13)	Current position (.16)	Overall effectiveness in this congregation (.16)
	Spiritual life (.15)	Current position (.15)
	Relationships with fellow clergy (.13)	Relationships with fellow clergy (.14)
	Support of denominational officials (.13)	

ministry. This seems clearly to be the case. When I correlate the three commitment measures that we previously considered with responses to the various questions about satisfaction, there are several interesting relationships. In Table 6.3 I list, in order of strength of relationship, those areas of dissatisfaction that are correlated with doubting one's commitment to ministry.[4] None of the correlations are especially strong; however, all are statistically significant.

Dissatisfaction with salary and benefits tops each of the three lists, and dissatisfaction with family life is second for two measures of commitment and in fourth place for considering leaving ministry altogether. That these two areas of dissatisfaction are the most important correlates of flag-

4. Note that for this table only, I have reversed the direction of the satisfaction responses so that a low score means greater satisfaction. This makes it easier to interpret their relationship to the commitment items that are also scored so that a low score means high commitment. Thus, the positive correlations in the table express a positive relation between low commitment and low satisfaction.

ging commitment is not surprising. The two are no doubt related; money matters frequently create stress in family relationships. In fact, those clergy who are dissatisfied with their salary and benefits are, unsurprisingly, also the ones most likely to report that their spouse resents the family's financial situation. The correlation between the two measures is quite strong. And as we saw earlier, spousal resentment of financial matters is strongly related to doubting the call.

In addition to salary and benefits and family life, pastors who expressed some doubt of their call also expressed moderate levels of dissatisfaction with their spiritual life, their relationships with fellow clergy, and their overall effectiveness in their position. While these correlations are statistically significant, most are relatively weak.

The relationship of the satisfaction items to commitment proved to be slightly stronger for the other two commitment measures: considering leaving pastoral ministry for another church-related job or leaving altogether for a secular job. Excepting family life, the top four correlations for considering leaving pastoral ministry for another church-related job had to do with aspects of pastors' current congregation: salary and benefits, housing, relationship with lay leaders, and the position itself. These were also important for considering leaving ministry altogether, along with dissatisfaction with one's own effectiveness in the congregation. Lack of support from denominational officials was weakly related to considering leaving pastoral ministry for another church position. Dissatisfaction with relationships with fellow clergy was also weakly related to thinking about leaving pastoral ministry, whether for another church-related position or for a career in another field.

Other Correlates of Satisfaction

There are some differences by denominational tradition in degree of satisfaction. Pastors in mainline Protestant denominations are the most likely to express satisfaction with their overall effectiveness, closely followed by Catholics, while conservative Protestant and black pastors express less satisfaction with their effectiveness but are more satisfied than the others with their spiritual life. Conservative pastors express highest satisfaction with their relationships with lay leaders — an important relationship in congregations with a congregational polity — the polity characteristic of a majority of the conservative Protestants in our sample. They also are more satisfied than the others with their family life. Pastors of historic black churches express the greatest dissatisfaction with their relationships with lay leaders, and Catholic priests express the greatest satisfaction with their relationships with fellow clergy. There are no significant differences by denominational tradition for the other satisfaction items.

Bivocational pastors, for the most part, express somewhat greater satisfaction on most of the items than those whose only vocation is ordained ministry. The responses of mainline Protestant bivocationals, however, reveal an important insight into their position: While they express relatively high satisfaction with their salary and benefits (since, it is assumed, they are earning income from other sources in addition to their congregation), they are also less satisfied with the support they receive from their denominational officials and especially with their relationships with lay leaders and their fellow clergy. Neither of the latter creates a problem for most conservative Protestants or historic black church pastors. It is likely that the dissatisfaction of mainline bivocationals represents the relatively low esteem in which bivocational pastors are often held in these denominations. Most mainline denominations have considered full-time, mostly seminary-trained pastors to be the ideal, even in small, financially struggling congregations. Indeed, several denominations have provided subsidies to these congregations to enable them to be served by a full-time pastor. But in recent years, for various reasons, denominations have often reduced or discontinued these subsidies, making it necessary for struggling congregations to turn to part-time or bivocational pastors. These pastors, however, are sometimes viewed as "second best," an unwelcome but necessary compromise. Correctly or incorrectly, many mainline bivocationals and part-time pastors believe that they do not get adequate denominational support and that their fellow clergy and even the lay leaders of their congregations do not always value them.

Pastors' age, experience, gender, and ethnicity are also correlates of satisfaction. Older pastors and those who have served longer in ministry express greater satisfaction with their congregations, as do white male clergy. Satisfaction with individual effectiveness as a leader, with spiritual and family life, and with denominational support and relationships with fellow clergy also increases with age and experience. Clergywomen express higher satisfaction with denominational support and relationships with fellow clergy than do male clergy, but they are less satisfied with both their spiritual and family life than male clergy are. Congregational size and location are not correlated with satisfaction; neither is pastors' marital status.

Thus far we have looked mostly at how various personal and social characteristics of pastors relate to their level of satisfaction. Clearly, however, what often most affects satisfaction are contextual or situational issues: issues in the congregations that the pastors serve or having to do with their relationships with family, fellow clergy, or lay members. In Table 6.4, I examine how situational issues correlate with the four dimensions or areas of satisfaction mentioned previously that I derived from factor analysis of the eleven satisfaction items (see note 3 for the items making up each of the four). I constructed a scale for each dimension and then computed correlations between the scales and various situational issues. Some of the items used are less obviously related to all four dimensions, especially several of the ones in the external support column. Nevertheless, all of the correlations shown are statistically significant.[5] The table is admittedly complex, and I will not comment on all of the relationships. Instead, I will highlight several themes that the table suggests.

Spousal resentment of the family's financial situation has the strongest negative relationship to pastors' level of satisfaction with characteristics of their current position and with external support. It is also moderately important for those things that make for personal and spiritual satisfaction. These relationships highlight once more the importance of clergy salaries and benefits and their effect on family relationships.

Stress as a result of congregational criticism, congregational conflict, and a perception that the congregation makes too many demands are, not surprisingly, contributors to dissatisfaction, especially with pastors' congregations and with their personal and spiritual lives.

Relational issues, whether positive or negative, are important or moderately important correlates of each of the satisfaction themes, especially for pastors' personal and spiritual satisfaction and satisfaction with their current position. For a pastor to have close friendships with congregational members is a quite controversial topic in discussions of clergy ethics. Some denominations strongly discourage pastors from having close

---

5. In addition to the four satisfaction factors used to organize the table, we also constructed an index of overall satisfaction, summing the responses for each pastor to the several satisfaction items. Most of the same relationships that are evident in the table are present when we correlate the overall satisfaction scores with the items included in the table.

Table 6.4
Selected Correlates of the Four Satisfaction Dimensions*

Situational Issues	Congregational Characteristics	Aspects of the Position	External Support	Personal-Spiritual Life
Ministry's effect on one's family	.23	.25	.16	.26
Spouse's resentment of time ministry takes	ns	-.21	ns	-.16
Spouse's resentment of financial situation	ns	-.49	-.29	-.25
Work preventing time with one's children	ns	ns	ns	-.30
Feeling lonely and isolated	-.19	-.32	-.17	-.32
Having close relationships with congregation members	.17	.16	.13	.16
Stress as result of criticism	-.21	-.20	-.14	-.30
Congregational conflict	-.16	-.23	ns	-.15
Congregation making too many demands	-.15	-.19	ns	-.25
Lack of agreement over the clergy role	-.18	-.28	ns	-.18
Not having a private life apart from clergy role	ns	-.16	-.21	-.28
People relating to me differently as a pastor	-.14	-.24	-.22	-.22
Having sufficient time for recreation, relaxation, and reflection	ns	ns	-.26	-.29
Feeling gifts are right for the congregation one is serving	.19	.14	ns	ns
Serving congregation that challenges one's creativity	.19	.14	ns	ns
Difficulty of reaching people with gospel	ns	-.15	ns	ns

*all correlations are significant at =.05; ns = not statistically significant

friendships with their members, either because such friendships can be perceived as favoritism or because of the potential that they may offer for inappropriate sexual relationships. The latter concern has taken on special importance in light of what appears to be an increase of clergy sexual misconduct in contemporary society.[6] Nonetheless, as I will discuss further in the next chapter, I believe that, despite their potential for mischief, friendships with parishioners and non-parishioners as well as with fellow clergy are essential for a pastor's mental and spiritual well being — as long as they have clear boundaries. Without them, the ministry can be a lonely and debilitating experience.

Other correlates of satisfaction — not unrelated to isolation and concern over friendships within the congregation — have to do with the clergy role. These are issues that we have already seen to have an impact on clergy commitment. They include lack of agreement over the pastor's role, the perception that people relate to them differently because they are clergy, and the difficulty of having a private life apart from one's work as a pastor. Disagreement over the clergy role, as we saw, is also a leading contributor to congregational conflict. Other role issues seem to create social distance between clergy and members by putting clergy on a pedestal, holding them to a higher standard than laity set for themselves, and treating them as somehow different from other men and women. It has been reported, no doubt apocryphally, that there are three restrooms at one popular Catholic shrine: one for women, another for men, and yet another for clergy!

Finally, time issues are also somewhat important for satisfaction: having sufficient time for recreation and renewal correlates positively, while work preventing clergy spending time with their children and resentment on the part of spouses of the time ministry takes both correlate negatively. These also probably add to the perception that ministry has a negative effect on pastors' families.

Physical and Emotional Health:
Are Clergy in Danger of Burnout and Exhaustion?

Thus far, we have seen that the commitment and satisfaction levels of the pastors in our survey are high, if not uniformly so, and we've considered some of the factors that create problems. But what about pastors' health?

6. I emphasize that sexual misconduct *appears* to have increased. In the absence of trend studies, we really don't know if there is more misconduct now than in the past. It could be that it is simply more often reported today than previously.

Are some of the same factors that affect satisfaction also operative when it comes to how clergy feel and to their physical and emotional health? Earlier I considered how clergy's ability to maintain a boundary, however porous, between work and non-work time had a significant positive relationship to their emotional and physical health. There I introduced three scales: one measuring positive feelings and energy, a second measuring emotional health, and a third assessing physical health. In each case, the scale is based on the pastor's self-assessment. Here I consider them further. The three scales should provide some insight into issues of burnout and fatigue that lead to depression, physical exhaustion, and dropping out of the pastorate.

In general, as with commitment and satisfaction, clergy score high on all three health-related measures. Each scale has a minimum score of 3 (indicating very poor health) and a maximum of 15 (indicating excellent health). The average (mean) score for the scale measuring positive feelings and energy is 11.8; for emotional health, it is 13.8; and for physical health, it is 13.3. These high average scores indicate that clergy generally view themselves as quite healthy. Of the three scales, only the physical health scale is affected by the pastor's age: older pastors, as might be expected, assess their health less robustly than younger ones do. As I reported earlier, Catholic priests are significantly less positive about their physical health, and mainline Protestants score lowest on the scale measuring positive feelings and energy. Denominational differences on the emotional health scale are not significant.

Although the large majority of clergy score high on all three scales, we can gain some purchase on issues that are related to health by looking at factors that may be correlated with those who scored lower. In addition to age, one would suspect that some of the same culprits that contribute to lower commitment and satisfaction also affect a pastor's health as we have measured it. That in fact proves to be the case as one can see in Table 6.5 on page 180. As before, the table includes only those issues that are significantly correlated with the three health measures.

Not surprisingly, many of the same relationships that affect commitment and satisfaction are also related to the three health measures. The first four have much to do with difficulties experienced around the clergy role: a sense of loneliness and isolation, the difficulty of having a private life apart from the role, the perception that pastors are treated differently from other people, and lack of agreement about the role. The next five have to do with the congregation: high demands on the pastor, stress be-

Table 6.5
Factors Associated with Clergy Health*

	Positive Feelings and Energy	Emotional Health	Physical Health
Feeling lonely and isolated	-.36	-.31	-.21
Difficulty having private life apart from clergy role	-.30	-.25	-.16
Perceiving different treatment as clergy	-.27	-.25	ns
Lack of agreement over clergy role	-.21	-.22	-.15
Congregation making too many demands	-.27	-.23	-.14
Stress from congregation's challenges	-.34	-.35	-.09
Congregation critical of pastor	-.18	-.21	-.13
Stress from congregation's criticisms	-.23	-.29	-.24
Feeling loved and cared for by congregation	.24	.20	ns
Little time for recreation, relaxation, reflection	-.32	-.17	-.15
Work preventing time with children	-.30	-.16	-.20
Spouse resenting time ministry takes	-.18	-.15	ns
Spouse resenting financial situation	-.25	-.26	-.10

*All correlations are statistically significant at ≤.05

cause of challenges, and criticism of members and the stress that this causes. There is also one positive relationship. Pastors who feel loved and cared for by the congregation also have positive feelings and energy and score high on emotional health. Three of the final four are related to the difficulty of having a private life apart from the clergy role: time for recreation, relaxation, and reflection; time with children; and spousal resentment of the time that one's ministry takes. Spousal resentment of the family's financial situation also correlates to negative feelings and lower emotional health. What I conclude from this is that although clergy health (as measured by the three scales) is generally good, the issues that the table shows to be related, mostly negatively, to health raise important flags.[7]

7. I have shown the entire list of significant relationships, since we can learn from each of them. When I used multiple regression analysis and looked at the effects of these

They are issues that denominations, lay members of congregations, and clergy themselves need to address.

How are the health scales related to commitment and satisfaction? Clergy who express positive feelings and energy and who assess their emotional health positively are significantly less likely to express doubts about their call to ordained ministry or to consider leaving pastoral ministry for another type of ministry position or to leave pastoral ministry altogether. Which is cause and which is effect is impossible to say. There is no significant relationship between the three commitment measures and the pastor's physical health.

The relation of health and satisfaction is a bit more complex, as we can see in Figure 6.3 on page 182, where I show correlations between the health scales and those measuring various aspects of satisfaction, including a measure of overall satisfaction, an index constructed by summing the responses for each pastor to the various individual items.

As is evident, the health scales are all significantly related to satisfaction — some more strongly than others — with one exception. There is no significant relationship between pastors' self-assessed physical health and satisfaction with one's denominational support, nor would I have necessarily expected that there would be. Indeed, the correlations between physical health and the other satisfaction measures are generally weaker, even if statistically significant.[8] What the table makes clear is that satisfaction with various aspects of one's ministry is strongly related to having positive feelings and energy and positive emotional health. Expressed negatively,

---

various measures, taken together, on each of the health scales (adding age, gender, total hours worked per week, and body mass index to the model as background variables), some of the relationships dropped from statistical significance. For positive feelings and energy, none of the background variables were significant; however, having time for recreation, relaxation, and reflection, stress due to congregational challenges, and feelings of loneliness and isolation continued to be important. For emotional health, having a life apart from the clergy role, stress due to congregational challenges, and feelings of loneliness and isolation continued to be important. Finally, for physical health, age, work preventing time for one's children, spouse resentment of ministry time and of the family's financial situation, and stress from congregational criticism had negative effects. Experiencing love and care from one's congregation had a positive effect.

8. In another multiple regression analysis, which looked at the relation of the health scales with the satisfaction measures, when I controlled for the pastors' age, the relation between physical health and satisfaction "washed out." In other words, physical health, as might be expected, declines with age.

Figure 6.3
Correlations between Health Scales and Satisfaction Measures

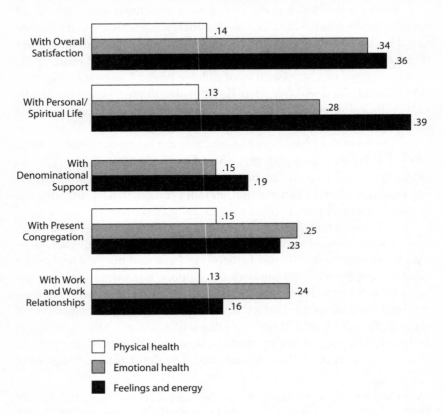

negative feelings and energy and negative emotional health — indicators of stress and burnout — are significantly related to low satisfaction with ministry. The same is true for commitment.

Commitment, Satisfaction, and Lay Perceptions of Good Fit

The study of Lutheran Church — Missouri Synod pastors we mentioned at the beginning of this chapter concluded that a mismatch between clergy and congregations was one of the primary causes of clergy stress and

Table 6.6
Perceptions of Good Match with
Commitment, Satisfaction, and Health

	Good Match
Doubted call	-.31
Considered leaving for other church position	-.19
Considered leaving for secular position	-.19
Satisfaction with work and relationships	.29
Satisfaction with present congregation	.27
Satisfaction with the denomination	.16
Satisfaction with personal and spiritual life	.27
Overall satisfaction with ministry	.34
Positive feelings and energy	.36
Emotional health	.21
Physical health	ns

burnout. Are the pastor's commitment to ministry, satisfaction, and health affected by lay members' belief that there is a good fit between the pastor and congregation? On the basis of the LCMS study and findings from the GoodWork Project we mentioned in Chapter 2, I would expect that laity's sense that the pastor is a good fit — a measure reflecting the alignment of the pastor's work with major stakeholders — would be positively related to the pastor's commitment, satisfaction and health. Table 6.6 shows the correlations between the various measures.

Doubting one's call and considering leaving ministry, either altogether or for another religious position, are negatively related to lay members' perception of a good fit, and the various measures of satisfaction, and two of the three health scales are positively related to a good fit in the eyes of lay members. Although I do not know from our measures what criteria laity use in making their judgments regarding a pastor's fit with the congregation, it is clear that their views are important to how clergy fare within the congregation. Lay perceptions matter! As a denominational executive told us, "I think a large part of the secret of clergy success in ministry is the match of pastors and congregations, getting the right person in the right place."

Commitment and Satisfaction in Other Occupations

Before concluding this discussion, I want to consider one additional question. Are the findings about commitment and satisfaction that I have reported unique to clergy? What of other occupations and professions? Considerable research has been done on work satisfaction generally, and much of it shows that American workers, especially professionals and managers, are highly satisfied with their work. The National Opinion Research Center regularly asks this question in their General Social Survey (GSS), a major national study conducted every other year. In cumulative GSS surveys from 1972-2000, 54 percent of all professionals and managers reported that they were "very satisfied" with their jobs, and another 35 percent claimed to be "moderately satisfied." Only about 3 percent were "very dissatisfied." These attitudes are not very different at all from what I found for clergy. Similarly, in a comparison of Japanese and American workers, American workers expressed much greater satisfaction with their jobs than Japanese workers: almost 70 percent of American workers would take the same job again, but less than one-fourth of Japanese say that they would do so (Lincoln and Kalleberg 1990: 70-72).

Despite these generally positive expressions of worker satisfaction, however, other research has called attention to flagging commitment and dissatisfaction, especially among several professional occupations. A 1997 study examining physicians' responses to managed care found that "more than one-third (35%) of physicians are either somewhat or very dissatisfied with the overall practice of medicine." Only 24 percent were very satisfied (Collins, Schoen, & Sandman 1997). As I have noted, the GoodWork Project focused on the work experiences of geneticists and journalists. Geneticists found considerable satisfaction and fulfillment in their work. Their major stakeholders and society generally supported their work and thought it was important. In contrast, journalists were often at odds with the financial interests of corporate media owners and with the lowbrow tastes of much of their audience. The researchers concluded that few if any geneticists, but quite a few journalists, would like to leave their respective professions (Gardner et al. 2001). A former dean of Yale Law School wrote of "a crisis of morale" among lawyers that is the product of growing doubts about the capacity of a lawyer's life to offer fulfillment to the person who takes it up (Kronan 1993: 2). A 1990 graduate of Harvard Law School polled his classmates ten years later. Some were content with their careers in law, but many who had not already abandoned their profession vowed to do so "with the very next infusion of cash or gumption" (Kurson 2000). Too, both public school teachers and nurses are in notoriously short supply, with much of the blame placed on low salaries and difficult working conditions.

What we have in these various accounts is quite similar to what we noted regarding clergy: There are sharp differences of opinion. On the one hand are the reports of considerable satisfaction with their occupations from a majority of American workers, including professionals. But, on the other hand, we find waning commitment as well as dissatisfaction among some workers. Evidently the mixed messages that we have found among clergy are not unique to them.

Conclusion

I began this chapter asking which of two common perspectives is more accurate: the one that views ministry as a troubled profession, perhaps even one in crisis; or the one that sees the profession as a deeply satisfying calling to which it is worth giving one's life? As I have noted, our data give some support to both perspectives, but most to the second. That is, most of America's pastoral leaders — represented by the sample that we surveyed — are deeply committed to their calling to ordained ministry. If they consider a change, it is more likely that they would pursue their call in another church-related occupation rather than dropping out. They are likewise generally satisfied with most aspects of their work. In short, they echo Eugene Peterson's comment with which we opened this chapter. And, if we can accept self-reported measures of health, clergy express positive feelings and energy and are emotionally and physically fit; though, like most Americans, they are also overweight as a group.

But what of those who dispute this essentially positive view? When we first completed our survey and published some of the early analyses of the data, including these positive findings about commitment, satisfaction, and health, we were not only surprised ourselves, but we met with considerable skepticism from others. Are clergy really as committed, happy, and healthy as our findings suggest?

To try to clarify these findings, we asked participants in focus groups how, given the general perception of crisis, they would explain these positive results. Several immediately suggested that our respondents most certainly were lying! That, or they simply had to be in serious denial. Without going that far, I would not be surprised if some clergy that we surveyed may have found it difficult to tell a stranger who was interviewing them that they had doubts about their calling or that they were dissatisfied with the work to which they have devoted their lives. This was what led me to see what could be learned from those who said they have doubted their call "once in a while," from those who are "somewhat satisfied" with various aspects of their ministry, and from those whose self-reported health was not altogether rosy. Other clergy whom we asked about the findings reminded us that our sample was drawn from those who are active pastors, not those who have left either for another church-related position or have dropped out.[9] As I have said, I do not doubt that this colors our findings. Yet, that active clergy are as highly committed and satisfied as the data show gives a reason to challenge the overly grim view of ordained ministry as a profession in crisis.

At the same time, we should not ignore those who see pastoral ministry as troubled, especially when clergy themselves express this view. Our findings give some support to this view, and I have tried to highlight those things that weaken commitment, foster dissatisfaction, and affect health negatively. At the risk of redundancy, I list once more the most serious issues that our analysis uncovered:

- Inadequate compensation, at least for many clergy in small and mid-sized congregations;
- Congregational conflict and criticism that is allowed to fester and remain unresolved;
- Stress from congregational challenges and demands, especially as they prevent pastors from spending quality time with their family or finding adequate time for recreation, reflection, and renewal;
- Pastoral role issues, especially the difficulty of maintaining a private life apart from one's role as pastor, as well as being treated differently because one is a pastor;
- The experience of loneliness and isolation.

9. In another *Pulpit & Pew* project, Dean Hoge and Jacqueline Wenger (2005) have interviewed individuals who have dropped out of Protestant pastoral ministry (either for another ministry position or for a secular position). Many of the factors that I found to have a negative impact on clergy were among the primary reasons that many dropped out. Hoge (2002) found some similar patterns among recently ordained Catholic priests who also chose to leave the priesthood.

The data suggest that the problems are not as widespread or bleak as some reports maintain. Even so, they should not be ignored, because they can have a significant negative impact on clergy, their congregations, and their families. Dispirited, drained clergy foster dispirited congregations, whose energy for ministry and mission is likewise drained. And the reciprocal is also true: dispirited and contentious congregations increase the likelihood that a pastor's commitment and satisfaction with his or her work will flag. Thankfully, these do not seem to be the situations in which a majority of clergy find themselves. Most would agree with John Newton, who famously said that while being a pastor can be at times "the worst of all jobs," it is also "the best of all callings."

Chapter 7

"A Manner of Life Worthy of the Gospel": Exploring the Meaning of Excellence in Ministry and Pastoral Leadership

"All art is craft. It must be made as well as thought. What is lost is the truth that all craft contains the potential to rise to art."

Henry Glassie, *The Spirit of Folk Art* (1989)

"Only live your life in a manner worthy of the gospel of Christ so that, whether I come and see you or am absent and hear about you, I will know that you are standing firm in one spirit, striving side by side with one mind for the faith of the gospel, and are in no way intimidated by your opponents."

Philippians 1:27-28

I open this chapter with Henry Glassie's quote because it implies that art is not distinct from craft but rather is a higher and more excellent expression of the knowledge, skill, and creativity that belong to a particular craft. In previous chapters, I have offered a portrait of those engaged in the craft of pastoral leadership — focusing mainly on their characteristics, their work, and how they are faring spiritually, emotionally, and physically. Now, both in this chapter and the next, I want to try to pull things together, addressing more fully the meaning of excellent ministry generally and especially excellent pastoral leadership. What practices characterize such ministry? And, in the next chapter, what can be done to call forth, nurture, and support it; that is, how to release its potential so that it rises to an art? The answers to such questions go beyond what can be learned from a quantitative survey, though what we have learned thus far provides many important clues. My main sources of answers, however, will be the focus group interviews with pastors, laity, and denominational officials and conversations in the several *Pulpit & Pew* advisory groups as we hammered out the meaning of excellence. Throughout the chapter I will also include my own perspective, which has emerged from the data analysis and reflection on my own experiences in the church and with clergy. What follows, then, is more qualitative than quantitative, more subjective than reflecting conclusions based on hard, objective data.

There are several points that I will address:

- First, I will review several assessments of the state of ministry today, especially pastoral ministry, that bear on our topic;
- Second, I will argue that, while recent discussion of excellence in the corporate world contains important insights applicable to churches and pastoral leaders, in last analysis it is seriously flawed and deficient as a perspective for excellent Christian ministry;
- Third, I will distinguish between normative and contextual descriptions of excellent ministry, noting that they are not mutually exclusive and that they are both important;
- Finally, I will point to several characteristics that, based on our research, describe excellent ministry and pastoral leadership both normatively and contextually.

Before turning to these themes, one point relating to terminology is worth making. Throughout the chapter, I refer sometimes to "excellent ministry" and at other times to "excellent pastoral leadership." By the first, I mean excellence in the life and work to which all Christians — clergy and laity — are called by virtue of their baptism. When I speak of excellent pastoral leadership, I refer to the work of pastors who lead congregations in such a way that the congregations and their members exhibit excellence in their life and practices. The two are obviously closely related, and I haven't tried to separate discussion of them into different sections of the chapter.

Assessments of Excellence in the Church: A Mixed Picture

Paul Wilkes recently published two books reporting his study of excellent Protestant and Catholic congregations (Wilkes 2001a and 2001b). Each contains case studies of congregations and parishes, large and small, urban and suburban that were nominated by various sources as excellent congregations. In an article in the *Boston Sunday Globe,* Wilkes (1999) reflected on his visits to many Protestant and Catholic churches across the country as he gathered data for his books. Writing especially to Catholics, he maintains that "in too many of our parishes, we have [clergy] who are sadly ordinary, . . . who had they ended up in any other field would be seen as second-rate practitioners."

Echoing Wilkes's assessment, Andrew Greeley (2004) contends that "The big problems in the priesthood . . . are not celibacy or sexual frustration, but the constraints on excellence in an envy-ridden, rigid and mediocre clerical culture that does a poor job of serving church members." Though Wilkes suggests that the quality of recruits is the problem, Greeley faults what he calls a "clerical culture," the operative assumptions and justifications that shape priests' understanding of their work and their practice. A majority of priests, he suggests, blame their problems on required celibacy, or the failures of their bishops, or the lack of commitment of their parishioners, or on secularism in the larger society. Only a few priests, approximately 25 percent in a recent survey, view the problem as the result of their own insensitivity, inadequate leadership, or poor preaching and liturgy. Whether the problem is a decline in the quality of recruits or a dysfunctional clerical culture that shapes performance, both Wilkes and Greeley lament the absence of excellent pastoral leadership in the practice of many priests.

Can the same be said of Protestant clergy? Sounding a note similar to Wilkes and Greeley, Lynne and Bill Hybels had this to say about many Protestant pastors and their congregations:

> Preaching is insipid and unrelated to daily life. Fellowship means little more than superficial conversations in the church lobby after a service. Communion is an autopilot ritual, and prayer a formality. Surprises — in terms of programs or sermons or policies or life transformations — seldom occur, and a sense of the miraculous is an outdated notion. The "haves" give little thought and even less help to the "have nots."

> The church operates as an isolated island of subculture, wondering
> why it is ignored and unappreciated by the community at large.
> (Hybels and Hybels 1995: 49)

They are not alone in their assessment of the poor quality of Protestant
pastoral leadership. Others have expressed similar opinions, often blaming
it on a decline in the quality of those entering ministry. As we have noted
previously, it is quite difficult, given existing data, to substantiate such
claims for either Protestants or Catholics. In a recent book, sociologist
Mark Chaves (2004: 39-43) marshals some evidence of a decline in the academic ability of entering seminarians in recent years. He points, for example, to data showing fewer Phi Beta Kappans and Rhodes Scholars among
clergy than in the past. Also, average Graduate Record Examination verbal
and analytical scores of entrants to seminaries, especially males, have declined — this at a time when the average scores of test-takers overall have
increased. Academic ability, however, is only one indicator of quality, and
it is not always the most predictive of excellent pastoral leadership.[1] Others
wonder if the shrinking number of younger entrants to ministry and the
church's increasing reliance on older, second-career clergy are also not evidence of a decline in the quality of pastoral leadership (e.g., Wheeler 2001).
They worry that the "best and brightest" of our youth are not attracted by
the prospects of leading declining congregations or being part of a profession that has lost status and authority. And they worry that even when
younger ministry candidates enter seminary, many of them have little
prior knowledge of congregational life or denominations, having experienced their call to ministry during their college years, often through involvement in a non-denominational campus religious group.

There is truth in these worries about declining quality; yet, the data
to make such claims are sparse and mostly impressionistic, especially when
it comes to the actual performance of clergy as leaders. As the historian
William Hutchison once commented, "Laments concerning 'ministerial
decline,' laid end to end, would form a wide and solid line from 1630 to

---

1. I recall a chapel sermon by a seminary faculty member with the title "God Loves a
C Student." In the sermon, he opined that C students were much more likely to be effective
pastoral leaders than students who made A grades but were more concerned about the latest
theological currents than in ringing doorbells to share the gospel with the unchurched.
Echoing Paul's words to the church at Corinth, he argued that God uses that which is simple
and foolish to shame the wise and powerful.

1930 [the period about which Hutchison was writing] and, if valid, would document the ending of all ministerial influence in America sometime before the Revolution" (1989: 12). What Hutchison said about declining ministerial influence is also applicable to laments about declining ministerial quality. Nevertheless, in the course of our research we did observe clergy whose work seemed to be at best average rather than excellent and others who seemed below average and often in trouble.

These less-than-excellent clergy and congregations, however, are not the whole story. In his research, Wilkes, as we did, discovered that there are parishes, congregations, and clergy with what he calls a "lust for excellence. They had an 'edge,'" he said, "tempered by constant self-analysis, and were open to both the workings of the Holy Spirit and ideas that bubbled up from . . . the people of God."

What, more fully, does this "lust for excellence" mean when describing ministry and pastoral leadership? My aim here is *not* to describe an impossible ideal of excellence or to portray highly charismatic clergy "superstars." Rather, it is to offer a perspective on excellence that sets the bar high, but not impossibly so.

Is "Excellence" the Right Word?

An issue that has provoked debate from the start of our work is whether "excellence" is the right word to use in discussing ministry and pastoral leadership. Not only does the word appear only minimally in Scripture, but also critics believe that it has been co-opted and often trivialized by those who write about and consult with members of the business world. Excellence, the critics say, has come to be equated with material success and measured primarily by the size and profitability of an organization, attributes that have little to do with a biblical and theological understanding of church and ministry. It is instructive to remember that not too long ago many would have held up Enron as a prime example of corporate excellence!

Much of the criticism of the corporate model of excellence is justified; nevertheless, some of the attributes ascribed to excellent business organizations seem quite applicable to Christian ministry, both of the congregation and the pastor. Consider the following description from Peters and Waterman in their 1982 bestseller *In Search of Excellence*. Among various attributes, excellent leaders and their organizations:

- Establish a clear vision that sets direction and boundaries, but give participants a free rein and necessary support to pursue the vision;
- Pay attention to the smallest details;
- Instill in all employees the values of the organization;
- Provide staff and leaders with the training needed to do their jobs well;
- Listen to participants and value their input.

While we might change a few words here and there ("members" would replace "employees," for example), these qualities do not seem antithetical to excellent congregations or pastoral leadership. For example, Peters and Waterman's emphasis on listening to participants, valuing their insights, and developing a clear vision that sets direction and boundaries seems to characterize the shared leadership of clergy and laity that we described in Chapter 5. There we saw that such a leadership style is positively correlated with various measures of congregational effectiveness. A Chicago-area pastor echoed this when he spoke of another minister in his denomination with whom he disagreed theologically but nevertheless admired for helping his congregation gain a clear sense of its identity and purpose: "I think he is an excellent pastor and that the church is doing great ministry because [he and his lay members] are clear about their congregation's identity. They are willing to be who they are [rather than trying] to be everything for everybody."

Peters and Waterman also stress the importance of doing things well, especially the little things. An article reporting research on the practices of world-class swimmers has the title "The Mundanity of Excellence" and makes a similar point. The author found that what gives excellent swimmers their edge — what makes them excellent — is not in last analysis some special talent or gift for swimming, although they are of course gifted. Rather it is their attention to doing well the day-to-day things that often seem mundane and even insignificant — for example, being punctual and regular in their practice time, being disciplined in following a set practice routine, working consistently and carefully until good techniques become second nature, and so forth (Chambliss 1989).[2] Without such at-

---

2. This insight into the importance of practicing the little as well as big things until they become habitual is actually very similar to Aristotle's views on excellence in his *Nichomachean Ethics*. For him, moral excellence (e.g., exhibiting justice, fairness, and courage in one's actions), as with physical excellence (e.g., excelling in some sport, exhibiting

tention, no amount of talent gives otherwise gifted swimmers the edge that they need. Such attention to doing the little, day-to-day things well until they become second nature seems equally applicable to pastors and congregations who wish to be more than sadly ordinary, whether small or large.

Similarly applicable to excellent pastoral leadership are Peters and Waterman's emphases on providing effective training for leaders, listening to members, and communicating effectively. All of these are important qualities for anyone aiming to lead a congregation and build up the body of Christ in its ministry.

Yet the critics are right. There are problems with the business model of excellence when it is applied to ministry uncritically and without serious qualification. In last analysis, the model privileges market values — success defined as growth, hard work, strength, efficiency, and avoidance of weakness or vulnerability. Most of these values are simply inappropriate for churches and especially for small congregations. In many small congregations, excellent ministry happens, but not as defined in market terms. Furthermore, reflecting consumerist values, the model encourages what we named in Chapter 5 as transactional leadership, a quid pro quo exchange in which the leader's primary aim is to satisfy the expressed needs of customers, clients, or members in exchange for their approbation, cooperation, and support (Burns 1978: 4). Market values and transactional leadership may be important for excellent business leadership, but they have serious limitations when applied to the church. So we need to look for other sources for an understanding of excellence appropriate to Christian ministry and pastoral leadership.

So What Is Excellent Ministry?

Clergy, we have maintained, are "producers of culture," producers of beliefs, feelings, and practices in congregational life that aim at being faithful to the gospel in the congregation's particular time and place. In the book from which we have drawn this perspective, Wendy Griswold describes

---

physical strength), is a habit that one learns. If one is to become physically excellent, excelling in some sport, one must repeatedly practice those actions necessary for that sport. So also, one becomes morally excellent by regularly practicing those actions characteristic of a morally excellent person until they become habitual.

two understandings of culture. One perspective, emphasizing culture's universal value, sees it as "the best that has been thought or known"[3] in art, literature, history, and philosophy. Appreciation of this universal or high culture is humanizing and civilizing. It "cultivates" the human mind and sensibilities and provides meaning and direction to life. A second perspective is contextual. Rather than a single universal or high culture, this view holds that there are multiple cultures that represent the complex whole of all that is produced in particular times and places. Some cultural products are explicitly produced in response to context, such as art or literature or special organizational forms; others are implicitly produced, such as informal but patterned relationships and practices that grow out of a group's life together. The important point of the second view is its emphasis that all that is produced is contextual, shaped by its particular time and place. These two views of culture provide a helpful way of thinking about excellent ministry and pastoral leadership.

The first view suggests a normative perspective on excellent ministry and pastoral excellence, a way of describing excellence by which all ministry practice is guided and judged. It is primarily the Bible but also the Christian tradition — the wisdom of the church that comes down to us through the centuries — that provide the church with a "high culture" of excellent ministry practices, the best that has been thought or known. Thus we look to Scripture — often to the book of Acts, or to Paul's letters, or to the Pastoral Epistles — to understand the practices of the early church. These writings tell us what ministry was at the outset of the church's life and provide a standard of excellence for today. Beyond Scripture, we can look also to the church fathers and mothers — to Gregory, Ambrose, Augustine, Teresa, and Catherine — or to particular denominational traditions and their perspectives on ministry — Calvinist, Lutheran, Wesleyan, or Pentecostal, for example. Either from Scripture alone — the perspective of most conservative Protestants and, historically, Protestants generally — or from Scripture and the way it has been interpreted through the tradition — a more Catholic approach — we find a "high culture" of excellent ministry practice that forms the "cultural objects" or "tool kit" side of Griswold's cultural diamond. Excellent ministry is that which draws on, produces (or better, reproduces) this high culture.

---

3. A phrase from the English educator and man of letters Matthew Arnold (cited in Griswold 1994: 5).

The second view, however, pushes us to view excellence more contextually, taking into account the other sides of the cultural diamond: pastor, congregation, and social world as they interact with the normative perspective. "One size does not fit all," as we heard again and again in our focus groups. Thus in understanding and producing excellent congregational ministry, we must consider the characteristics of the pastor, his or her particular congregation — its size, location, "life cycle" stage as a congregation, and its denominational tradition (or lack thereof). We must also consider relevant characteristics of the broader social world in which the congregation is located. Given the constraints of these particular contextual characteristics, excellent pastoral leadership involves asking what are the best and most appropriate ministry practices possible at this time and in this place for a particular pastor and his or her congregation. What does it mean for *this pastor* and *this congregation* to be faithful to the gospel in this context?

These two views, while quite different, need not be mutually exclusive. There is essential wisdom about excellence in the Bible and in the church's traditions. They hold up the highest and best about Christian ministry and standards of excellence that both guide and critique ministry practices in any time and place. They are the primary normative "tool kit" available to pastors and congregations for shaping their congregational "clay jars." Yet, there are also the constraints of particular ministry contexts that shape practice, understanding that the highest and best must always be adapted to meet the needs and challenges presented by particular contexts.

These two perspectives were often present in our various discussions of excellence, including the focus groups. There were strong advocates of a normative perspective that describes a view of excellent ministry applicable to all situations. There were equally strong advocates of a more nuanced, contextual view. On both sides, however, there was consensus that the business model of excellence is inadequate. It contains helpful insights, but in its totality, it is not an apt expression of excellent ministry.

A Normative View:
Excellence Shaped by Jesus' Cross and Resurrection

Among various efforts to define or describe excellent ministry normatively, I found both provocative and helpful some comments by Christine

Pohl, who teaches Christian ethics at Asbury Seminary in Kentucky. In a reflection paper prepared for *Pulpit & Pew's* theological colloquium, she had the following to say about excellent ministry:

> Within faithful Christian communities . . . understandings of excellence and practices of excellent ministry will often be complex and somewhat ambiguous given at least the following factors: First, at the center of our proclamation and our hope is a crucified Savior. . . . Second, the Kingdom of God privileges "the poor, crippled, lame, and blind," and faithful followers of Christ have a distinctive call to welcome "the least" to our tables and into our congregations. . . . Third, while pursuing holiness (or excellence), Christians recognize the persistent reality of human sinfulness. We all depend on God's forgiveness and healing, as our struggles with sin or its consequences are part of daily congregational life. And finally, our own motives and efforts in ministry are often a strange mixture of sin and grace, skill and frailty. (Pohl 2001)

The four factors that Pohl lifts up express core insights from the gospel that stand in stark contrast to an understanding of excellence based primarily on the values of market capitalism. Rather than efficiency, success, power, status, and strength, they reflect an excellence grounded in the experience of Jesus, whose path to the Easter triumph led through Gethsemane and Golgotha. Members of our theological colloquium began to refer to this as "cruciform excellence," an excellence grounded in the bedrock conviction that God's excellence — God's power, righteousness, and love — is most fully visible in Jesus' life and ministry, culminating in the cross and resurrection. In the book *Resurrecting Excellence: Shaping Faithful Christian Ministry* (Jones and Armstrong 2006), which offers a theological complement to this book's sociological perspective, the authors use the term "resurrecting excellence" to capture the meaning of excellence that Jesus' experience reveals. By itself, they believe, the concept of cruciform excellence is overly negative, too lacking in hope, and too prone to encourage clergy and congregations to view themselves as victims when things go wrong. Whichever term is used, holding together cross and resurrection transforms the meaning of excellence. In Jesus' supreme act of obedience, his self-emptying, and self-giving for the sake of others, Christians see God's excellence fully revealed in vulnerability, in a love that reaches out to all, but especially to those at the margins of society, a love that death cannot overcome. The resurrection is God's honoring of — God's seal of approval on — Jesus' cruciform way of life. The resurrection is also God's promise and hope-filled message to those who participate in Christ's continuing ministry in the world.

This vision is at the heart of excellent Christian ministry, lay as well as ordained, and it stands in sharp relief from much that is celebrated in the business model of excellence. When Paul uses his clay jar metaphor, he emphasizes that the jars are made of clay so that "it may be made clear that this extraordinary power belongs to God and does not come from us" (2 Cor. 4:7). And he goes on to describe his personal afflictions and the persecution he had experienced — hardly the kind of marks of excellence that would find much favor among leaders in the corporate world. To repeat: the business model is not without its virtues, some of which are clearly applicable to Christian ministry, but Jesus' experience radically shapes, deepens, and extends the meaning of excellence, placing it within the horizon of God's saving work in Jesus' life, death, and resurrection.

Paul's letter to the Philippians makes this point when he calls the Philippians to live their lives in a manner worthy of the gospel of Christ. Living in a city heavily populated with retired Roman soldiers, Philippian Christians would have had a view of excellence shaped by military virtues, much as those of the market shape ours. By calling them to shape their lives by the gospel, Paul holds up to them a different standard of excellence.[4]

Two further implications of a normative perspective were strongly emphasized in our various discussions. First, excellent ministry is *corporate or communal in character*. As Christine Pohl continues,

> In [I Corinthians 12] Paul describes the right functioning of the church as the body of Christ in which there are many parts but one body, and all parts are important. "To each," Paul says, "is given the manifestation of the spirit for the common good." In this same chapter, [he] recognizes weakness in the midst of a rightly functioning body and notes that, within the community of the church, when one suffers, all suffer together. [Then] at the end of his description of the right functioning of the body, Paul writes, "And I will show you a still

4. He makes the standard even more explicit in Philippians 2:1-11, by use of words from what is probably an early Christian hymn.

more excellent way." This . . . way is the way of love [that Paul describes in those memorable words of Chapter 13]. [Later] he asks, "What should be done, then, my friends?" And he answers, "Let all things be done for building up [the Body]."

Excellent ministry, therefore, is deeply communal; it involves practices that are focused on building up and strengthening the whole body, which itself is called to be an agent of reconciliation in the world. As Pohl says, "[Excellent ministry] is less about exceptionally gifted individuals and more about a community that recognizes and depends on each person's contributions and bears one another's burdens."

This communal understanding of ministry reflects the important paradigm shift to which we called attention previously — a shift from an individualistic, pastor-centered view of ministry to one that emphasizes the work of the whole people of God. How widely this shift has permeated thinking about ministry, both Catholic and Protestant, was brought home to us both in our survey and in our focus groups.[5] As we saw in Chapter 5, there was a strong positive correlation between lay reports of shared ministry and their belief that there was a good match between the pastor and congregation. In the focus groups, when the participants, both pastors and laity, were asked to draw a picture of what excellent ministry looked like to them, almost invariably the drawings were corporate rather than individual in character. Although the figure of the pastor often had a distinctive place in the drawings — sometimes up front, sometimes in the center of a circle of members, sometimes encouraging and supporting from behind — most drawings showed people doing ministry together, whether they were worshiping or serving others. Pastors who were able to equip and turn loose their members to engage in the congregation's ministry were regularly held up as exemplars of excellent leadership. It is clear from the drawings that the "people of God" ecclesiology has captured the imagina-

---

5. See also D'Antonio et al. (1996) and D'Antonio et al. (2000). Both of these books report a wide acceptance by Catholic laity of the corporate or "People of God" paradigm for church life. A study of clergy in nine Protestant denominations (Monahan 1999) reported that lay members were sharing in the core work ministry with their pastors in the majority of congregations in the study. Such sharing was generally accepted by clergy and laity, with very little role ambiguity reported by the pastors who completed the survey. That is, sharing ministry with laity did not cause the clergy to experience role confusion for the clergy; nor, according to clergy reports, did it create role confusion for lay members.

tion of many in contemporary church life regardless of whether it is always practiced.

A conservative Protestant pastor in California saw excellent ministry happening "when people are won to faith in Christ, where there is spiritual growth, becoming more like Jesus Christ. And eventually they begin to use their own spiritual gifts and jump into ministry themselves. I'm really passionate about leadership development," he added, "so I'm . . . looking to see those people raised up to be leaders themselves."

Another California pastor gave an example of excellent ministry practiced by a group of "very ordinary people" who were equipped and encouraged by their congregation to participate in what were called "TLC (Tender Loving Care) Groups." The pastor told of going to a hospital where a church member had been taken after being critically injured in an automobile accident. When he arrived, a TLC Group was already present. For two weeks before the man died, the group "recycled, staying with the man's wife, hugging her, always there. . . . I look at how removed I was from that whole thing [and see] that it's the body happening, the body of Christ released and empowered to do the Kingdom's work."

A Chicago pastor described a congregation in which its coordinator of ministry volunteers "will take individual members and try to figure out what their skills are and where they can fit in the ministry. And if it's within the parish context, that's terrific. But if it's in the wider community, that's also terrific. They're seen as a representative of that congregation in whatever aspect of community life it is."

Donald Miller (Miller 1997: 80) describes a similar practice in "new paradigm" churches, congregations that are often independent or affiliated with such movements as the Vineyard Christian Fellowship, Calvary Chapel, and Hope Chapel. Although pastors in these churches are often strong, sometimes authoritarian leaders, they nevertheless, to use Miller's words, "democratize the sacred"; that is, they do not jealously guard their clerical prerogatives. They aim instead to multiply members who will exercise their gifts for ministry in service of the church's mission. These pastors are not interested in attracting followers who will sit at their feet.

There is in these examples an important and freeing lesson for all pastors. The pastor neither has to do everything that a congregation or parish needs to be done, nor does he or she have to be good at everything that is required in the congregation. The pastor brings his or her gifts and works to discover and nurture complementary gifts of others in the congregation as together they pursue the congregation's mission. In an interview, Father Jack Wall, a Catholic priest in Chicago, expressed it as follows: "The pastor has to be the person who believes most deeply that things can happen in the congregation and to recognize that how it happens is not wholly dependent on the pastor. After all, what happens is of God. . . . [Also] we must trust the laity. . . . The vocation of our lay members and their gifts provide the richness that defines the mission of the congregation" (Schier n.d.). The point is that the excellence encouraged in Scripture is, in last analysis, communal. Its goal is ministry by the whole people of God, clergy and laity together, participating in Christ's continuing ministry in the world.

A second implication of the normative perspective follows from the first: *Excellent ministry involves change and life transformation.* Or, using James MacGregor Burns's category, it is transformational rather than transactional. To quote him, "The transforming leader recognizes and exploits an existing need or demand of a potential follower [that is, he or she does not avoid transactional concerns]. But, beyond that, the transforming leader looks for potential motives in followers, seeks to satisfy higher needs, and engages the full person of the follower" (1978: 4). One pastor put it this way: "You can see something is different because that ministry is there. If . . . nothing is happening," he continued, "then it's not good ministry." In its concern with transformation, excellent ministry involves, as the pastor continued, "a balance between nurture that happens in the congregation and a real sense of connection with the world beyond." That is, transformation occurs not only inside the congregation but it affects the community outside as well. And, reflecting the grounding of ministry in Jesus' resurrection, a number of participants told us that a mark of excellent ministry is where hope is alive, supplying an energy source for the community it serves. As a Chicago pastor expressed it, "Good ministry has to offer hope in some capacity. We fall prey to the studies that say that the church is dying, and we have to resist that. If our churches are not hopeful places where the gospel that is preached is not about whether the church has lost members or gained members, or about anything that drags people down, then we're just perpetuating a business or something. The church has to offer hope, and not just for people personally but also for the community it serves, and it has to be a place where people find resources for dealing with the world."

The pastor's comment is a reminder that although excellence

grounded in Jesus' cross and resurrection is no guarantor of success as the corporate world defines it, neither is it devoid of hope. As an example, a denominational official in Indianapolis saw excellent ministry in the case of a pastor who was trying to help his congregation gain a new vision of its ministry and mission while at the same time nurturing its current members through the painful transition. "It's a hard time for the church and the pastor, but the pastor is doing a super job. He expresses his anxieties to me, but he is not anxious with them."[6] He also told of another pastor who had struggled valiantly for about seven years to help his urban congregation reach residents of its changed neighborhood. While they were not successful in bringing residents into the church's membership, they have been quite effective in serving the needs of the neighborhood through outreach programs. "We're very likely going to have to close this ministry," he said, "but when I look at it, it has been a good ministry . . . and I value [the congregation's] creativity, their willingness to risk, their willingness to change. The fact that it hasn't borne fruit in the way we would define as successful doesn't mean to me that it hasn't been a good ministry." Neither case would likely be defined as excellent in terms of a market understanding of success; however, both can be viewed as excellent when we use the cross and resurrection as criteria.

In summary, while excellent ministry viewed from the perspective of Jesus' experience does not privilege the world's criteria of success, neither does it condone careless, unimaginative, uncreative pastoral leadership or congregational life — the kind of sadly ordinary ministry that Paul Wilkes lamented. Rather Jesus' cross and resurrection provide a normative lens for understanding and shaping faithful congregational life and pastoral ministry. Whether successful or not in quantitative terms, excellent ministry is that which is lived out in a manner of life worthy of the gospel. And, as such, it is both communal and transformative.

---

6. His description of the pastor's being non-anxious in the presence of members reflects Edwin Friedman's insight that leading congregations in difficult, often conflictual experiences requires the leader to be a "non-anxious presence," not transferring anxiety that he or she may be feeling about the congregation to the members, expressing it instead to the denominational official (Friedman 1985: 27).

Excellence in Response to the Context

Several of the examples cited above, especially the ones from the Indianapolis denominational official, provide a helpful transition into the second way of thinking about excellent ministry based on Griswold's two views of culture. If the cross and resurrection provide a normative way of describing the best and highest expression of excellence for Christians, the examples remind us that its concrete embodiment in the life of the church must nevertheless be understood contextually. Christian ministry does not take place in isolation from the social world, from broader currents in the culture in which it takes place, as we emphasized in Chapter 2. The various characteristics of this social world — its pluralism, special interest groups, consumerism, and de facto congregationalism — present contextual challenges to pastoral leadership and affect the way in which congregational culture is produced.

The context also includes characteristics of each local congregation and its setting. As I have emphasized, variations in congregations — in their size, location, ethnicity, resources, life cycle stage, and/or denominational tradition — are important in shaping how excellent pastoral leadership is understood and carried out. For example, in a small congregation, excellent ministry will often be described in terms of the care, support, and fellowship that members share with each other and with those in their surrounding community. In such congregations a pastor is most likely to be valued as an excellent leader if she or he genuinely knows and loves the congregation, visits in members' homes, workplaces, and hospital rooms, and is present with them in significant moments in their lives. A pastor of a small rural church in Alabama expressed this vividly: "People don't care how much you know until they know how much you care." Such a pastor may or may not be an especially dynamic preacher or gifted administrator — though preaching and administration are clearly important — but the pastor is nevertheless considered to be an excellent leader because the people know that she or he cares deeply for them and will be present with them when a need arises.

The same pastor might not be equally valued by members of a large urban or suburban church, who often value dynamic preaching, inspiring worship, and a full array of well-designed programs and outreach ministries. Because the congregation is large, members don't necessarily expect that the senior pastor will know them in any deep way; although, when illness, death, or other needs arise, they will look to the congregation for such care — if not from the senior pastor, then at least from a staff member or a lay caregiver such as a Stephen Minister.[7] If the senior pastor is both a gifted preacher and a warm, caring pastor, she or he will be doubly appreciated; but for many large congregations, quality preaching and programs take precedence when they think of excellent pastoral leadership.[8]

Similarly, a congregation's location — urban, suburban, or rural — makes a difference in the pastoral gifts and practices that count for excellent pastoral leadership. Some pastors are able to function much more effectively in one type of setting than in others. The same is true when it comes to the congregation's particular life cycle stage (if we can legitimately apply that term to congregations) or to particular challenges that the congregation may face. Some pastors are gifted in starting and developing new congregations but not especially gifted in staying with them over the long haul as the congregation grows and matures. In contrast, others may not be particularly effective at starting a new congregation. They lack the necessary entrepreneurial skills. But they are quite gifted in working with an established, mature congregation or one that is in need of being re-energized. A Baptist official described the former type as church "planters." The latter, whom he described as "growers," know how to take an already "planted" congregation and build it into a strong congregation that will last over time.

Other contextual factors are also important. Congregations that represent different denominational traditions will often understand excellence differently because they hold contrasting views concerning the core task of the church. As we noted in Chapter 3, the culture of conservative Protestants is more likely to lead them to place a premium on biblical preaching and teaching, having a born-again experience, winning others to Christ, and helping members grow as disciples; whereas both mainline Protestants and Catholics are more likely to value worship and the celebration of the sacraments and social outreach and view the Christian life as a journey, the purpose of which is reconciliation with God and neighbor. Al-

7. Stephen Ministries is a national, non-denominational program by means of which lay members are trained and certified as caregivers in the congregation. They visit in hospitals and in the homes of shut-in members, and they provide support to members in times of need, such as sickness or bereavement.

8. See Lummis (2003) for a discussion of differences in lay views of desired pastoral attributes.

though these perspectives may not, in last analysis, be contradictory, they do imply somewhat different congregational practices and leadership characteristics — one giving strong emphasis to evangelism and less to social outreach; the other emphasizing nurture, teaching, outreach, and, where necessary, prophetic witness. Similarly, as we saw in the discussion of pastoral authority, some conservative Protestants, especially those in the Pentecostal tradition, do not place a high value on a seminary-educated clergy. Instead, they value the pastor's religious zeal as a mark of excellence much more highly than his or her formal education.

In these and others ways, what is considered excellent ministry, including pastoral leadership, is affected by the characteristics of congregations and their contexts. The living out of cruciform or resurrected excellence must be contextualized. Different contexts call for and/or value particular pastoral gifts, and not everyone has these gifts in equal measure. Thus some pastors may be excellent leaders in one context, but they would not valued as such in some other. Different contexts also call for different ministry practices, and not all leaders and members have the gifts or agility to respond in ways that are needed in the context.

In sum, excellent ministry must be understood dually: both normatively and contextually. There are normative standards of excellence that we find in the Bible and in the church's traditions. Jesus' cross and resurrection provide a way of describing what is at the heart of a normative understanding of excellent ministry: the highest and best example of ministry that one can know and follow. The Bible and the church's traditions add to this normative perspective. But giving expression to this standard of excellence requires that it be instantiated within particular contexts in response to the opportunities and challenges that come from the broader culture and in particular local congregational settings. One size does not fit all.

Some Marks of Excellent Ministry

Despite the complexity that various contexts introduce, we can lift up some characteristics or marks of excellent ministry that seem to exemplify it in many different settings. While they do not exhaust the possibilities, they are characteristics that, from our discussions and focus group interviews, I have come to believe are of special importance for any ministry that aims at a Christ-shaped excellence in the face of particular contextual challenges.

Resiliency and Spiritual Disciplines

As we were reminded by a number of focus group participants, the practice of excellence that comes from following Jesus can be costly. It stands in contrast to one of the conclusions of the GoodWork Project. As we saw, Harvard researchers found that it is easier for professionals to do good work — that is, to use their expertise in ways that are consonant with their ethical convictions — when there is alignment between the professionals' values and those of their primary stakeholders. There will be many times, however, when clergy and their congregations, or clergy as distinct from many members of their congregations, will experience misalignment between their own religious and moral convictions and those of the larger society or even those of a majority of their congregation. A North Carolina pastor expressed it this way: "The gospel at its greatest point of clarity regularly stands over against the decisions that the world recommends." Following the gospel often calls pastors and congregations to be willing to rub against the grain of things that they encounter. For example, many pastors and laity in the American South who joined in the struggle for racial justice in the 1960s learned the costs of opposition to the dominant culture. More recently, those who have taken strong, principled stands — some supporting and others opposing — on issues such as abortion, stem cell research, homosexual unions, or war and peace have also often faced sharp criticism. But it is not only about these big social issues that painful challenges occur. Recall the earlier finding about the prevalence of congregational conflict, often, though not always, focused on the pastor and her or his leadership style and practices.

Thus ministry that tries to follow "a manner of life worthy of the gospel" requires that pastors and congregations develop *resiliency* — a toughness combined with elasticity that enables them to endure without breaking when facing the tough challenges and difficult tasks that come from trying to follow in Jesus' way. A folk saying describes a resilient person as being "like a black gum tree against thunder." The tree bends in the storm, but it does not break. This is an apt description of the resiliency characteristic of excellent Christian ministry, a quality essential for dealing with what one pastor called "the inevitable toxicity that exists at times in ministry, but *without becoming toxic oneself*" (emphasis added). He spoke of the importance of being able to deal with unhealthy situations in a healthy and positive way, exhibiting "honesty, integrity, and even a certain amount of cheerfulness at the right time," qualities, I believe, that reflect resiliency.

Developing resiliency is a fruit of engaging in regular spiritual disciplines, disciplines in which clergy and lay Christians proactively put themselves in position to be renewed by God's grace. Just as the act of eating can make one realize how hungry she or he is, spiritual disciplines, interviewees said, awaken a desire for God. Through these disciplines pastors and laity find the nourishment and strength — the grace — to face the challenges of the day. A priest in Arizona who practices a daily discipline of prayer and meditation and takes a monthly day for renewal was described by his bishop as one who "knows his people deeply, is interested in their well-being, available to them in sickness, often at the hospital, present with them in times of death. And he is regularly in the midst of the fray." "It is his regular discipline of prayer and meditation," the bishop said, "that sustains him in his work and makes him an excellent pastor." A conservative Protestant pastor in North Carolina told us, "If I do not practice a regular discipline of prayer, if I am not 'plugged in,' I have nothing to offer to the congregation. I have no resources, no power. I know for myself that except the Lord build the house, I labor in vain."

These comments resonate with those that Adair Lummis heard when she asked what lay members look for in a pastor. Denominational officials told her over and over that laity look for a pastor who is spiritually authentic, who is a dynamic spiritual leader. Said one, whose comment was echoed by others, "They want somebody who has a faith of his or her own, somebody who has some spiritual depth, who knows his or her own faith, and *can articulate it*" (Lummis 2003: 10, emphasis in the original).

In considerable contrast to these examples and comments, recall that the clergy in our survey expressing the *greatest dissatisfaction* with their spiritual life were also the ones significantly more likely to doubt their call to ministry, to have seriously considered dropping out, and to report feeling lonely, isolated, and drained in fulfilling their functions in their congregation. In short, they lack the resiliency and spiritual depth that are essential for the practice of excellent ministry.

Agility and Reflective Leadership

Closely related to resiliency is another characteristic of excellent ministry in a rapidly changing society. In our project discussions, we came to call it *agility*, implying nimbleness and resourcefulness in response to new challenges. Elsewhere (Carroll 1991) I have described this characteristic as *reflective leadership*. Reflective leadership deepens the meaning of agility to mean not only responding nimbly but also faithfully, thoughtfully, innovatively, and appropriately (all the adverbs are important) in the face of a constantly changing world, one sometimes experienced as being like "white water." Such a world confronts congregations and clergy with ongoing challenges that require new ways of thinking and responding, ways of responding that Ronald Heifetz (1994: 8) calls "adaptive" rather than "technical." Technical responses are responses to routine problems that are clearly definable and have relatively fixed solutions. In contrast, "adaptive work consists of the learning required to address conflicts in the values that people hold, or to diminish the gap between the values people stand for and the reality they face. Adaptive work requires a change in values, beliefs or behavior" (p. 22). Many of the challenges that pastors and their congregations face today require adaptation, not technical responses, if they are to reshape their congregation's culture in faithfulness to the gospel.

Adaptation, as a characteristic of an agile or reflective response, is not the same as accommodation. As I said in the earlier discussion of pastoral leadership, it is not simply giving in (accommodating) to a difficult situation. Rather it involves holding in creative tension the challenges of the present situation *and* the goods of the Christian faith, both Scripture and tradition. In so doing each informs the other in an ongoing dialogue or argument. In this reflective conversation, Scripture and tradition remain living resources that are newly interpreted in the encounter with present challenges as pastors and congregations seek ways of responding in faithfulness to the gospel. Recall once more Alasdair MacIntyre's point that living traditions always involve a continuous argument about what it means to live by them. In the same process, however, responses to present challenges must avoid simple accommodation. What is needed is not a "knee-jerk" reaction but rather an effort to respond to the new challenges faithfully, informed and guided by engagement with Scripture and tradition and with the leading of the Holy Spirit. In a similar vein, Craig Dykstra speaks of a distinctive kind of "pastoral imagination," "a way of seeing into and interpreting the world which shapes everything a pastor thinks and does." The pastoral imagination involves "the constant interplay of attention to Scripture; sorting through the gospel's call and demand on them and their congregations in their particular context" (2001: 1-2). A North Carolina pastor described this "as the wisdom of both pastoral leaders and parish leaders to understand what chapter they happen to be in, in terms of the larger picture of ministry in which the congregation is set. It's so easy to get wrapped up in issues that are in front of us at this moment." An example of what I mean by agility or reflective leadership or pastoral imagination was provided by one of our advisory group members.[9]

In the early 1990s, a new pastor was appointed pastor of St. Mark United Methodist Church in downtown Atlanta. The church has a proud heritage as a once thriving, progressive congregation. At the time of the new pastor's appointment, however, he was told that he was to help make an assessment as to whether the church should be closed. It had lost many members to suburban congregations and those who had stayed were increasingly elderly. The large sanctuary was typically three-quarters empty on Sunday mornings.

One Saturday afternoon during his first year at the church, the pastor heard a commotion outside. He discovered that Atlanta's annual "Gay Pride" parade was passing in front of the church building. Down the street, a few members of Atlanta's fundamentalist First Baptist Church held a counter demonstration on the church ground, publicizing their conviction that homosexuality was sinful.

For a long while the pastor, himself a conservative in style and belief, pondered what he had seen. Eventually he initiated conversations with his administrative board with the suggestion that St. Mark offer refreshments for the next year's marchers along with a banner that would read: "Welcome to St. Mark." Needless to say, not everyone was enthusiastic. For several meetings the board considered the proposal and together they engaged in serious Bible study of passages generally considered to condemn same-sex relations, along with other passages about hospitality to the stranger. They also consulted the United Methodist *Discipline* which, though forbidding ordination of homosexuals and same sex unions, nonetheless declares that the church's ministry extends to all people, regardless of sexual orientation.

At length the leaders agreed, and the pastor's proposal was put into action at the next Gay Pride parade. The response was remarkable. Many marchers applauded as they passed; a few cried; and a small number turned up the following Sunday for worship. Finding a welcome, they

---

9. Professor Brooks Holifield of Candler School of Theology provided the example at one of our advisory group meetings.

passed the word to others, and the membership roll began to move upward. Today the church flourishes with large numbers of gay and lesbian members alongside the still aging remaining congregants. The church has also developed a strong program of outreach to the needy in downtown Atlanta.

This reshaping of the congregation's culture is an example of the agility and imagination required for reflective leadership and, by extension, for excellent ministry. In it, the pastor and lay leaders did not make a hasty response either to welcome or to exclude its gay and lesbian neighbors. Rather they engaged in a reflective and prayerful conversation with the church's traditions and denominational policies and their own admittedly ambivalent feelings. Out of this conversation, they made an adaptive response to the new situation in which they found themselves, a response that they believed was both faithful to the gospel's emphasis on hospitality and appropriate to the church's current circumstances. What had been a dying congregation has found new life as it practiced hospitality to a group that some would treat as pariahs.

Agility or reflective leadership as practiced by the pastor and his congregation is not something that we can find laid out in a manual to follow. Some pastors and laity attempt to use the Bible, the tradition, the latest work from a church growth or conflict management specialist, or simply what has worked for them in a previous congregation or situation to provide a formula for responding. As helpful and important as these resources may be as guides for action, treating them as blueprints to be imposed is, more often than not, not very useful. Indeed, doing so fails to respect a congregation's distinctive needs and challenges.[10] Congregations not only differ significantly in their cultures and often require different responses, but many challenges that face them are also novel and without precedent.

---

10. Kevin Miller (2004), recounting an incident where he learned that one's previous congregational practices are not necessarily appropriate for another congregation, no matter how similar the congregations seem, cites a paragraph from Dietrich Bonhoeffer's *Life Together*. Bonhoeffer warned that "God hates visionary dreaming; it makes the dreamer proud and pretentious. The man who fashions a visionary ideal of community demands that it be realized by God, by others, and by himself. He enters the community of Christians with his demands, sets up his own law, and judges the brethren and God Himself accordingly. . . . When things do not go his way, he calls the effort a failure. When his ideal picture is destroyed, he sees the community going to smash. So he becomes, first an accuser of his brethren, then an accuser of God, and finally the despairing accuser of himself."

As the Atlanta example makes clear, congregational leaders must often think and respond "outside the box." They must find their own way of responding with agility "in a manner worthy of the Gospel."

Because there is the potential for mistakes and failure as well as success, agility or reflective leadership also involves both humility and a willingness to learn from one's failures as well as successes. After describing several pastors, each of whom had led their congregations to make difficult and not always successful choices in response to their changing communities, the denominational official in Indiana cited earlier in this chapter concluded that what is common to each of them "is that they are open to learning. They are eager to share and reflect on their own ministry. They are not afraid of looking at their own role and their own leadership style as they are present in the midst of change. They take an appropriate amount of responsibility for what's happening in their congregations without overly identifying with what's happening. And they are lifelong learners."

Trust and Personal Authority

A third characteristic of excellent pastoral leadership, one that I have discussed previously and need only to highlight here, is *trust*. "Trust me," the slick salesman says; but as the ancient warning to prospective consumers puts it, *caveat emptor,* "let the buyer beware." Just the opposite must be the case for pastors: *credat emptor,* "let the 'buyer' trust." A pastor is not likely to be or be perceived as an excellent leader if she or he does not have the trust of her or his members. He or she is especially unlikely to be able to lead a congregation through difficult changes without being a trusted leader. In the discussion of authority in Chapter 5, I contrasted personal or informal bases of a pastor's authority with formal authority. To recall the distinction, the latter is typically based on ordination by a denomination or a congregation and often on having the requisite educational credentials. Informal or personal authority, in contrast, is tacit acknowledgement by a pastor's congregation that he or she has won the congregation's trust, having demonstrated integrity, wisdom, and genuine care in dealings with the congregation. Formal authority is quite important; yet, for difficult changes to be addressed, it needs to be complemented by informal or personal authority.

Trust in the pastor's leadership is engendered by recognition that the pastor is a person of deep faith, one whose life is grounded spiritually as we discussed earlier in relation to resiliency. But it is also engendered when laity recognize that their pastor genuinely cares for them — not always an easy task. As a denominational leader told Adair Lummis, "Deep down with all of the crap you get, you have to be able to say what the little book by Bonhoeffer [*Life Together*] said years ago, 'I love these people.' And if people know they are loved, they will follow pretty well where you are going" (Lummis 2003: 13). Recall the words of the small church pastor cited earlier: "People don't care how much you know until they know how much you care." Another rural pastor commented, "God is more than a sermon that I just preached. When you have children in your community who are hungry, families where the water is cut off, then you can't stop with the sermon. You have to show that you care." A judicatory executive in California made this point negatively by describing what he called "bad ministry," which he described as "ministry that does not have an ear for the people. . . . What I mean by that is some pastors felt that their calling was for preaching and teaching, and they didn't care to visit anyone. . . . They only had a very narrow view of what was needed in a particular church, and it was hurtful to the people in the pews because they felt that their pastor didn't care at all. He preached wonderful sermons, but then where's the caring?" Both spiritual depth and a genuine love of one's people are prerequisites for the personal authority that enables one to lead.

Staying Connected

A fourth characteristic essential for practicing excellent pastoral leadership is a *willingness to stay connected,* to avoid the isolation that leads to burning out and dropping out. As I have noted earlier, in many conversations with pastors and denominational leaders and in our national survey, the issue of clergy friendships emerged as of considerable importance for sustaining ministry in challenging times. Having close friends is in itself not a guarantor of excellent pastoral leadership; however, without the support, companionship, mutual critique, and joy that friends offer, without those with whom one can be vulnerable and share deeply, it is difficult, if not impossible, to sustain the kind of excellent ministry that follows in Jesus' path.

In the preceding chapter, we saw how feeling isolated was a contributor to lack of satisfaction in ministry and to pastoral health problems. And it was also a key factor related to doubting one's call and considering dropping out of ministry or actually doing so. For Protestant pastors who have dropped out of ministry, just over half reported that they felt lonely or isolated (Hoge and Wenger 2005). Similarly, Catholic priests who had resigned from the priesthood within five years of being ordained listed the loneliness of the priestly life as second only to celibacy among the problems facing priests today (Hoge 2002: 170). The two are related. For priests, the celibate lifestyle precludes having a spouse and children as primary friends with whom to share interests, joys, and frustrations. Loneliness and isolation are inevitable unless the priest has friendships within the parish, with fellow priests, or with others outside the parish. Protestant clergy at least have the possibility of spouses and children as friends; yet, when friendships are limited to spouse and children, it often places too great a burden on those individuals. As we saw from the survey, feeling isolated and being dissatisfied with family life are highly and significantly correlated. Isolation that results from the lack of friendships beyond one's family is not the only contributor to Protestant clergy family dissatisfaction, but it is an important one.

As I have noted, the topic of friendships with members of one's congregation is a hotly debated one, made more contentious in recent years because of highly publicized incidents of clergy sexual misconduct. In spite of the opportunities that such friendships offer for abuse, I am convinced that they should not be avoided. Excellent ministry is difficult, if not impossible, if a person cuts her- or himself off from close friendships both within and outside the congregation.

The theologians in our project use the term "holy friendships" to describe what they believe is characteristic of friendships that both reduce the possibility of abuse and also support excellent ministry (Jones and Armstrong 2006). In their view, holy friendships grow out of an individual's relationship with God that, like resilience, is nurtured in spiritual disciplines of prayer, meditation and worship. Through these practices, individuals discover the friendship of God, who respects us, is patient with us, and seeks only our well-being. A holy friendship with God, they believe, is the ground for the friendships that Christians establish with one another. In such friendships, each respects the other's boundaries and seeks the other's well-being. This makes possible deep and honest sharing, support of one another in good and bad times, and enjoyment of each other's companionship. Such an understanding makes it possible for clergy to enter into deep friendships with parishioners, fellow clergy, and those outside the congregation.

In a reflection paper prepared for our project's theological colloquium, Lillian Daniel (2001), a United Church of Christ pastor, described her own experience of developing such friendships, the boundaries that she felt necessary to establish for herself, and also the satisfaction that her friendships have brought her. "I know that I have friends in my church," she wrote. "I am also aware that there are limits to those friendships, ways in which we are set apart from one another. The major focus of my life — my ministry — is a topic that is, for the most part, off limits [to friends from within the congregation]. I must find other friends with whom to vent about the frustrations of work, from staff conflicts to various vocational vacuums." She then went on to describe a deep friendship she established with two other clergywomen similar to her in age. "Together we have been through two ordinations, three births, two job changes, one wedding, and a coming out story. . . . We disagree politically and theologically. We have radically different understandings of our calls. Yet nothing could have prepared me . . . for the way in which God has used our friendship for both holy encouragement and prophetic correction." She also expressed deep appreciation for a group of mostly older clergymen who have befriended and mentored her in important ways.

In the same paper, she told of serving on her denomination's Committee on Ministry and having to deal with issues of pastoral misconduct. "As we heard case after case of sexual misconduct, a common theme came through. They generally told stories of loneliness and isolation from their peers."

Staying connected, being proactive in establishing appropriate "holy" friendships both within one's congregation and especially with fellow clergy, is a powerful resource that supports and sustains excellent pastoral leadership.

Self-Directed, Career-Long Learning

Finally, those who practice excellent pastoral leadership are both self-directed and career-long learners. They are not so much a "learned" clergy as a "learning" clergy. They take the initiative in asking such questions as these: What am I learning from my successes and failures in pastoral leadership? What new things do I need to know to do the job God has called me to do? What intellectual and practical resources do I need in order to face challenges that come over the course of my career?

As we have seen, not all congregations or denominations value learning — at least when it is symbolized by a graduate theological degree such as the Master of Divinity. Although I am a strong believer that graduate theological education is essential, I know that some traditions and congregations prefer to educate their pastors through mentoring and discipleship.[11] This may, for a very few, imply that they devalue all learning, but I doubt it. Even when formal theological education is frowned on, few congregations would want a pastor with no education and who is unwilling to learn. The willingness to be a learner, formally or informally, is, I believe, a sine qua non of excellent pastoral leadership, and it will only grow in importance as the level of education of American society continues to rise.

In a study in which she interviewed an admittedly non-random sample of talented pastors, Barbara Wheeler (1984) found that clergy considered as "pacesetters" or "innovators"[12] were less likely to be drawn to formal programs of continuing education and more likely to favor independent or self-initiated forms of learning. They did not avoid formal programs, but they selected them carefully or designed their own to meet their specific needs. Such self-initiated, career-long learning is, I believe, an important characteristic of excellent pastoral leaders.

One place that such learning is evident is in the midst of one's ministry practice. As was noted in the discussion of agility above, reflective leaders regularly ask themselves what they are learning from both their successes and failures. They listen to the "talkback" from the situation — in the midst of practice as well as in retrospect. In doing so, they are often led to reframe or redefine the situation they are facing in ways that help them to adapt to their challenge more effectively. Donald Schön (1983), who wrote about "reflective practice" in some detail, says that when reflecting-in-action, "the practitioner allows himself to experience surprise, puzzle-

---

11. Donald Miller, in studies of "new paradigm" churches both here and in the developing world (Miller 1997 and 2003), points to discipling and mentoring as the preferred method of developing new pastoral leaders in their belief that this reflects the New Testament pattern of Jesus and Paul.

12. Some of the pastors were selected for their intellectual ability, others for their organizational strength, and yet others for their spiritual maturity and depth (Wheeler 1984: 4).

ment, or confusion in a situation which he finds uncertain or unique. He reflects on the phenomena before him, and on the prior understandings that have been implicit in his behavior. He carries out an experiment that serves to generate a new understanding of the phenomena and a change in the situation. When someone reflects-in-action," Schön continues, "He becomes a researcher in the practice context" (68). Regular efforts to reflect-in-action and reflect-on-action are an important part of the continuing learning that characterizes excellent pastoral leadership. Doing so often leads one to resources that help one address the particular challenge one is facing — what has come to be called "just-in-time" learning.

As important as reflection in and on one's action is, pastors also need the nourishment that comes from more systematic opportunities for continuing theological education: establishing regular habits of reading, taking part in either independent or formal or continuing education opportunities, and, where circumstances permit, taking regular sabbatical leaves for reflection and renewal.

As for regular habits, we saw previously that on average clergy spend about four hours a week reading other than for specific sermons. As I noted in the examination of the most-read authors, few professional theologians made the lists. Instead, the most popular authors reflect a heavy concern with issues of ministry practice. In an additional analysis of recently read books using questionnaire responses from the U. S. Congregational Life Survey (Carroll 2003), I found this pragmatic focus further reflected. Ideas for preaching, techniques of church leadership, and strategies for church growth dominated the list of recently read books. These are areas of work that not only occupy much of a pastor's time; they are also ones about which clergy often complain that they were ill prepared by their seminaries. As I noted in our earlier discussion of most-read authors (see Chapter 4), pastors also read authors who write about spirituality, especially pastoral spirituality — authors whose work helps them reflect on their vocation.[13]

The overall impression that these findings give is that many clergy do not read very deeply or widely. With some notable exceptions, what they read is relatively light fare and pragmatically focused. While this is not surprising, given the pressures pastors face and the busy lives they lead, I sug-

---

13. For more on pastors' reading habits, see the *Christian Century* article "Pastors' Picks" (Carroll 2003).

gest that, if this is all that clergy read, they not only are selling themselves short, but their congregations as well. Pastoral leadership can be greatly enriched and moved beyond being merely ordinary when clergy regularly stretch their minds through reading, and not only works of serious theology and biblical interpretation, but also novels, poetry, and works of social analysis and criticism.

Beyond regular reading, excellent pastoral leaders will seek out continuing theological education opportunities that address the issues they are facing, not only in their present congregations, but also issues they are encountering at the particular career stage in which they find themselves. The issues and challenges that one faces vary at different stages in one's journey through ministry: the early years, mid-career, late career, and retirement. No one is adequately prepared upon leaving seminary for the many-faceted roles that a pastor must play, or for the surprises that await a pastor when he or she changes congregations and encounters a different culture and different expectations for the pastoral role. Nor is one prepared for the challenges that come from the rapid social and cultural changes characteristic of the world in which we live today. Throughout his or her career, the pastor who practices excellence in ministry will be regularly growing, deepening his or her knowledge of Scripture and theology, expanding his or her understanding of the world in which we live and the changes taking place around us, and developing new skills of communicating, teaching, counseling, and leading. The more things change, the more pastoral leaders and their congregations must change — growing and adapting to the new realities and challenges that they face.

Unfortunately, for some pastors resistance to continual learning throughout their career is not a matter of fearing the idolatry of career-management. It is rather a matter of laziness. Learning seems to have stopped when they crossed the stage at graduation and received their diploma. One of our advisors said that in his experience, some pastors who have been in the ministry for twenty years don't really have twenty years of experience. They have one year of experience that they repeat twenty times. Another judicatory executive described some pastors as having a "four-year bag of tricks. They move on to a new congregation at least every four years," he said. "There they recycle their bag of tricks once again, and then move on." These are stereotypes, of course, but sadly there is a lot of truth in them. For whatever reason, some clergy's personal and professional growth is badly stunted and they end, to use Paul Wilkes's words, as "sadly ordinary."

So, this last point is an exhortation to pastors who would be more than sadly ordinary: Tend your career with care. Take the initiative to nurture and nourish it — not for the sake of professional advancement, though that may be part of your motivation, but because excellent ministry demands it as a way of keeping one's call fresh and alive and being able to live a manner of life that is worthy of the gospel.

Here, then, is at least a partial description of what our research and reflection suggests about excellent ministry and the characteristics of excellent pastoral leadership. More could be added; additional characteristics could be put forward; however, these are some of the most notable. Each of them is an important way in which cruciform or resurrected excellence is lived out in various contexts of ministry, working to produce congregational cultures that are faithful to the gospel and effective within their particular contexts.

Conclusion

In concluding this chapter, I acknowledge that this description of excellence in ministry raises the bar rather high, but not so high as to be impossible to achieve. Although one would like to believe that all congregations and pastors can exhibit the marks of excellence described here, I am realist enough (and perhaps also sufficiently Calvinist) to acknowledge that some will not do so — some because they are lazy and unwilling to pay the price of discipline and hard work required, others because they lack some of the gifts and graces that excellence requires, and yet others because they lack needed training, support, and encouragement from their congregation, denomination, or fellow clergy. My hope, nevertheless, is that pastors and congregations are able to move beyond being sadly ordinary, that they become so adept in the craft of ministry that, to return once more to our pottery metaphor, they become master potters, whose craft has risen to its potential as an art. What will help this transformation to occur? This is the question to be addressed in the final chapter — admittedly with only partial answers.

Chapter 8

Strengthening Pastoral Leadership and Nurturing Excellence: Some Strategies

"Let us not forget that Jesus did not call prophets but disciples, ordinary people willing to lay down their nets and journey through dust-ridden towns."

Charles Marsh, *The Beloved Community*

The preceding chapters have offered a portrait of U.S. pastoral leaders and their work early in the twenty-first century. I've called them "God's potters," called to the craft of shaping congregational "clay jars," congregations that in their life together and practices reveal God's extraordinary power. In a complementary perspective drawn from cultural sociology, I have referred to pastors as "producers of culture." In their preaching, teaching, worship leadership, pastoral care, and institutional leadership, pastors draw from a "tool kit" of resources — scripture and tradition, symbols, rituals, and practices — that help to construct and shape the congregational culture through which members find meaning for their lives, belonging in a community of faith, and empowerment in the face of the challenges of their social context.

Cultural production in congregations is a complex and dynamic process, as Griswold's model of the "cultural diamond" illustrates. While clergy take the lead in the process, they are not the only shapers of the culture that is produced. Lay members bring their own dispositions and experiences to the process; the larger social world in which both clergy and laity are embedded also works its influence; and pastors and laity both draw on resources from the Christian tradition and past congregational practices. In this book, however, I have focused primarily on clergy, those men and women called and set apart in the pastoral office to use the knowledge and wisdom of their craft to lead God's people in ministry. Only in a limited way have we also been able to gain glimpses of the fuller picture of how congregations are shaped in the dynamic interaction of clergy and laity in the context of their social world.

We have, however, considered some of the important challenges that clergy and congregations face in the current social and cultural context — challenges that make their work different, if not more difficult, than in earlier times. Although the goals of the church have not changed, I have tried to show how the ways to reach those goals have changed. We have also seen that present-day pastors are a diverse lot personally, socially, and theologically. The settings in which they work are also quite diverse — from a twenty-member rural chapel to a fifteen-thousand-member suburban megachurch. Despite the diversity of congregations and clergy, today's pastors share several core tasks in common, regardless of denominational tradition, but we have also considered ways that the several traditions shape those core tasks differently. We took note of the importance of the match or fit between a pastor and his or her congregation, as well as the significance of the pastor's style of leading for congregational life and functioning — that is, for shaping and constructing the congregation's culture.

We have seen that pastors today generally appear to be highly committed to their calling, satisfied with many things about their work, and relatively healthy physically and emotionally — despite reports to the contrary; though we have also noted some of the factors that lead to questioning of the call, dissatisfaction, and poor health. We were able to gain some understanding of aspects of their work that create problems, that cause clergy to doubt their call, create stress for themselves and their families, and consider dropping out of pastoral ministry. Inadequate compensation — though not the only culprit — looms large among issues that create difficulties for some pastors and their families. Finally, I have discussed what we learned in our survey and focus groups about excellent ministry, both normatively and contextually, and I pointed to some of the marks that I believe to be characteristic of excellent pastoral leadership. In doing so, I have tried, in a small way, to reclaim excellence as a category appropriate for ministry, one that goes beyond its use and misuse in the business world and instead takes Jesus' life and ministry — especially his death and resurrection — as its pattern. This kind of excellence calls not for superstar clergy or congregations that function like well-oiled machines, but, in Charles Marsh's words in this chapter's epigraph, for "disciples, ordinary people willing to lay down their nets and journey through dust-ridden towns."

The portrait that I have painted in these chapters has been deliberately broad in order to provide as full a picture as possible of today's pastoral leaders. As I said at the outset, I made this choice both by necessity and design. To be able to answer the questions about ordained ministry that I set out to explore, I believed it important to err on the side of breadth, even if it meant sacrificing some depth. Even with this broad approach, I have left gaps that others will need to fill in future research and reflection and with in-depth studies of particular aspects of pastoral practice. For now, however, I conclude with a few proposals that grow out of what has been learned — proposals that my colleagues in this project and I believe will help to strengthen pastoral leadership and call forth, nurture, and support excellent ministry both now and in the days ahead. Given the diversity of clergy and their congregations, I realize that some of our proposals may not fit everyone; yet, I believe that they are relevant for the majority, and it is to them that I make them.

Recruiting for Excellence

Since there were limits to what we could reasonably cover in our research, we did not explore recruitment into ordained ministry in any detail; yet, I am very much aware that recruitment is a critical issue facing the church and will play a crucial role in shaping the future of pastoral leadership — especially if we hope to encourage the kind of pastoral excellence described in the preceding chapter. There was a time in the recent past that many Protestant denominations — in sharp contrast to Catholics whose priest shortage began earlier — experienced a surplus of pastors (Carroll and Wilson 1980) and paid little attention to (and even discouraged) active recruitment of new clergy. That time has passed, and recruitment has once more become a priority for Protestants as well as Catholics — rightly so if the churches want pastors who are more than sadly ordinary.

In our survey, we asked two questions about recruitment that, for reasons of chapter coherence and length, I chose not to include in what was reported in earlier chapters. We asked, "In the past five years, how many from your present congregation have decided to enter some form of ordained religious leadership?" and "In the past two years, how many persons have you personally encouraged to become a pastor or priest?" Without now attempting to look in detail at the clergy's responses to these questions, let me simply report that the results were not especially encouraging. Although a majority of pastors said that they have encouraged one or more people from their congregation to consider a call to ministry in the past two years, half of the congregations and parishes have had no one from their community pursuing some form of ordained ministry in the past five years. Focus group participants suggested a number of factors that have affected recruitment. One is the loss of infrastructural support that has, in the past, encouraged recruitment, such as the declining number of parochial schools, church camps, and denominational colleges that once were important channels into ministry. Familial support for sons and daughters considering ordained ministry has also waned. "Catholic families used to count it as a badge of honor to give at least one son to the priesthood, and they supported and honored celibacy as a high calling. That is no longer the case," said one priest. And in *Pulpit & Pew's* research on Asian American pastoral leadership (Tseng 2005), researchers reported that many Asian American parents actively discourage their children from considering a call to ministry. They want them to pursue high-status, high-paying professions, and pastoral ministry is not considered to be one of these.

What then is needed to strengthen recruitment of women and men who have the requisite gifts and graces to be excellent pastors? Although what I will suggest applies both to Catholics and Protestants, Catholics face considerably steeper obstacles to resolving their priest shortage because of the restriction of the ordained priesthood to celibate males. A change in either the celibacy or gender requirement would almost surely ease the shortage to a considerable extent.

Traditionally, recruitment to ministry has begun in congregations, often with parental support and encouragement. Since parental support can no longer be taken for granted, special efforts are required of congregations. They can become fertile seedbeds for recruitment when clergy and lay leaders create the conditions that encourage both young and older members to consider whether God may be calling them to ordained leadership. I believe this best happens when several conditions are present:

First among these is a congregation with what some have referred to as a "culture of call" (Pelusa-Verdend 2002) — that is, a congregation that understands and teaches that all baptized Christians are called to ministry as members of the people of God. As I have said, the emphasis on the call to ministry of all Christians is one of the most important changes in the understanding of ministry of the past half century — not only for Catholics since Vatican II, but also for Protestants, who historically affirmed the priesthood of all believers but did not always practice it.

Although God does not call all Christians to ordained ministry, God does call some — through what, following H. Richard Niebuhr, I referred to in Chapter 1 as the "secret call." Hearing that call, however, is often quite difficult amidst the cacophony of competing claims and multiple career opportunities that vie for many people's attention. I believe, however, that these individuals are more likely to be open and attentive to God's special call if they are in congregations that encourage all members to consider that they are called, as the people of God, to participate in Christ's continuing ministry in the world. In that kind of culture, where the general call to ministry is taken seriously, God's special call is more likely to be heard and encouraged.

Second, in creating a culture of call, it is important that pastors and lay leaders regularly hold up the vocation to ordained ministry as a viable life commitment, asking members, either collectively or individually, to consider whether God may be calling them to it. Sermons and teaching occasions that present a theology of ministry, the meaning of God's call to all Christians, and the special calling to ordained ministry are important aids in creating a "culture of call" in a congregation. Just as important, however, is identifying and personally encouraging individuals with great promise for pastoral leadership to consider whether God may be specially calling them.

Whether they are young people in high school or college who are considering their career options or older members of the congregation who are exploring a career change that may involve ordained ministry, a "nudge" from the pastor and others in the congregation can be crucial for their decision-making. Some pastors are reluctant to do this, either because they think calling is God's prerogative and not theirs or because they know that ordained ministry is a challenging and often difficult calling, and they are not at all sure that they want to encourage anyone to take it up. In either case, to put it bluntly, they need to get over their reluctance. Pastors and laity can recognize those who seem to have the requisite gifts and graces to be excellent pastors and encourage them to listen for God's special call. Also, one can be honest with potential candidates about the challenges of being a pastor, even as one can also be honest about the opportunities that ordained ministry offers for a fulfilling, satisfying life.

I would suggest, however, that pastors and laity exercise serious discernment in deciding whom to encourage. Not everyone who believes that God may be calling them to ordained ministry has been blessed with the requisite gifts and graces for the task. They lack what Niebuhr referred to as God's providential call — that is, the special gifts or talents needed to be good pastors. Some have unresolved psychological issues; for others ministry may be a way of trying to escape a bad personal or familial situation; yet others may simply seem to lack the spiritual insight, intellectual capacity, or personal and social skills needed for functioning effectively as pastors. When we encourage and/or ordain those who have no apparent gifts for ministry, even though they may be "good" people, we are very likely to be making a major mistake. Though it is difficult to discourage such individuals, at least until they recognize and are working to resolve the particular issues that may be keeping them from being effective pastors or demonstrate that they have the requisite gifts for ministry, they need to be dissuaded from pursuing ordination. Both they and the congregations that they may eventually serve will likely be spared frustration and disappointment.

Third, beyond commending ministry to others in sermons, teaching occasions, or counseling, recruitment will be enhanced by the personal example of pastors who themselves exhibit the kind of excellence described in the preceding chapter. Seminary students often single out a particular minister, either the pastor in their home congregation, a campus minister, or some other person whose passion for ministry has been contagious and who has provided a positive role model that they wish to emulate. Most pastors can also testify to the example of some minister in their past who helped them to imagine themselves in a similar pastoral role.

Fourth, recruitment is not the responsibility solely of the congregation. It requires the efforts of various types of organizations, events, and groups that also contribute to creating a culture of call. These include denominational youth conferences and camps, campus ministries, seminary programs, and other events where the call to ministry — the call to the general ministry of all Christians and the special call to ordained ministry — is presented. The recently established summer youth institutes in theological seminaries, with funding support from Lilly Endowment, have provided the opportunity for young people to engage in theological exploration as well as consider what God may be calling them to be and do with their lives. These, along with the various other extra-congregational organizations and events, can work synergistically with congregations to enhance serious consideration of ministry generally and ordained ministry in particular.

Finally, all of these efforts at recruitment will be substantially aided by the church's willingness and ability to provide the necessary material support for ordained clergy — salaries, health care benefits, and pensions — that enable them to enjoy a well-lived life. We have commented on these issues previously and will return to them below. In this connection, there is a special need to make it possible for recruits to ordained ministry to complete their theological education without the substantial educational debt that many current seminary graduates accrue.[1] It is true that other professionals also complete their education with a heavy debt, often much more than seminarians; however, many of them can reasonably expect that their earnings will be adequate to repay these debts in a timely manner without significant strain on themselves or their families. This is not true for clergy, whose low salaries, especially in the early years of ministry, often create considerable strain on them and their families. It would be surprising if this did not discourage at least some from answering the call to ordained ministry when they stop and count the cost. As the cost of theological education continues to rise,[2] seminaries, denominations, congregations, and individual lay members can significantly aid recruitment of good candidates for ministry by finding ways to increase scholarship support for such

---

1. A third of the clergy in our survey who have been in ministry fewer than ten years have educational indebtedness that they are continuing to pay off; 16 percent of those with ten to twenty years in ministry still have educational debt. An Auburn Seminary study found that Master of Divinity graduates in 1991 averaged slightly over $11,000 of indebtedness (Ruger and Wheeler 1995). No doubt the average has increased over the past decade as educational and other costs have continued to rise.

2. Daniel Aleshire, the Executive Director of the Association of Theological Schools, estimates that the cost, on average, of educating a Master of Divinity student is approximately $100,000, or more than $30,000 per year (Theological Educators Speak 2004).

students, either through direct scholarships or by increasing seminary endowments for scholarship aid.[3]

Theological Education for Excellence

Nurturing excellence in ministry also obviously has implications for the shape and quality of theological education. Although forming pastoral leaders whose lives reflect the kind of excellence that we described in the previous chapter is clearly not the sole responsibility of theological schools, nonetheless much of the groundwork for excellence is either laid there or it is unlikely to happen. If the seminary is doing its job, it will insure that its graduates know the Christian story, know how to communicate the story effectively in differing contexts, can lead the congregation in meaningful and spiritually challenging worship, are learning how to lead congregations in terms of the congregation's needs and social context, and are growing spiritually, having developed disciplines that support that growth.

In the not-too-distant past, theological schools could assume that students who enrolled were already at least partially formed in some of these areas prior to matriculation: that they came from Christian homes, had been actively involved in a congregation, and perhaps had attended a denominational college or had a broad exposure to the humanities, including courses in a religion department in a liberal arts institution. This kind of pre-seminary socialization can no longer be assumed. Many students now come from secular institutions with backgrounds in technical studies such as business, communications, computer science, or engineering. Many younger students also come with little experience in congrega-

3. The Evangelical Lutheran Church in America (ELCA) and the United Methodist Church are both seeking to raise money to provide direct scholarships to students attending Lutheran and Methodist seminaries respectively. The Presbyterian Church (PCUSA) Pension Board has created a loan forgiveness program for pastors who commit to serving small (often rural) congregations for a specified number of years. A group of PCUSA laity and clergy in one southern state have also created scholarship funds to make it possible for promising college graduates to spend a trial year in a seminary to explore whether ordained ministry is a possibility for them. This program is patterned after an earlier trial-year program administered by the Fund for Theological Education with support from the Rockefeller Brothers Fund.

tions. Rather, they have had a Christian experience and call to ministry through participation in a campus ministry or parachurch organization such as InterVarsity Christian Fellowship or Campus Crusade for Christ, and now they are trying to find out how and where to live out their calling. The point is that what seminaries formerly could assume about their students' prior formation is no longer applicable for many of their students. Thus considerable remedial work is required, and this competes with time that could be spent on other necessary seminary studies.

Given the diverse backgrounds and needs of those pursuing ordained ministry, no single model of theological education will be appropriate to all. My personal preference would be that all candidates have the experience of a residential theological education where they can be immersed in the culture of the school, interacting regularly with faculty and peers in and outside the classroom, encountering each other's ideas and shaping their own perspectives in response, growing spiritually in a shared worship life, and forming friendships likely to endure throughout their careers.[4] Experiencing such a culture is especially important for those with little prior ministry formation. Yet, this ideal is increasingly difficult to realize, both because of the costs of theological education and the number of older, second-career students who are reluctant or unable to engage in a residential educational process. Also, the growing use of lay pastors to serve in small congregations requires educational models other than residential.

To meet the needs of this diverse constituency, a number of schools have resorted to various types of distance education (Web-based learning, satellite programs, and so forth) or they have made it possible for students to commute to classes on a part-time basis or to take evening classes while holding another job. Although such practices may be necessary and cost-efficient, given the constituency, it is nonetheless difficult to see how they make it possible for a student to experience the formative power of a school's culture to the degree that residential education does, and that, I maintain, is a serious deficiency. Short of banning such practices, which is highly unlikely, schools need to be especially diligent to develop formative experiences for their non-residential as well as residential students so that they are given the opportunity to be shaped by their education and life together in more than superficial ways. Much to my regret, I know of denominational leaders, desperate to fill pulpits of small congregations in

---

4. For examples of the formative power of seminary culture, see Carroll et al. (1997).

their judicatories, who encourage students in their care to enroll in nearby, non-residential seminary programs, regardless of the seminary's educational quality or denominational tradition, because doing so allows them to serve full time as pastors while enrolled in the school. Quality and denominational tradition aside, these students' involvement in the educational process is often limited solely to class attendance, in which they have little opportunity to interact with or get to know faculty or fellow students.[5] While such students get their credentials, they and the churches they serve are seriously shortchanged in the process. These practices work against nurturing excellence in ministry and my sense is that in virtually all cases they should be discouraged.

Although it would be controversial given additional cost and time, adding a fourth year to the current three-year, full-time seminary curriculum would make an important contribution to forming excellent pastoral leaders. This is already the practice in Lutheran seminaries. During the first two years, Master of Divinity students would engage core subjects — biblical study, the history of the church's traditions, theology, ethics, and social analysis — in considerable depth, along with an introduction to basic ministry practices. During a third year — similar to Lutheran practice — students would leave the school to work full-time in a ministry setting such as a congregation under the supervision of a seasoned mentor-pastor and lay members who provide regular support and feedback. It would be important, given the large number of small congregations in Protestant denominations, that internships be established in small as well as mid-sized and large congregations. In these various settings students would be exposed to a full range of pastoral duties, gaining firsthand experience in various ministry practices, with opportunities to reflect on their experiences and performance with their mentor, lay committee, and on occasion with peers serving in other settings. As well as reflection and receiving feedback and critique on their practice, interns would also be encouraged to address questions of how scripture and tradition inform issues they encounter in the congregation, or how their practice is shaped, influenced, or challenged by the social context and culture of the congregation. Experi-

5. In the process of conducting research for a study of seminary cultures (Carroll et al. 1997), I met a seminary student who commuted sixty miles each way three days a week. He arrived just in time for class and often left shortly afterwards, occasionally taking time to use the seminary's library. When asked, he could name only two fellow students and was not sure of the name of one of his professors.

ences during the internship would inform selection of coursework for the final, fourth year, especially pursuing issues encountered in their congregational experience.

Because the current three-year model gives most students only limited exposure to congregational life and leadership, many complain that they leave seminary with little sense of how to lead a congregation, including understanding congregational dynamics and dealing constructively with inevitable conflicts that arise. Catholics previously overcame this problem by assigning newly ordained priests to be assistants in parishes, serving under the mentorship of a seasoned pastor. The priest shortage, unfortunately, has made this pattern difficult, if not impossible. Thus, for both Protestants and Catholics, the four-year model with its intern year is a way of partially remedying these lacunae.

Although this model adds an additional year and extra costs to the seminary experience, I maintain that it would significantly help students and seminary faculty bring together interactively the necessary theoretical bases of ministry practice with the insights that arise from that practice — fostering habits of reflection on practice and agility discussed in the preceding chapter. Also, teaching would be enlivened by the fresh insights and questions from practice that students bring back from their intern year, and students would have had opportunity to learn firsthand the art and craft of ministry practice from their clergy and lay mentors. It also can have reciprocal benefits for the mentors, and it is not simply that the host congregation gains an additional staff member for a year. Rather the opportunity to mentor interns can push both clergy and lay mentors to be more reflective about the work of ministry, to think more clearly about what they do and why they do it. Although this proposal may seem overly idealistic, it is important to ask whether its potential for giving the church better-prepared, well-formed pastors with a greater likelihood for excellence is not well worth the additional time and cost.[6]

Short of adding this fourth year, or, better, in addition to it, it is encouraging to note that some denominations and organizations are now

---

6. At present, Lilly Endowment as a part of its "Transition-into-Ministry" program is currently making possible on a limited scale a more elaborate version of the intern year — actually a two-year program — that places two or more new seminary graduates into a single congregation where they work under the supervision and mentorship of the congregation's pastor and senior staff. For a description of this and other Transition-into-Ministry models, see an interview with the project's coordinator, David Wood (Schier n.d.).

treating the three to five years following seminary graduation as a transitional learning period in which new ministers engage with a seasoned pastor-mentor and with peers in reflection on their ministry experiences, do further study growing out of the questions raised by their practice, grapple with issues of their identity as pastors, and engage in corporate spiritual disciplines.[7] For example, the Evangelical Lutheran Church in America has established a three-year "First Call" program that provides this additional mentoring and peer support for new ordinands. United Methodists have a somewhat similar requirement during a three-year probationary period following seminary graduation, in which probationers meet regularly with peers and mentors for worship, study, and reflection on their experience before they move on to ordination.

Other programs have been specially designed to deal with ministry in small congregations, which can be challenging for new pastors whose previous experience has been as members of, or interns in, large churches. The pottery image is appropriate as we think of the importance of these transition-into-ministry programs. When these programs are done well, new ministers are, in the language of the crafts, apprentices under the tutelage of a master potter. Guided by their mentors and critiqued and supported by their apprentice peers, they have hands-on opportunity to practice the crafts of preaching, teaching, leading, giving pastoral care, managing conflicts — learning how to form congregational clay jars that reveal God's power. Furthermore, such experiences can help apprentice pastors to cultivate necessary spiritual disciplines and habits of lifelong learning that are critical to excellence in ministry throughout one's career. And they develop friendships that can sustain them over the long haul and combat the loneliness and isolation that many current clergy lament.

A somewhat similar opportunity for reflection on practice is available in the Doctor of Ministry programs that many seminaries offer as a continuing education degree for clergy. These programs usually require that a pastor have at least two years of post–M.Div. ministry experience prior to enrollment. They not only give practicing clergy occasion to en-

---

7. The Catholic Church used to accomplish this experience of learning-in-practice following seminary by assigning newly ordained priests to serve for several years as assistant pastors in parishes led by a seasoned pastor. Unfortunately, the priest shortage has made this "probationary" period increasingly rare, and new priests are often put in charge of large parishes with little training or experience in parish administration (Hoge 2002). This is one reason that some newly ordained priests drop out.

gage in further theological study and practice corporate spiritual disciplines, but they also offer peer group reflection on real-life issues that students have encountered in their ministry. Furthermore, the programs typically require a disciplined action-reflection project/thesis on some aspect of the pastor's ministry. While Doctor of Ministry programs as a group have a reputation for being lightweight, and some can be justly faulted for this, and though some clergy undoubtedly pursue the degree primarily for the status it confers, graduates of more demanding programs regularly express gratitude for the opportunity their studies provided for engaging in disciplined reflection on experience and cultivating an ongoing habit of reflective practice.

All of this is to say that excellent pastoral leadership is not only grounded in disciplined study of Scripture, church history, theology, ethics, and the practices of the church and its ministry — which is a major responsibility of first-degree theological education — but it is also an art and a craft learned by reflection on practice and aided by engagement with wise mentors and peers, not only during a probationary period but throughout one's career. Both of these kinds of education — formal schooling and apprenticeship — are needed. In the early years of the church in America, some denominations, especially Presbyterians and Congregationalists, placed heavy emphasis on a learned clergy, and they founded colleges and theological seminaries to provide that education. Others, such as the Methodists, also founded colleges, but they did not require (and often even distrusted) formal seminary education. Instead, early Methodist circuit riders, often with little formal education, carried their Bibles and theological books with them in their saddlebags, reading as they traveled their circuits. Where possible they rode with fellow pastors, questioning each other about their spiritual health, discussing their reading, and considering issues pertaining to the congregations in their charge. Theirs was an apprenticeship, a learning-through-practice, aided by mentors and peers. What I am suggesting is the necessity of holding these two models of learning together: formal, basic theological study coupled with apprenticeship and continuous reflection on one's practice throughout one's career. Neither is adequate without the other.

Congregational and Denominational Practices
That Support Excellence

Previously we considered the importance of clergy compensation. Here I wish to reinforce what has been said. While focusing primarily on compensation, I note the significance of other forms of support as well.

As discussed previously, for the majority of Protestant and Catholic clergy, compensation is generally low, especially when one takes into account the years of education that many denominations expect of their pastors. It is primarily in large and very large congregations that senior pastors are well compensated; this is not generally true for those in small and some mid-size churches. This raises several critical issues that call for attention.

First, even though the majority of Protestant congregations are quite small, as we have seen, most U.S. churchgoers participate in mid-size and large congregations. How aware, I wonder, are they of the truly low salaries that many small-church clergy receive, a situation sometimes compounded by lack of health care or pension benefits? I suspect that most laity, operating from their perspective as members of a mid-size or large congregation point of view, see the compensation that their pastor receives and assume that this is true of the majority. "Why," they may ask, "should there be complaints about clergy salaries? Our pastor certainly is well paid and receives many perks." Although this may be true for their pastor, their misperception about clergy salaries generally needs to be corrected by regular efforts to remind laity, denominational officials, and clergy themselves of the actual circumstances that many, indeed the majority, of clergy in small and mid-sized churches face.

Second, there is the two-tiered (one is tempted to say two-class) system that the small church–large church divide in salaries creates. As we also saw earlier, because of the relatively small number of large or mega Protestant congregations (again, Catholics are an exception), most clergy will spend their careers in small churches. Many of these congregations offer fulfilling ministries to their pastors, and some pastors prefer them to being pastors of large congregations. Yet, do these pastors not deserve to be compensated adequately for their work, which is often every bit as demanding as the work of pastors of large congregations — at times even more so due to the lack of staff assistance?

Redressing the inequity that exists in compensation is an exceedingly thorny and complex issue, especially when a difficult economic climate, coupled with membership losses, has shrunk the resources of many congregations; yet, inequity in compensation needs to be addressed if churches are to attract good candidates and support those already in ministry. Denominations with connectional polities have had a better record of this than those with congregational polities, especially in small and mid-size congregations, often establishing minimum compensation levels for full-time pastors and even providing subsidies to some promising congregations to bring their salary up to the minimum. Connectional denominations have also been able to make annual claims on their congregations for financial support of ministry — not only to provide minimum salary support in small sister congregations, but to subsidize theological students and schools and provide other forms of support for pastors and their families. Denominations with congregational polities have been less able to establish minimum compensation expectations for their congregations or to lay claim to financial support of theological education and the needs of clergy beyond the congregation.

Although many congregations today, whether in connectional or congregational polities, are struggling financially with declining membership and growing maintenance costs for aging buildings, there is a great need to raise the awareness of lay members of the cost of recruiting, educating, and supporting excellent pastoral leaders and of the considerable sacrifice that many clergy and their families are making in order to respond to God's call. But raising awareness that fails to lead to concrete action is not enough. Not only do congregations need to examine the support they provide to their own pastors, but also important are denominational assessments (in connectional denominations), voluntary contributions (in congregational polities), and individual gifts by lay members in support of theological education and ministry. These provide essential resources for student scholarships, clergy continuing education, and denominational programs that make possible equitable salaries for a denomination's clergy.

Of course, no one enters pastoral ministry because of the salary it promises; yet the issue of justice in compensation cannot be ignored. In a culture driven by consumption, one that all too often measures personal worth by net worth and style of life, is it surprising that very few bright, achievement-oriented college students give ordained ministry a second thought when making vocational decisions? Is it surprising, too, that many clergy and their spouses become bitter or discouraged over their relatively low salaries? Why, too, should we be surprised that worries over career advancement often diminish a pastor's sense of calling? It is quite difficult to keep a call to ministry vital and healthy when there are constant worries about finances. As one pastor expressed it, "Nobody goes into ministry for the money, but we do have to pay the mortgage, put food on the table, pay for child care, and save for college education."

All of this suggests that there is a great need for critical theological reflection on the meaning of money in our society, including what constitutes fair compensation for clergy. Clergy should not be left to bear Christian witness to the virtue of a simple lifestyle primarily because their salaries leave them no option. If small and large congregations are to have the good leadership for which they ask, they will need to pay for it either directly or with assistance from their denominations. Doing so will help to encourage good pastors to stay in ministry for the long haul. It may also make ordained ministry a more attractive vocational choice for promising candidates.

Support for equitable salaries is not the only way that denominations and congregations can support excellent ministry. Making sure that clergy take regular days off and providing them with the opportunity and financial support for continuing education and periodic sabbatical leaves are also essential. As we saw, these practices are more fully institutionalized in the Catholic Church and mainline Protestantism than in conservative Protestant and historic black denominations. And they are also affected by church size: The benefits are more likely to be offered in larger congregations. Because of their importance in reducing stress and burnout, in dealing with issues that arise at various stages of a pastor's career, and in providing occasions for clergy to engage in reflection and renewal, these benefits are critical if congregations and denominations wish to support and sustain imaginative and faithful pastoral leadership.

One other matter applies both to denominations and to congregations: working hard at the mostly inexact science of matching clergy and congregations. We have seen how important this is not only for congregational effectiveness but also for clergy commitment, satisfaction, and health; but, as we have emphasized previously, clergy are not "interchangeable parts." They cannot be fit in anywhere there is a need. This adds to the problem created by the current shortage of clergy, especially among Catholics and also in some Protestant denominations. The fact that clergy are not interchangeable makes matching clergy and congregations especially difficult when there is a shortage of candidates. Add to this the restrictions that some clergy with working spouses place on mobility, and the problem is even more complex. Nonetheless, matching clergy and congregations as much as is possible is very important.

We know some of the obvious things that make for a good match: for example, the importance of educational and theological compatibility between the pastors and congregation. Also in recent years, considerable thought has gone into making the deployment process more intentional — whether by consultation with laity and clergy in denominations that assign pastors to congregations or, in those where the congregation calls their pastor, by an often elaborate process of congregational self-study and discernment to determine the kind of pastor they need. But deployment is still very much an inexact science — the more cynical might call it a gamble. Although there is no way to guarantee a good match between congregation and pastor, even as there is no way to guarantee a good match between spouses, those engaged in calling or assigning pastors to congregations and clergy considering becoming pastor of a particular congregation will do well to ask hard and searching questions about the potential for a positive relationship to develop.

Despite the best process, there will still be mismatches, some of which will end in parting of ways, but others that may, in time, mature into a happy and satisfying relationship. In such cases, clergy who are able to adapt their style to fit the congregation will be much more likely to exercise effective leadership than those who are rigid and inflexible. This calls for the kind of agility that I described in the preceding chapter. Likewise, it calls for congregations that are open to change, to new ways of thinking, and new or different congregational practices that do not violate their core convictions about their calling and purpose. Agility and openness on the part of clergy and congregations do not guarantee a good match, but without them, a good match will be much less likely.

Clergy Taking Responsibility for Excellence

Were I to stop here without asking what responsibility clergy themselves have in the pursuit of excellence in ministry and pastoral leadership, I would clearly be remiss. Much that has previously been said, especially in the preceding chapter, bears directly on this question and need not be elaborated on here. Clergy need to take responsibility for

- Developing regular spiritual disciplines;
- Developing a pastoral imagination through ongoing habits of reflection on their practice;
- Being lifelong learners who pay special attention to the kind of learning needed for the particular career stage they are facing;
- Nurturing what we called "holy" friendships both within and outside the congregation;
- Maintaining appropriate, though not rigid, boundaries between their personal and family life and their work;
- Being diligent in self-care concerning their physical and emotional health.

All of these form a kind of litany of obvious but extremely important practices necessary for developing and sustaining pastoral excellence.

There is, however, one additional issue that my colleagues and I believe to be especially important. I have emphasized the importance of clergy meeting together for friendship, study, and mutual support, and there is no way that I would deny the importance of such gatherings. Yet it is our impression that some of the expressions of dissatisfaction, low morale, and even health problems that are the conversation topics of many informal clergy gatherings and discussions among denominational leaders about the pastors in their care are fostered and exacerbated by an unhealthy clerical culture — "a culture of complaint" or a "culture of denial." In no way do I wish to minimize the problems that many clergy face that lead to dissatisfaction and low morale; nevertheless, there is a kind of "can you top this?" gamesmanship that is often played in such gatherings.

In the preceding chapter, I cited Andrew Greeley's comments about an unhealthy clerical culture that leads priests to blame forces outside of themselves — either in the church or the larger culture — for many of their problems. The problem is not limited to priests. Protestant pastors, as well, develop an unhealthy clerical culture. It is a culture often characterized by competitiveness and envy. Comments such as the following can be heard in many informal clergy gatherings and conversations: "How did he get assigned (or called) to St. Peter's by the Sea? Why do I always get stuck in places like this? It's not fair!" "Can you believe the salary they are paying her? She hasn't been ordained half as long as I." "I wish my congregation provided me with such a posh parsonage!" "What? They're furnishing you with a car? You've got to be kidding!" There's also denial. If there are problems, as with Greeley's priests, they are the fault of the laity, or one's bishop, or of trends in the broader society over which pastors have no control: "It's impossible to do effective ministry today. Our society is too secular, hedonistic, and consumer-driven." "My parishioners lack any real commitment. Their faith is shallow. They show up only when they feel like it or when there's not something else competing for their time." "We can't start any new ministries in our congregations. There simply aren't enough members willing to take responsibility for them." "I really worked hard at my preaching for the first few years, but nobody seemed to appreciate my sermons. So I've quit trying so hard." Someone has called this kind of griping the "ain't-it-awful syndrome."

Denominational officials also participate in this culture of complaint and denial, often blaming the poor performance of the congregations in their judicatories on the declining quality of candidates for ministry, or poor pastoral leadership, or lack of vision in the congregations. And, turning the clergy's denial upside down, recall, as in Chapter 6, that some clergy and denominational leaders in focus groups told us that pastors expressing high levels of commitment to their call and satisfaction with their ministry are themselves in denial. "They're lying through their teeth," as one said. This makes it difficult to tell who is in denial. Is it this latter group who gripe about the problems of ordained ministry and question the veracity of their colleagues' expressions of commitment and satisfaction? Or is it those colleagues who can't bring themselves to tell an interviewer that they have serious questions about their call to ministry and/or are really dissatisfied with the vocation to which they have devoted their lives?

I realize that this description of clerical culture is painted in broad strokes and risks caricature; and I admit that I have, perhaps, overstated the case — but not by much. To be sure, there are problems that all clergy face. Pastoral ministry is not easy, as I have been at pains to point out at many places in the preceding chapters. The problems that pastors face are not all of their own making, nor are they likely to go away. And the kind of excellent ministry and leadership to which God calls congregations and pastors often runs against the grain of our broader culture. Furthermore, clergy and their denominational leaders need supportive contexts in which to vent the real frustrations that they experience.

But such contexts will be much more healthy when clergy use them for friendship and mutual support and as places where, speaking the truth in love, they call each other to account for competitiveness and envy and sloppy work and refuse to let each other wallow in denial; where they help a colleague reflect on and gain perspective on the difficult issue (or parishioner) that she or he is facing rather than jumping in to share other horror stories that feed the denial and frustration; and where they pray and study together. Healthy clergy groups produce a culture of excellence — one that is not only critically realistic and honest about the difficulties of pastoral leadership, but one that is positive and hopeful about its promises and joys. Such groups can play a significant role in nurturing excellence that is grounded in Jesus' cross and his resurrection.

Potters, like other artisans, often acknowledge those in their craft who are masters. These individuals exhibit excellence in their work; they realize the craft's potential as an art; and they are able to teach and mentor others, helping them move towards excellence. There are also apprentices, individuals in the early stages of learning, who look to the masters for guidance. And there are journeyman potters — those who are competent but not yet excellent. They move (journey) from one place to another, contributing to each what they are able to do best, whether it be digging and preparing the clay, turning the pots, applying the glaze, or firing the kiln. There are clergy who also fit this middle category. They are journeymen (or journeywomen) who move from congregation to congregation, using their gifts of leadership. Some, unfortunately, fall into the "sadly ordinary" category and remain there. Many, however, have important contributions to make as they grow and expand their capacity to exercise their gifts of ministry. My hope is that both "apprentice" and "journeyman" clergy can be helped to grow in this way, to go beyond the ordinary and learn to exhibit the excellence of masters, fashioning and shaping their congregational clay jars so that they reveal God's extraordinary power. For this to happen seminaries, denominations, congregations, and clergy themselves will all need to play their roles in calling forth, nurturing, and sustaining excellence.

Research Methods

National Telephone Survey of Pastors

Describing pastoral leadership at the beginning of the twenty-first century is a daunting task. Particularly difficult is capturing the immense variety of clergy engaged in pastoral leadership. Previous clergy studies have typically used samples drawn from lists provided by denominations — usually the larger denominations that have up-to-date records of names and addresses of their pastors. From these lists, some form of random sampling is then used to select those to be surveyed. Although this is a very legitimate way to study issues of pastoral leadership in a limited number of denominations or perhaps a single denomination, especially if stratified random sampling is used to insure representation of important subgroups within the denomination(s), it is not adequate for assessing the state of pastoral leadership as a whole. The *Yearbook of American and Canadian Churches* for 2004 lists some 160 U.S. denominations — some quite large and many others very small, many of whom do not have accurate information about their pastors. Even if adequate lists existed for each of these groups, drawing a sample from this large universe would be a challenge. One would also exclude pastors of the many nondenominational or independent churches, including most "storefront" churches.

Since our purpose was to take stock of the whole of U.S. pastoral leadership, we needed a different type of sampling method that would have the likelihood of including clergy from all groups, large and small, including pastors of independent congregations. Following the lead of Mark Chaves in the National Congregations Study (Chaves 2004), we used what is called hypernetwork or multiplicity sampling.[1] Quoting Chaves: "The key insight is that organizations attached to a random sample of individuals constitute a random sample of organizations even in the absence of a comprehensive list of units in the organizational population. One simply starts with a random sample of individuals and asks them to name the organization(s) to which they are attached" (214).

The random sample of individuals used for our purposes was the General Social Survey (GSS), conducted in 2000 by the National Opinion Research Center (NORC). A well-known and respected survey of Americans, the GSS uses cluster sampling methods to insure that its participants are a random sample of individuals from across the United States. We cooperated with the U.S. Congregational Life Survey being undertaken by researchers from the Research Services Office of the Presbyterian Church (USA) who contracted with NORC to develop a random sample of congregations. To do so, NORC interviewers asked participants in the 2000 GSS if they had attended religious services at least once a year and, if so, to indicate the name and address of that place of worship. After eliminating duplicate nominations of congregations, congregations for which no address could be located after exhaustive search, others that had closed since the 2000 survey, and those groups that do not hold regular worship services, 1,292 congregations remained in the sample.

NORC callers found that sixty-one of the 1,292 congregations did not have a current pastor, including twelve Jehovah's Witness groups who would not name one person to be interviewed from their leadership council, or the congregations did not or would not answer the telephone or return calls during the nineteen-week field period. This left 1,231 eligible congregations for the purposes of our pastor survey.

An interview protocol was developed and pretested by the Pulpit & Pew staff in consultation with our advisory groups and a diverse group of researchers and with assistance from the NORC staff. Alternative wording was developed for some questions to make the guide appropriate for Catholics, Protestants, and those in other religious traditions. The final protocol, including the response percentages for each question, can be found in Appendix B.

---

1. See MacPherson (1982) for a description of hypernetwork sampling.

Materials describing the project, including a letter inviting participation and an Interview Preparation Worksheet, were sent to the pastor of each congregation in the Spring of 2001. The worksheet asked the pastor to prepare in advance answers to some questions that required information that might not be readily at hand during a telephone interview. This was followed by a telephone call from a NORC interviewer either to conduct the interview or arrange an appointment to do so at a later time. Through persistent efforts by the interviewers, 883 forty-five minute interviews were completed: 72 percent of the eligible pastors. These included 832 Catholic and Protestant clergy and fifty-one clergy from other religions. Altogether some eighty-one faith groups or denominations are represented in the sample. Due to the small and heterogeneous sample of the "other religions" group, we decided to exclude their responses from our analysis.

Because we were interested in a sample that reflected pastors of large and small congregations, it was necessary to weight the sample. As Chaves (2004: 215) notes, "The probability that a congregation will appear in this sample [including the Pulpit & Pew sample] is proportional to its size. Because congregations are nominated by individuals attached to them, larger congregations are more likely to appear in the sample than smaller." To correct for this, as Chaves did in the National Congregations Study, we weighted the data inversely proportional to congregation size. For example, for clergy in a one-thousand-member congregation, a weight of $\frac{1}{1000}$ is applied, and for those in a one-hundred-member congregation, a weight of $\frac{1}{100}$ is applied, and so on. This corrects for the overrepresentation of pastors of large congregations and makes it possible to treat each pastor, whatever his or her congregation's size, as one unit in the population. Unless otherwise noted, all of our analysis is based on the weighted sample. Our membership measure is the average weekly attendance rather than the number of members on the congregation's role.

U.S. Congregational Life Survey

As noted in the Preface, at the time that we collected pastoral leader data through the NORC survey, our research partners in the U.S. Congregational Life Survey, Cynthia Woolever and Deborah Bruce of the Presbyterian Research Services Office, surveyed attendees at the main worship services of the churches served by our pastors. This survey was done the weekend of April 29, 2001. The response rate of congregations that returned completed attendee surveys was 36 percent (434 congregations) of the sample of congregations that NORC had been able to locate and verify. When we compared their survey congregations to our sample of pastors, we were able to match attendee and pastor responses for 351 of the participating congregations. Some non-response bias is present in the combined data due to the lack of very large churches in the congregational sample. There were also too few congregations from historic black denominations for separate analysis; thus, when we use the USCLS data, we have grouped black congregations with either mainline or conservative Protestants, as appropriate. Woolever and Bruce have summarized results of their study and their methods in two books (Woolever & Bruce 2002, 2004).

Focus Groups

As noted in the Preface, we conducted twenty-three focus groups in seven sites across the U.S. to gain qualitative data that would supplement the quantitative survey data and to gain further insight into several puzzles that we had noted in the initial analysis of the NORC survey data. We contracted with Professor Richard Kruger of the University of Minnesota[2] to assist us in designing the focus group process, selecting appropriate sites, identifying the types of participants needed for the groups, framing the questions to be asked, and training the moderators and assistant moderators who would conduct the groups in the seven sites. Participants in the focus groups were white and African American clergymen and -women from a variety of denominations. Denominational officials and laity were also involved, as were representatives of small, large, urban, suburban, and rural congregations.

Following the training session, moderators selected participants for their groups, conducted the interviews, recorded and transcribed the sessions, and prepared a summary analysis of their findings which they shared in a subsequent meeting. Pulpit and Pew staff also read and coded the group transcripts, using coding themes that corresponded to the topics that were to be developed in this book. We have used the focus group data primarily to augment and enrich the quantitative findings.

---

2. For a very helpful guide to conducting focus groups, see Kruger and Casey (2000).

Questions asked in each focus group included the following (with instructions as to the amount of time to be allotted to each question):

1. Please tell us your name, the name of your church and the location of your church.

2. What is your first impression when you hear the words "good ministry"?

3. Can you give a brief example of good ministry? This might be a time when you have experienced or observed good ministry. (No names please)

4. Draw a picture of "good ministry," including the pastor in the picture.

   (When finished each person was asked to hold up his/her diagram and explain how it works)

   PROMPT, as needed, the respondent to get at both pieces of the following information:

   • What is the core work of the congregation?

   • What is the role of the pastor in making good ministry happen?

   (After all pictures were described, moderators asked this key follow-up question for the entire group:)

   • How do you know this is good ministry? (PROMPT: What metaphors/images best capture the pastor's role?)

5. Respondents were given a handout with twenty qualities and practices of good pastoral leadership and asked to rate the importance of each quality and practice listed. They were then asked to check which three of the twenty qualities and practices they felt are the most important. In other words, which three if missing would jeopardize good ministry from taking place?

   (Moderators then tabulated results for all practices and characteristics on an enlarged version of the worksheet, and asked for discussion of reasons for the importance of and lack of importance of as many items as seemed appropriate.)

6. What nourishes and strengthens good pastoral leadership? What gets

in the way of good pastoral leadership? (PROMPTS: At the congregational level? At the denominational level?)

7. What one thing would you change to help foster good pastoral leadership? (PROMPT: If you could tell the dean of a seminary, a denominational executive, congregations, pastors, etc.)

8. This focus group is a part of a larger study on pastoral leadership. In an earlier survey of clergy, the findings revealed some areas that are a puzzle to us. Help us determine how to interpret these findings. I have them listed on a handout (distributed to the group).

9. Of all the things we've talked about today, what to you is the most important?

10. Have we missed anything? Is there anything else we should have talked about?

Appendix B

Interview Protocol
and Response Frequencies

The following is the interviewer protocol for the phone survey of pastors conducted during 2001 by the National Opinion Research Center for Pulpit and Pew.

Beginning with Question 11, we show survey frequencies for responses to each question next to response categories. These frequencies are based on weighted data and include only the 832 Catholic and Protestant responses. See Appendix A for further information regarding weighting. Some frequencies may not total to 100 percent due to rounding. For some questions (which are noted), frequencies were categorized after the data collection process; thus the response categories shown were not used during the interview process. Several questions that asked for qualitative responses are listed, but the responses are omitted. Throughout the interview guide where rating scales were used, most scales were scored from 1 (most satisfied, most important, etc.) to 4 (least satisfied, least important, etc.). However, for purposes of analysis in the preceding chapters, I reversed the scoring to make 1 mean least satisfied, least important, etc. and 4 to indicate the opposite. In the protocol that follows, I have the wording as it was in the original interviews.

PASTORAL LEADERSHIP SURVEY

First, I'd like to be sure that I have the correct contact information:

1. I have the following name for your congregation. (Preloaded) Is this correct?

    1. Yes (SKIP TO Q. 3)   2. No

2. What is the correct name for your congregation? _____

3. I have the following information for your denomination. (Preloaded) Is this correct?

    1. Yes (SKIP TO Q. 5)   2. No

4. What is the correct denomination? (refer to Job Aid) _____

5. I have the following street address for your congregation. (Preloaded) Is this correct?

    1. Yes (SKIP TO Q. 7)   2. No

6. What is the correct address for your congregation? _____

7. I have the following phone number for your congregation. (Preloaded) Is this the best phone number to reach you?

    1. Yes (SKIP TO Q. 9)   2. No

8. What is the best telephone number to reach you? _____

9. Are you the congregation's principal leader?

    1. Yes   2. No

(IF THE CONGREGATION CURRENTLY HAS A PRINCIPAL LEADER AND THE RESPONDENT IS NOT THAT PERSON, THANK THE RESPONDENT AND ASK HOW YOU MIGHT GET IN CONTACT WITH THE PRINCIPAL LEADER.)

Your Faith Background

10. What was your denomination growing up, if any, before you were 12 years old?

11. Which of the following describes the church attendance of your father before you were 12 years old?

1. Occasional (2 or 3 times a year)	14%
2. About once per month	8%
3. Weekly attendance	56%
4. Did not attend	19%
5. Not applicable	3%

12. Which of the following describes the church attendance of your mother before you were 12 years old?

1. Occasional (2 or 3 times a year)	13%
2. About once per month	7%
3. Weekly attendance	72%
4. Did not attend	8%
5. Not applicable	1%

13. How would you best describe your church attendance at age 16?

1. Occasional (2 or 3 times a year)	11%
2. About once per month	6%
3. Weekly attendance	74%
4. Did not attend	9%

14. Were you involved in church-based youth activities at age 16?

1. Yes	71%
2. No	29%

15. Did you have a leadership role in church-based youth activities at age 16?

1. Yes	60%
2. No	40%

16. What is <u>your</u> present denomination if any? (IF RESPONDENT IS ROMAN CATHOLIC, ASK Q. 17. IF RESPONDENT IS A MEMBER OF A PROTESTANT DENOMINATION OR INDEPENDENT, GO TO Q. 18.)

17. (FOR CATHOLICS) When it comes to your approach to religious faith, as distinct from your denominational affiliation, would you say that you are a conservative, moderate, or progressive Catholic, or do none of these describe you?

1. Conservative	7%
2. Moderate	52%
3. Progressive	33%
4. None	6%
5. Other	2%

18. (FOR PROTESTANTS) When it comes to your approach to faith, as distinct from your denominational affiliation, would you say that you are a pentecostal, fundamentalist, evangelical, mainline, or liberal Protestant, or do none of these describe you?

1. Pentecostal	12%
2. Fundamentalist	9%
3. Evangelical	33%
4. Mainline	16%
5. Liberal	11%
6. None	9%
7. Other (please specify)	10%

Family Matters

19. Which of the following best describes your current marital status?

1. Never married (SKIP to Q. 22)	10%
2. In first marriage	73%
3. Divorced or separated (SKIP to Q. 22)	4%
4. Widowed (SKIP to Q. 22)	1%
5. Remarried after death of spouse	1%
6. Remarried after divorce	10%
7. Other (please specify)	< 1%

20. What kind of work does your spouse normally do? (That is, what is his/her job category?)

1. Professional, technical	40%
2. Managers, administrators, sales workers	15%
3. Clerical and related workers	10%
4. Craftsmen and related workers	< 1%
5. Operatives, except transport	1%
6. Transport, equipment operators, laborers	< 1%
7. Farmers, farm laborers	< 1%
8. Service workers	6%
9. Not in labor force	27%

21. How many children do you have living at home in each of the following age groups? (Write in the number in each age group.)

1. I have no children at home.	55%

The following frequencies represent the percent of all pastors who indicated that they had at least one child in that age range living at home:

2. Aged 0-4 years	8%
3. Aged 5-11 years	17%
4. Aged 12-18 years	27%
5. Aged 19 years or more	15%

Your Background in Ministry

22. Are you ordained?

1. Yes	88%
2. No (SKIP TO Q. 30)	12%

23. At what age did you first seriously consider that you were called to become an ordained minister or priest? _____

High school (age 18 and under)	44%
College (age 19-22)	17%

| Post-college (age 23-29) | 17% |
| Second career (age 30 and over) | 22% |

(Respondents gave their age in years; responses were later coded into these ranges.)

24. How old were you when you received full ordination as minister/pastor/priest? _____

Age 25 and under	24%
Age 26-30	31%
Age 31-39	27%
Age 40 and over	18%

(Respondents gave their age in years; responses were later coded into these ranges.)

25. Overall, how many years have you been in the ordained ministry full- or part-time for which you were paid a salary? _____

Less than 10	26%
10-20 years	27%
21-30 years	27%
31+ years	20%

(Responses were coded into these categories.)

26. In how many different positions, including your current one, have you served as a paid ordained pastor/priest? _____ (FROM WORKSHEET)

In first position	21%
In second position	16%
In third position	23%
In fourth position	13%
In fifth or greater position	27%

(Responses were coded into these categories.)

27. Did you work full-time at other occupations before entering ordained ministry?

| 1. Yes | 70% |
| 2. No (SKIP TO Q. 32) | 30% |

If yes, for how long?	First career pastor	30%
28. _____ years	1 to 5 years in other occupations	19%
29. _____ months	6 to 10 years in other occupations	12%
	11 or more years in other occupations	40%

(Responses were coded into these categories.)

30. What kind of work did you do before becoming a minister? That is, what was your job called? Please specify. _____

31. What is the highest level of theological training you have obtained?

1. None	9%
2. Certificate from denominational training program, Bible college, or seminary	11%
3. Bible college degree	3%
4. Master of Divinity or Bachelor of Divinity	50%
5. M.A., S.T.M., Th.M., or other Master's degree	8%
6. Doctor of Ministry degree	7%
7. Ph.D. or Th.D.	4%
8. Other _____	7%

Your Current Position

32. How would you describe your current position?

1. Senior pastor, priest, or minister	54%
2. Solo pastor, priest, or minister	38%
3. Interim pastor, priest, or minister	2%
4. Co-pastor	2%
5. Other (Specify) _____	4%

33. In what year did you become pastor of this congregation? _____ (Responses were later coded into these categories.)

1 to 5 years in current position	47%
6 to 10 years	21%
11 to 15 years	11%
16 to 20 years	8%
More than 20 years	13%

34. Do you presently serve as pastor of other congregations in addition to this one?

1. Yes	12%
2. No (SKIP TO Q. 37)	88%

35. How many? _____

Serves one church	88%
Serves two churches	8%
Serves three or more churches	4%

Tent-Maker or Bivocational

36. Do you work at any job other than as pastor of this congregation (and other congregations related to it)?

1. Yes	28%
2. No (SKIP TO Q. 38)	72%

37. What kind of work do you do?

1. Professional, technical. Please specify. _____	61%
2. Managers, administrators, sales workers	12%
3. Clerical and related workers	1%
4. Craftsmen and related workers	7%
5. Operatives, except transport	2%
6. Transport, equipment operators, laborers	2%
7. Farmers, farm laborers	7%
8. Service workers	9%

Other Staff

38. Other than you, how many of the following paid staff, full- or part-time, are employed by your congregation? (FROM WORKSHEET)

The following frequencies represent the percentage of pastors reporting at least one person in the category.

	Full-time	Part-time
Ordained professionals	23%	15%
Lay professionals	23%	38%
Clerical/secretarial	28%	39%
Custodial/maintenance	18%	55%

Encouraging Others into Ministry

39. In the past <u>five</u> years, how many from your present congregation have decided to enter some form of ordained religious leadership? _____

One or more	50%

40. In the past two years, how many persons have you personally encouraged to consider becoming a pastor/priest? _____

One or more	77%

Time Spent in Ministry Tasks

41. Approximately how many hours in a typical week do you spend in work related to your employment in this congregation? (FROM WORKSHEET) _____

> (In the final interviews this question was not asked; the answer was derived from Q. 42)

42. In the worksheet that you received in the mail, we listed a number of pastoral tasks and asked you to estimate how much time in a typical week you devote to each task, including preparation where applicable. When I read the list, please refer to your worksheet and tell me how much time you estimated spending for each task. (FROM WORKSHEET)

	Median Hours
1. Preaching	10
2. Worship and sacramental leadership, including funerals and weddings	4
3. Teaching people about the faith	4
4. Training people for ministry and mission	1
5. One-on-one time working to convert others to the faith	2
6. Pastoral counseling and spiritual direction	3
7. Visiting members, sick, and shut-in	3
8. Visiting prospective members	1
9. Administering the work of the congregation, including staff supervision	4
10. Attending congregational board and committee meetings	2
11. Thinking about and promoting a vision and goals for the congregation's future	2
12. Involvement in denominational, interdenominational, interfaith affairs	1
13. Involvement in community affairs and issues beyond the congregation	1
14. Other. Please specify: _____	0

As you look back over this list of pastoral tasks and other demands on you as a pastor:

43. Which three of the tasks do you do best?

1. Preaching	83%
2. Worship and sacramental leadership, including funerals and weddings	42%
3. Teaching people about the faith	54%
4. Training people for ministry and mission	6%
5. One-on-one time working to convert others to the faith	8%

6. Pastoral counseling and spiritual direction   27%

7. Visiting members, sick, and shut-in   27%

8. Visiting prospective members   5%

9. Administering the work of the congregation, including staff supervision   19%

10. Attending congregational board and committee meetings   3%

11. Thinking about and promoting a vision and goals for the congregation's future   13%

12. Involvement in denominational, interdenominational, interfaith affairs   4%

13. Involvement in community affairs and issues beyond the congregation   2%

44. In what three areas do you think you most need to improve?

1. Preaching   20%

2. Worship and sacramental leadership, including funerals and weddings   7%

3. Teaching people about the faith   16%

4. Training people for ministry and mission   28%

5. One-on-one time working to convert others to the faith   31%

6. Pastoral counseling and spiritual direction   21%

7. Visiting members, sick, and shut-in   21%

8. Visiting prospective members   27%

9. Administering the work of the congregation, including staff supervision   29%

10. Attending congregational board and committee meetings   9%

11. Thinking about and promoting a vision and goals for the congregation's future   20%

12. Involvement in denominational, interdenominational, interfaith affairs   18%

13. Involvement in community affairs and issues
beyond the congregation   23%

45. In your ministry in the congregation, with which
two age groups do you spend most of your time working?

    1. Children (to age 12)   15%

    2. Youth (age 12 to 18)   20%

    3. Single Young Adults   9%

    4. Married Young Adults   26%

    5. Middle-Age Adults   68%

    6. Older Adults   57%

46. Within the last seven days, how much time did you spend in the following
activities? (FROM WORKSHEET) _____   Median Hours

    1. Prayer, meditation, Bible reading, and other
spiritual disciplines   7

    2. Reading other than for sermons   4

    3. Searching the web, chat groups, e-mail   1

    4. Family life (time, other than at meals, spent
on family activities)   8

    5. Household chores (laundry, shopping, etc.)   4

    6. Physical exercise for your health   2

    7. Recreation (other than exercise)   2

    8. Commuting to work   1

    9. Eating out with friends   2

47. Other than the Bible, what three authors do you read most often in relation
to your work as a pastor? (FROM WORKSHEET)

    1. _____

    2. _____

    3. _____

48. What journals do you most often read? (List up to three — FROM WORKSHEET)

      1._____

      2._____

      3._____

Time Away from Ministry

49. Do you regularly take a day off each week?

      1. Yes   66%

      2. No   34%

50. How often during the past year did you take part in some form of continuing theological education lasting at least a full day?

      1. None   22%

      2. Once or twice   33%

      3. Three to five times   28%

      4. Five or more times   17%

51. Does your current congregation provide you with a sabbatical leave?

      1. Yes   30%

      2. No (SKIP TO Q. 53)   70%

52. How long was it for? _____ (Respondents gave the number of months; responses were later coded into these categories)

      Less than one month   12%

      One month   33%

      Two months   6%

      Three months   23%

      Four months   3%

      Six months   13%

      Seven months   1%

      12 months or more   9%

The Congregation

53. Do you and your lay leaders engage in an annual evaluation of your performance?

1. Yes	58%
2. No	42%

54. Do you have regular performance evaluations by an appropriate denominational official?

1. Yes	29%
2. No	61%
3. Not applicable as not part of a denomination	10%

55. How important would you say that the denomination of this congregation is for the way that it organizes its programs or ministries?

1. Great importance	41%
2. Somewhat important	33%
3. Somewhat unimportant	5%
4. Of little importance	8%
5. Of no significance, not in a denomination	14%

56. In your work as a pastoral leader, which occupies more of your attention on a week-to-week basis? Is it:

1. Dealing with the problems and needs of individual members	13%
2. Dealing with the problems, needs, and direction of the congregation as a whole	32%
3. Each of these in roughly equal proportion	55%

57. Which of these statements most accurately describes your congregation?

1. Our congregation has no clear vision, goals, or direction (SKIP TO Q. 59)	1%
2. We have some ideas but no clear vision (SKIP TO Q. 59)	21%
3. We have a clear vision but not enough commitment to achieving it	49%

4. We have a clear vision and a strong
commitment to achieving it   29%

58. If the congregation has a clear vision, how compatible with the vision are its current programs and structures?

    1. Very compatible   44%

    2. Somewhat compatible   52%

    3. Somewhat incompatible   4%

    4. Not at all compatible   < 1%

Do you (1) strongly agree, (2) somewhat agree, (3) somewhat disagree, or (4) disagree that:

59. This congregation is always ready to try something new?

    1. Strongly agree   27%

    2. Somewhat agree   49%

    3. Somewhat disagree   17%

    4. Disagree   8%

60. The current morale of this congregation is high?

    1. Strongly agree   53%

    2. Somewhat agree   37%

    3. Somewhat disagree   6%

    4. Disagree   3%

61. Members of the congregation have a sense of excitement about the congregation's future?

    1. Strongly agree   54%

    2. Somewhat agree   38%

    3. Somewhat disagree   6%

    4. Disagree   3%

62. The congregation's leaders are willing to change programs and structures to meet new challenges?

    1. Strongly agree   46%

    2. Somewhat agree   41%

3. Somewhat disagree   11%

4. Disagree   3%

63. Over the last two years, has there been any conflict in this congregation?

     1. No conflict that I'm aware of (SKIP TO Q. 65)   32%

     2. Some minor conflict   47%

     3. Major conflict   5%

     4. Major conflict, with leaders or members leaving   16%

     5. Don't know (SKIP TO Q. 65)   < 1%

64. What was the conflict about?

     1. Finances   7%

     2. Changes in worship styles   8%

     3. Changes in music styles   3%

     4. Changes in other programs of the congregation   7%

     5. Doctrines   < 1%

     6. Pastoral leadership style   22%

     7. Lay leadership style   14%

     8. Conflicts between staff and/or clergy   4%

     9. Sexual misconduct   4%

     10. Issues regarding homosexuality   1%

     11. Racial issues   < 1%

     12. Issues about a new building or renovation
of an existing building   6%

     13. Other, please specify _____   22%

A variety of factors affect a congregation's acceptance of its pastor's leadership. How important is each of the following in your current congregation? Is it of (1) great importance, (2) somewhat important, (3) somewhat unimportant, or of (4) little importance?

65. Being ordained

     1. Of great importance   58%

     2. Somewhat important   21%

3. Somewhat unimportant	7%
4. Of little importance	14%

66. Having a seminary degree or certificate

1. Of great importance	43%
2. Somewhat important	26%
3. Somewhat unimportant	12%
4. Of little importance	19%

67. Having a clear sense of call from God

1. Of great importance	87%
2. Somewhat important	10%
3. Somewhat unimportant	2%
4. Of little importance	2%

68. Being competent in the tasks of ministry, including preaching

1. Of great importance	88%
2. Somewhat important	11%
3. Somewhat unimportant	< 1%
4. Of little importance	< 1%

69. Having the trust of the majority of the congregation

1. Of great importance	91%
2. Somewhat important	9%
3. Somewhat unimportant	< 1%
4. Of little importance	0%

70. Your physical appearance

1. Of great importance	24%
2. Somewhat important	48%
3. Somewhat unimportant	16%
4. Of little importance	12%

71. Your gender

1. Of great importance	44%
2. Somewhat important	25%
3. Somewhat unimportant	16%
4. Of little importance	15%

72. Your race or ethnicity

1. Of great importance	17%
2. Somewhat important	28%
3. Somewhat unimportant	19%
4. Of little importance	36%

Commitment and Satisfaction and Job Stress

As you think about your experience, how important is each of the following in sustaining your commitment to pastoral ministry? For each of the following, would you say that it is of (1) great importance, (2) somewhat important, (3) somewhat unimportant, (4) of little importance?

73. Feeling that your gifts for ministry are right for the congregation you are serving

1. Of great importance	84%
2. Somewhat important	15%
3. Somewhat unimportant	1%
4. Of little importance	< 1%

74. Serving a congregation that offers challenges to your creativity

1. Of great importance	57%
2. Somewhat important	38%
3. Somewhat unimportant	3%
4. Of little importance	3%

75. Having close relationships with your congregation's members

1. Of great importance	65%
2. Somewhat important	31%
3. Somewhat unimportant	3%
4. Of little importance	1%

76. Financial well-being

1. Of great importance	25%
2. Somewhat important	53%
3. Somewhat unimportant	11%
4. Of little importance	11%

77. Opportunity to own your own housing

1. Of great importance	38%
2. Somewhat important	25%
3. Somewhat unimportant	11%
4. Of little importance	26%

78. Anything else? Please specify _____

1. Yes	26%

At the present, what is your level of satisfaction with the following. Are you (1) Very satisfied, (2) Somewhat satisfied, (3) Somewhat dissatisfied, or (4) Very dissatisfied?

79. Your overall effectiveness as a pastoral leader in this particular congregation?

1. Very satisfied	36%
2. Somewhat satisfied	59%
3. Somewhat dissatisfied	4%
4. Very dissatisfied	1%

80. Your current ministry position?

1. Very satisfied	74%
2. Somewhat satisfied	24%
3. Somewhat dissatisfied	2%
4. Very dissatisfied	< 1%

81. Housing or living arrangements?

    1. Very satisfied   74%

    2. Somewhat satisfied   19%

    3. Somewhat dissatisfied   6%

    4. Very dissatisfied   1%

82. Spiritual life?

    1. Very satisfied   42%

    2. Somewhat satisfied   53%

    3. Somewhat dissatisfied   5%

    4. Very dissatisfied   < 1%

83. Opportunities for continuing theological education?

    1. Very satisfied   50%

    2. Somewhat satisfied   39%

    3. Somewhat dissatisfied   12%

    4. Very dissatisfied   1%

84. Support from your denominational official?

    1. Very satisfied   52%

    2. Somewhat satisfied   35%

    3. Somewhat dissatisfied   10%

    4. Very dissatisfied   3%

85. Relations with fellow clergy?

    1. Very satisfied   52%

    2. Somewhat satisfied   36%

    3. Somewhat dissatisfied   10%

    4. Very dissatisfied   2%

86. Relations with lay leaders in your congregation?

    1. Very satisfied   71%

    2. Somewhat satisfied   30%

    3. Somewhat dissatisfied   1%

    4. Very dissatisfied   < 1%

87. Relations with other clergy and staff members in your church?

1. Very satisfied	73%
2. Somewhat satisfied	25%
3. Somewhat dissatisfied	2%
4. Very dissatisfied	< 1%

88. Your salary and benefits?

1. Very satisfied	51%
2. Somewhat satisfied	41%
3. Somewhat dissatisfied	6%
4. Very dissatisfied	2%

89. (IF MARRIED) Your family life?

1. Very satisfied	73%
2. Somewhat satisfied	23%
3. Somewhat dissatisfied	4%
4. Very dissatisfied	< 1%

Clergy face many problems today. Would you indicate how important the following problems are to you on a day-to-day basis? Is it (1) a great problem, (2) Somewhat a problem; (3) Very little problem; (4) No problem?

90. Lack of agreement over what the role of a pastor is.

1. A great problem	6%
2. Somewhat a problem	22%
3. Very little problem	32%
4. No problem	40%

91. Difficulty of having a private life apart from my ministerial role.

1. A great problem	8%
2. Somewhat a problem	33%
3. Very little problem	26%
4. No problem	33%

92. Finding time for recreation, relaxation, or personal reflection.

1. A great problem	17%
2. Somewhat a problem	43%
3. Very little problem	19%
4. No problem	22%

93. Relationships with other clergy and staff members in the church

1. A great problem	< 1%
2. Somewhat a problem	9%
3. Very little problem	29%
4. No problem	62%

94. Having people relate to me differently because I'm a pastor.

1. A great problem	3%
2. Somewhat a problem	28%
3. Very little problem	34%
4. No problem	34%

95. Difficulty of reaching people with the gospel today.

1. A great problem	25%
2. Somewhat a problem	53%
3. Very little problem	12%
4. No problem	10%

96. Looking back over the last five years how often have you doubted that you are called by God to the ministry?

1. Very often	4%
2. Fairly often	4%
3. Once in a while	31%
4. Never	62%

97. In the past five years how often have you thought of leaving pastoral ministry in a congregation to enter another type of ministry position?

1. Very often	6%
2. Fairly often	37%
3. Once in a while	58%
4. Never	2%

98. In the past five years how often have you thought of leaving pastoral ministry to enter a secular occupation?

1. Very often	2%
2. Fairly often	3%
3. Once in a while	24%
4. Never	71%

99. Thinking back over the past year, how often have people in your congregation made you feel loved and cared for?

1. Very often	66%
2. Fairly often	24%
3. Once in a while	10%
4. Never	0%

100. During the past year, how often have the people in your congregation listened to you talk about your private problems and concerns?

1. Very often	5%
2. Fairly often	12%
3. Once in a while	54%
4. Never	29%

101. During the past year, how often have the people in your congregation made too many demands on you? Would you say very often, fairly often, once in a while, or never?

1. Very often	7%
2. Fairly often	13%
3. Once in a while	49%
4. Never	31%

102. During the past year, how often have the people in your congregation been critical of you and the things you have done? Would you say very often, fairly often, once in a while, or never?

1. Very often	4%
2. Fairly often	5%
3. Once in a while	66%
4. Never	26%

103. Looking back over the past year how often have you experienced stress as a result of dealing with congregation members who are critical of your work?

1. Very often	8%
2. Fairly often	9%
3. Once in a while	56%
4. Never	27%

104. Over the past year how often have you felt lonely and isolated in your work?

1. Very often	6%
2. Fairly often	11%
3. Once in a while	51%
4. Never	32%

105. Over the past year how often have you experienced stress because of the challenges you face in this congregation?

1. Very often	13%
2. Fairly often	26%
3. Once in a while	48%
4. Never	13%

Effects of Ministry on Family

(IF RESPONDENTS HAVE CHILDREN LIVING AT HOME, ASK QUESTION 106, OTH-ERWISE SKIP TO Q. 107.)

106. Over the past year how often have you felt that your work in this congregation did not permit you to devote adequate time to your children?

1. Very often	10%
2. Fairly often	18%
3. Once in a while	45%
4. Never	27%

(IF RESPONDENTS ARE MARRIED, ASK QUESTIONS 107 AND 108. OTHERWISE SKIP TO Q. 109.)

107. Over the past year how often has your spouse voiced resentment over the amount of time that your ministry takes up?

1. Very often	3%
2. Fairly often	10%
3. Once in a while	42%
4. Never	46%

108. Over the past year how often has your spouse voiced resentment over the financial situation in which you find yourselves by being in pastoral ministry?

1. Very often	2%
2. Fairly often	7%
3. Once in a while	26%
4. Never	65%

Leadership Style

I am now going to read a series of statements. Please (and I want you to) select the statement that seems most like your style and vision of pastoral leadership.

109. Please choose one of the following two statements.

In the last analysis, the ordained ministry is a calling to a particular state and quality of life that sets one apart from the laity.   39%

Ordained ministers are no different from any Christians except that they have special training which equips them to lead the work of the church.   61%

110. Again, please choose one of the following two statements.

When deciding on a new program or ministry, we discuss the theological rationale for what we are considering.   27%

When deciding on a new program or ministry, we primarily take into consideration how well it meets the desires and needs of members or prospective members.   73%

111. Please choose one of the following four statements.

I make most of the decisions; lay members generally follow my lead.   5%

I try to inspire and encourage lay members to make decisions and take action, although I will take action alone if I believe that it is needed.   70%

Lay leaders come up with most of the initiatives in the congregation, although I try to exert a strong influence on their decisions.   12%

Lay leaders make most of the decisions about the congregation's directions and programs; my role is to empower them to implement their decisions.   12%

112. Please choose one of the following two statements.

I enjoy keeping things stirred up and challenging
my lay leaders with new ideas and programs. 28%

I generally prefer to keep things functioning
smoothly by introducing changes gradually. 72%

113. Please choose one of the following two statements.

It is essential in a rapidly changing world that
congregational leaders should seek to be innovative
in such things as worship and music styles. 61%

In a rapidly changing world, it is essential that
leaders keep their congregation focused on the
inherited traditions and practices of the church. 39%

114. Please choose one of the following two statements.

My lay leaders and I regularly take time to
discuss and define future needs and directions
of the congregation. 57%

The time my lay leaders and I spend together is
largely taken up with keeping things going,
keeping the congregation functioning effectively. 43%

Effects of Ministry on Family

115. (Ask if ever married) In general, would you say that your family has been very positively affected by your ministry in this congregation, somewhat positively affected, somewhat negatively affected, or very negatively affected?

1. Very positively 60%

2. Somewhat positively 31%

3. Somewhat negatively 8%

4. Very negatively 2%

116. In your current planning, at what age do you anticipate retiring from active pastoral ministry? _____

Your Health

117. In general, would you say your health is:

1. Excellent		35%
2. Very good		41%
3. Good		19%
4. Fair		4%
5. Poor		1%

118. What is your height?   Median: 5′ 10″

119. What is your weight?   Median: 192 lbs.

Body Mass Index Fitness:

Underweight	1%
Normal	21%
Overweight	48%
Obese	30%

120. During the past four weeks, how much of the time have you accomplished less than you would like with your work or other regular daily activities as a result of your physical health?

1. All of the time	1%
2. Most of the time	2%
3. Some of the time	10%
4. A little of the time	16%
5. None of the time	71%

121. During the past four weeks, how much of the time have you been limited in the kind of work or other activities you could do as a result of your physical health?

1. All of the time	< 1%
2. Most of the time	1%
3. Some of the time	6%
4. A little of the time	12%
5. None of the time	81%

122. During the past four weeks, how much of the time have you accomplished less than you would like as a result of any emotional problems (such as feeling depressed or anxious)?

1. All of the time	0%
2. Most of the time	1%
3. Some of the time	7%
4. A little of the time	14%
5. None of the time	78%

123. During the past four weeks, how much of the time have you done work or activities less carefully than usual as a result of any emotional problems (such as feeling depressed or anxious)?

1. All of the time	< 1%
2. Most of the time	< 1%
3. Some of the time	5%
4. A little of the time	15%
5. None of the time	80%

The following questions are about how you feel and how things have been with you during the past four weeks. For each question, please give the one answer that comes closest to the way you have been feeling. How much of the time during the past four weeks . . .

124. Have you felt calm and peaceful?

1. All of the time	13%
2. Most of the time	66%
3. Some of the time	18%
4. A little of the time	2%
5. None of the time	1%

125. Did you have a lot of energy?

1. All of the time	11%
2. Most of the time	63%
3. Some of the time	21%
4. A little of the time	3%
5. None of the time	1%

126. Have you felt downhearted and depressed?

1.	All of the time	0%
2.	Most of the time	1%
3.	Some of the time	10%
4.	A little of the time	38%
5.	None of the time	52%

127. Did you feel worn out?

1.	All of the time	1%
2.	Most of the time	5%
3.	Some of the time	38%
4.	A little of the time	37%
5.	None of the time	20%

128. Have you been happy?

1.	All of the time	24%
2.	Most of the time	67%
3.	Some of the time	8%
4.	A little of the time	1%
5.	None of the time	0%

Background

129. Respondent's Gender (INTERVIEWER, CODE WITHOUT ASKING UNLESS THERE IS DOUBT)

1.	Male	89%
2.	Female	11%

130. What is the highest educational qualification you have completed?

1. High school diploma or equivalent (SKIP TO Q. 132)	9%
2. Community college diploma (SKIP TO Q. 132)	5%
3. Bachelor degree from a four-year college or equivalent	19%

4. Master's degree   ·49%

5. Earned doctorate   11%

6. Other   7%

131. What was your undergraduate major? _____

132. Which of the following racial categories best describes you?

     1. White   81%

     2. African American   15%

     3. Asian American or Pacific Islander   1%

     4. American Indian or Alaska Native   < 1%

     5. Other, please specify _____   3%

133. Would you characterize yourself as Hispanic/Latino?

     1. Yes   3%

     2. No   97%

134. In what year were you born? (Responses were later coded into these categories.)

     Age 44 or less   27%

     Age 45 to 50   21%

     Age 51 to 60   31%

     Age 61 and over   21%

135. In what state were you born or, if not born in the United States, in what foreign country? _____

     U.S. born = 95%

136. Which of the following categories comes closest to the type of place you were living in when you were 16 years old?

     1. In open country or on a farm   27%

     2. In a small city or town (under 50,000)   31%

     3. In a medium-sized city (50,000-250,000)   15%

     4. In a suburb near a large city   13%

     5. In a large city   14%

137. What kind of work did your father do while you were growing up?

1. Professional, technical	29%
2. Managers and administrators, sales workers	18%
3. Clerical and related workers	1%
4. Craftsmen and related workers	12%
5. Operatives, except transport	4%
6. Transport, equipment operatives, laborers	19%
7. Farmers, farm laborers	20%
8. Service workers	4%
9. Not in workforce	3%

138. What kind of work did your mother do while you were growing up?

1. Professional, technical	14%
2. Managers and administrators, sales workers	7%
3. Clerical and related workers	7%
4. Craftsmen and related workers	1%
5. Operatives, except transport	1%
6. Transport, equipment operatives, laborers	1%
7. Farmers, farm laborers	1%
8. Service workers	10%
9. Not in workforce	60%

Finances

139. What is your current salary as a pastor prior to taxes, including fringe benefits & allowances but excluding housing, health insurance, and pensions? (FROM WORKSHEET)

Median = $25,777

140. Does your congregation furnish you with a parsonage/manse/rectory or provide a housing allowance?

1. Yes	39%
2. No (SKIP TO Q. 143)	61%

141. How much is that allowance?

　　Median = $1,000/month

142. How much is the fair rental value of your parsonage/manse/rectory (FROM WORKSHEET)

　　Median = $700/month

143. How much money do you have to set aside each month to repay in educational debts? (FROM WORKSHEET)

1. None	84%
2. $1 to $300	10%
3. More than $300	5%

(Respondents gave a dollar amount; data was later coded into these categories)

144. Does your congregation contribute to a pension program for you?

1. Yes	60%
2. No	40%

145. Do you receive health care benefits either from your congregation or your spouse's employer?

1. Yes	79%
2. No	21%

146. What is the total amount of any income that your family receives from sources other than your income from the church, such as a spousal salary, a second job, investments etc? (FROM WORKSHEET)

　　Median = $16,000

THANK YOU VERY MUCH FOR COMPLETING THE SURVEY

Works Cited and Consulted

Abbott, Andrew. 1988. *The System of Professions*. Chicago: University of Chicago Press.

Ammerman, Nancy T. 1997a. Golden Rule Christianity: Lived Religion in the American Mainstream. In *Lived Religion in America: Toward a History of Practice*, edited by David D. Hall, 196-216. Princeton: Princeton University Press.

———. 1997b. *Congregation and Community*. New Brunswick, N.J.: Rutgers University Press.

———. 2005. *Pillars of Faith: American Congregations and Their Partners*. Berkeley: University of California Press.

ATS. 2002-2003. *Fact Book on Theological Education*. Pittsburgh: Association of Theological Schools.

Bahari, Sarah. 2005. Marry us, friend (or family). *The News and Observer* (Raleigh, N.C.), March 22, E: 1, 3.

Balmer, Randall. 1989. *Mine Eyes Have Seen the Glory: A Journey into the Evangelical Subculture in America*. New York: Oxford University Press.

Barnes, Craig. 2004. Sometimes Ministry Stinks. *Leadership Journal*, September 28.

Berger, Peter L. 1992. *A Far Glory: The Quest for Faith in an Age of Credulity*. New York: The Free Press.

Bledstein, Burton J. 1976. *The Culture of Professionalism*. New York: W. W. Norton & Co.

Blizzard, Samuel W. 1985. *The Protestant Parish Minister: A Behavioral Science Interpretation*. Society for the Scientific Study of Religion Monograph Series, vol. 5. Storrs, Conn.: Society for the Scientific Study of Religion.

Bonn, Robert L. 1975. Moonlighting Clergy. *Christian Century*, September, 4-8.

Boser, Ulrich. 2005. A New Kind of Ministry. *US News: America's Best Graduate Schools 2006*. Available online at http://www.usnews.com/usnews/edu/grad/articles/brief/06div_brief.php.

Brooks, David. 2000. *Bobos in Paradise: The New Upper Class and How They Got There.* New York: Simon & Schuster.

———. 2005. Empty Nests, and Hearts. *The New York Times,* 15/January, Opinion.

Brown, Raymond. 1984. *The Churches the Apostles Left Behind.* Kansas City: Sheed and Ward.

Brunette-Hill, Sandi, and Roger Finke. 1999. A Time for Every Purpose: Updating and Extending Blizzard's Survey of Clergy Time Allocation. *Review of Religious Research* 41 (Fall): 48-64.

Bureau of Labor Statistics. 2000. Are Managers and Professionals Really Working More? *Issues in Labor Statistics,* Summary 00-12 (May).

Burns, James MacGregor. 1978. *Leadership.* New York: Harper Torchbooks.

CARA (Center for Applied Research on the Apostolate). 2003. Catholic Ministry Formation Enrollments: Statistical Overview for 2002-2003. Washington: CARA. Available online at http://cara.georgetown.edu/pdfs/Overview2003.pdf.

Carder, Kenneth L. 2001. Market and Mission: Competing Visions for Transforming Ministry. Available online at http://www.pulpitandpew.duke.edu/otherpub.html.

Carroll, Jackson W. 1985. The Professional Model of Ministry: Is It Worth Saving? *Theological Education* XXI, no. 2, Spring: 7-48.

———. 1991. *As One with Authority: Reflective Leadership in Ministry.* Louisville: Westminster John Knox Press.

———. 1998. Leadership and the Study of the Congregation. In *Studying Congregations: A New Handbook,* edited by Nancy T. Ammerman, Jackson W. Carroll, Carl S. Dudley, and William McKinney. Nashville: Abingdon Press.

———. 2000. *Mainline to the Future: Congregations for the 21st Century.* Louisville: Westminster John Knox Press.

———. 2000. *Reflections of a Clergy Watcher.* Durham, N.C.: Pulpit & Pew.

———. 2003. Pastors' Picks: What Preachers Are Reading. *The Christian Century,* 23 August.

Carroll, Jackson W., and Wade Clark Roof. 2002. *Bridging Divided Worlds: Generational Cultures in Congregations.* San Francisco: Jossey-Bass.

Carroll, Jackson W., Barbara G. Wheeler, Daniel O. Aleshire, and Penny Long Marler. 1997. *Being There: Culture and Formation in Two Theological Schools.* New York: Oxford University Press.

Carroll, Jackson W., and Robert L. Wilson. 1980. *Too Many Pastors? The Clergy Job Market.* New York: Pilgrim Press.

Chambliss, Daniel F. 1989. The Mundanity of Excellence: An Ethnographic Report of Stratification and Olympic Swimmers. *Sociological Theory* 7, no. 1: 70-86.

Chang, Patricia M. Y. 2003. *Clergy Supply and Demand in Selected Protestant Denominations.* Research Report from Pulpit & Pew: Research on Pastoral Leadership. Durham, N.C.: Duke Divinity School.

Chaves, Mark. 1999. The National Congregations Study. *Journal for the Scientific Study of Religion* 38: 458-76.

————. 2004. *Congregations in America*. Cambridge, Mass.: Harvard University Press.

Chaves, Mark, and James C. Cavendish. 1994. More Evidence on U.S. Catholic Church Attendance. *Journal for the Scientific Study of Religion* 33: 376-81.

Christopherson, Richard W. 1994. Calling and Career in Christian Ministry. *Review of Religious Research* 35, no. 3, March: 219-37.

Church Personnel Services: Pastoral Leadership Search Effort. 2003.

Cohen, Steven M. 2002. *Conservative Rabbis and Their Approaches to Religious Leadership: Evidence from Studies of Rabbis and Congregational Lay Leaders*. New York: The Jewish Religious Leadership Institute of the Jewish Theological Seminary.

Collins, Karen Scott, Cathy Schoen, and David R. Sandman. March 1997. "The Commonwealth Fund Survey of Physician Experiences with Managed Care." *The Commonwealth Fund*. 21/June/2002.

Constantine, Mark D. 2005. *Travelers on the Journey: Pastors Talk About Their Lives and Commitments*. Grand Rapids: William B. Eerdmans Publishing Company.

Cooke, Bernard. 1975. *Ministry to Word and Sacrament*. Philadelphia: Fortress Press.

Cozzens, Donald B. 2000. *The Changing Face of the Priesthood: A Reflection on the Priest's Crisis of Soul*. Minneapolis: Liturgical Press.

Daniel, Lillian. 2001. Collegial Friendship. Paper presented at the Pulpit & Pew Theological Colloquium. Durham, N.C.: Duke Divinity School.

D'Antonio, William V., James D. Davidson, Dean R. Hoge, and Katherine Meyer. 2001. *American Catholics: Gender, Generation, and Commitment*. Walnut Creek, Calif.: AltaMira.

D'Antonio, William V., James D. Davidson, Dean R. Hoge, and Ruth A. Wallace. 1996. *Laity American and Catholic: Transforming the Church*. Kansas City: Sheed and Ward.

Dayton, Donald, and Robert K. Johnston. 1991. *The Variety of American Evangelicalism*. Knoxville: University of Tennessee Press.

DeYoung, Curtiss Paul, Michael O. Emerson, George Yancey, and Karen Chai Kim. 2003. *United by Faith: The Multiracial Congregation as an Answer to the Problem of Race*. New York: Oxford University Press.

DiMaggio, Paul J., and Walter W. Powell. 1983. The Iron Cage Revisited: Institutional Isomorphism and Collective Rationality in Organizational Fields. *American Sociological Review* 48 (April): 147-60.

Dorsey, E. Ray, David Jarjoura, and Gregory W. Rutecki. 2003. Influence of Controllable Lifestyle on Recent Trends in Specialty Choice by U.S. Medical Students. *Journal of the American Medical Association* 290, no. 9, 3 September: 1173-78.

Douglass, H. Paul. N.d. *The City Minister at Work*. Unpublished manuscript.

Douglass, H. Paul, and Edmund de S. Brunner. 1935. *The Protestant Church as a Social Institution*. New York: Russell and Russell.

Dudley, Carl S., and David A. Roozen. 2001. *Faith Communities Today: A Report on Religion in the United States Today*. Hartford Institute for Religion Research. Hartford, Conn.: Hartford Seminary.

Dykstra, Craig. 2001. The Pastoral Imagination. *Initiatives in Religion*, Spring, 1-2, 15.

Eck, Diana L. 2001. *A New Religious America: How a "Christian Country" Has Now Become the World's Most Religiously Diverse Nation.* San Francisco: HarperSanFrancisco.

Eiesland, Nancy L. 2000. *A Particular Place: Urban Restructuring and Religious Ecology in a Southern Exurb.* New Brunswick, N.J.: Rutgers University Press.

Farley, Edward W. 1990. The Presbyterian Heritage as Modernism: Reaffirming a Forgotten Past. In *The Presbyterian Predicament: Six Perspectives,* edited by Milton J. Coalter, John M. Mulder, and Louis B. Weeks. Louisville: Westminster John Knox Press.

Finke, Roger, and Rodney Stark. 1992. *The Churching of America, 1776-1990: Winners and Losers in Our Religious Economy.* New Brunswick, N.J.: Rutgers University Press.

Forsyth, P. T. 1907. *Positive Preaching and the Modern Mind.* New York: A. C. Armstrong and Son.

Friedman, Edwin H. 1985. *Generation to Generation: Family Process in Church and Synagogue.* New York: The Guilford Press.

Gardner, Howard, Mihaly Csikszentmihalyi, and William Damon. 2001. *Good Work: When Excellence and Ethics Meet.* New York: Basic Books.

Glassie, Henry H. 1989. *The Spirit of Folk Art.* New York: Abrams.

Greeley, Andrew. 2004. *The Catholic Revolution: New Wine, Old Wineskins, and the Second Vatican Council.* Berkeley: University of California Press.

————. 2004. For Priests, Celibacy Is Not the Problem. *New York Times,* 3/3.

Gregory the Great. 1950. *Pastoral Care.* Translated by Henry S. J. Davies. Ancient Christian Writers: The Works of the Fathers in Translation, ed. Johannes Quasten and Joseph C. Plumpe, vol. 11. New York: Newman Press.

Griswold, Wendy. 1994. *Cultures and Societies in a Changing World.* Thousand Oaks, Calif.: Pine Forge Press.

Hadaway, C. Kirk, and Penny Long Marler. 1998. Did You Really Go to Church This Week? Behind the Poll Data. *The Christian Century,* 6/May, 472-75.

Hadaway, C. Kirk, Penny Long Marler, and Mark Chaves. 1993. What the Polls Don't Show: A Closer Look at U.S. Church Attendance. *American Sociological Review* 58: 741-52.

Hadden, Jeffrey K. 1968. *The Gathering Storm in the Churches.* Garden City, N.Y.: Doubleday.

Halaas, Gwen Wagstrom, M.D. 2004. *The Right Road: Life Choices for Clergy.* Minneapolis: Fortress Press.

Hall, Richard H. 1969. *Occupations and the Social Structure.* Englewood Cliffs, N.J.: Prentice-Hall.

Harris, Joseph Claude. 2005. The Disturbing Trends Behind Parish Change. *America,* 2/May, 11.

Hatch, Nathan O. 1989. *The Democratization of American Christianity.* New Haven: Yale University Press.

Healy, Anthony E. 2005. *The Postindustrial Promise: Vital Religious Community in the 21st Century.* Herndon, Va.: The Alban Institute.

Heifetz, Ronald A. 1994. *Leadership Without Easy Answers.* Cambridge, Mass.: Belknap Press of Harvard University Press.

Herberg, Will. 1955. *Protestant-Catholic-Jew.* Garden City, N.Y.: Doubleday Anchor Books.

Hernandez, Edwin, Milagros Peña, Kenneth Davis, CSC, and Elizabeth Station. 2005. *Strengthening Hispanic Ministry Across Denominations: A Call to Action.* Research Report from Pulpit and Pew: Research on Pastoral Leadership. Durham, N.C.: Duke Divinity School.

Hoge, Dean R. 2002. *The First Five Years of the Priesthood.* Collegeville, Minn.: Liturgical Press.

Hoge, Dean R., Jackson W. Carroll, and Francis X. Scheets OSC. 1988. *Patterns of Parish Leadership: Cost and Effectiveness in Four Denominations.* St. Louis: Sheed and Ward.

Hoge, Dean R., John E. Dyble, and David T. Polk. 1981. Organizational and Situational Influences on Vocational Commitment of Protestant Ministers. *Review of Religious Research* 23, No. 2 (December): 133-49.

Hoge, Dean R., and Jacqueline E. Wenger. 2003. *Evolving Visions of Priesthood: Changes from Vatican II to the Turn of the New Century.* Minneapolis: Liturgical Press.

————. 2005. *Pastors in Transition: Why Clergy Leave Local Church Ministry.* Grand Rapids: William B. Eerdmans Publishing Company.

Holifield, E. Brooks. 2002. The Heritage. Unpublished manuscript from a forthcoming history of pastoral leadership in America.

————. Forthcoming. *A History of Pastoral Leadership in America* (working title). Grand Rapids: William B. Eerdmans Publishing Company.

Holmes, Urban T. 1978. *The Priest in Community.* New York: Seabury Press.

Hout, Michael, and Claude S. Fischer. 2001. Religious Diversity in America, 1940-2000. Paper presented at annual meeting of the American Sociological Association.

Howell, Leon. 2003. *United Methodism @ Risk: A Wake-up Call.* Kingston, N.Y.: Information Project for United Methodists.

Huba, Stephen. 2000. Para-Clergy Help During Rabbi Shortage. *Cincinnati Post,* July 26. Available online at http://www.cincypost.com/news/2000/rabbis072600.html.

Hudnut-Beumler, James. 1999. *Finding God in the Suburbs.* Louisville: Westminster John Knox Press.

Hutchison, William R. 1989. Protestantism as Establishment. In *Between the Times: The Travail of the Protestant Establishment in America, 1900-1960,* edited by William R. Hutchison. Cambridge: Cambridge University Press.

Hybels, Lynne, and Bill Hybels. 1995. *Rediscovering Church: The Story and Vision of Willow Creek Community Church.* Grand Rapids: Zondervan.

Jacquet, Constant H., Jr. 1989. Women Ministers in 1986 and 1977: A Ten-Year View. In

Yearbook of American and Canadian Churches, edited by Constant H. Jacquet, Jr., 261-66. Nashville: Abingdon Press.

Jenkins, Philip. 2002. *The Next Christendom: The Coming of Global Christianity.* New York: Oxford University Press.

Jones, L. Gregory, and Kevin R. Armstrong. 2006. *Resurrecting Excellence: Shaping Faithful Christian Ministry.* Grand Rapids: William B. Eerdmans Publishing Company.

Jones, Malcolm. 2004. Wrestling With Angels. *Newsweek,* 6/December, 87.

Kahle, Roger R. 1999. Does the ELCA Face a Clergy Shortage? *The Lutheran,* January.

Kierkegaard, Søren. 1999. *Provocations: Spiritual Writings of Kierkegaard.* Edited by Charles E. Moore. Farmington, Pa.: Plough Publishing House.

Klaas, Alan C., and Cheryl D. Klaas. 1999. *Clergy Shortage Study.* Study Commissioned by the Board for Higher Education, Lutheran Church — Missouri Synod. Smithville, Mo.: Mission Growth Ministries.

Kronan, Anthony T. 1993. *The Lost Lawyer: Failing Ideals of the Legal Profession.* Cambridge, Mass.: The Belknap Press of Harvard University Press.

Kruger, Richard A., and Mary Anne Casey. 2000. *Focus Groups: A Practical Guide to Applied Research.* Thousand Oaks, Calif.: Sage.

Kurson, Robert. 2000. Who's Killing the Great Lawyers of Harvard? *Esquire,* August, pp. 82-94.

Larson, Ellis L. 1995. A Profile of Contemporary Seminarians Revisited. *Theological Education* 31 (Supplement): 1-118.

Larsen, Ellis L., and James M. Shropshire. 1988. A Profile of Contemporary Seminarians. *Theological Education* 31 (Supplement): 1-118.

Larson, Magalai S. 1977. *The Rise of Professionalism: A Sociological Analysis.* Berkeley: University of California Press.

Lawson, Linda. 1999. 'Tentmaking' Ministers Predicted to Become Southern Baptist Norm. *Baptist Press News,* August 11.

Lee, James Michael, and Louis J. Putz. 1965. Introduction. In *Seminary Education in a Time of Change,* edited by James Michael Lee and Louis J. Putz. Notre Dame, Ind.: Fides Press.

Lehman, Edward C., Jr. 1993. *Gender and Work: The Case of the Clergy.* New Brunswick, N.J.: Transaction Press.

————. 2002. *Women's Path Into Ministry: Six Major Studies.* Research Report from Pulpit & Pew: Research on Pastoral Leadership. Durham, N.C.: Duke Divinity School.

Lincoln, C. Eric, and Lawrence H. Mamiya. 1990. *The Black Church in the African American Experience.* Durham, N.C.: Duke University Press.

Lincoln, James, and Arne Kalleberg. 1990. *Culture, Control, and Commitment: A Study of Work Organization and Work Attitudes in the United States and Japan.* Cambridge: Cambridge University Press.

Lindner, Eileen, ed. 2004. *Yearbook of American and Canadian Churches.* Nashville: Abingdon Press.

Lischer, Richard. 2001. *Open Secrets: A Spiritual Journey Through a Country Church.* New York: Doubleday.

Lummis, Adair T. 2003. *What Do Lay People Want in Pastors? Answers from Lay Search Committee Chairs and Regional Judicatory Leaders.* Research Report from Pulpit & Pew. Durham, N.C.: Duke Divinity School.

Lynd, Robert S., and Helen Merrell Lynd. 1929. *Middletown: A Study in American Culture.* New York: Harcourt, Brace and Company.

MacDonald, Gordon. 2003. The Root of Leadership: How to Gain, and Maintain, Your People's Trust. *Leadership,* Winter, 53-58.

MacIntyre, Alasdair. 1984. *After Virtue,* 2nd ed. Notre Dame, Ind.: University of Notre Dame Press.

MacPherson, J. Miller. 1982. Hypernetwork Sampling: Duality and Differentiation among Voluntary Organizations. *Social Networks* 3: 225-49.

Malloy, David. 2004. Black United Methodists Address Lack of Youth in Church. *United Methodist News Service,* March 31.

Mamiya, Lawrence. 2005. *River of Struggle, River of Freedom: Trends in Black Churches and Black Pastoral Leadership.* Research Report from Pulpit & Pew: Research on Pastoral Leadership. Durham, N.C.: Duke Divinity School.

Marsh, Charles. 2005. *The Beloved Community: How Faith Shapes Social Justice, from the Civil Rights Movement to Today.* New York: Basic Books.

Marty, Martin E. 2001. Young Clergy: Where Are They? *Sightings,* March 26. Available online at http://marty-center.uchicago.edu/sightings.

May, Mark A., William Adams Brown, Frank K. Shuttleworth, Jesse A. Jacobs, and Charlotte V. Feeney. 1934. *The Profession of the Ministry: Its Status and Problems.* The Education of American Ministers, vol. II. New York: Institute for Social and Religious Research.

May, Mark A., and Frank K. Shuttleworth. 1934. *Appendices.* The Education of American Ministers, vol. IV. New York: Institute for Social and Religious Research.

McAnally, Thomas. 2001. Is the United Methodist Church Facing a Clergy Shortage? *United Methodist News Service,* April 5.

McDuff, Elaine M., and Charles W. Mueller. 2000. The Ministry as an Occupational Labor Market: Intentions to Leave an Employer (Church) Versus Intentions to Leave a Profession (Ministry). *Work and Occupations* 27:1, February.

McMillan, Becky R., and Matthew J. Price. 2003. *How Much Should We Pay Our Pastor? A Fresh Look at Clergy Salaries in the 21st Century.* Research Report from Pulpit & Pew. Durham, N.C.: Duke Divinity School.

McRoberts, Omar M. 2003. *Streets of Glory: Church and Community in a Black Urban Neighborhood.* Chicago: University of Chicago Press.

Mead, Sidney. 1956. The Rise of the Evangelical Conception of Ministry in America (1607-1850). In *Ministry in Historical Perspectives,* edited by H. Richard Niebuhr and Daniel Day Williams. New York: Harper & Row.

Memphis Declaration. 1992. Available online at http://www.goodnewsmag.org.

Miller, Donald E. 1997. *Reinventing American Protestantism: Christianity in the New Millennium.* Berkeley: University of California Press.

————. 2003. Emergent Patterns of Congregational Life and Leadership in the Developing World: Reflections on a Research Odyssey. Occasional Paper from Pulpit & Pew: Research on Pastoral Leadership. Durham, N.C.: Duke Divinity School.

Miller, Kevin. 2001. Can Pastors Really Be Happy? *Leadership,* April 15, 2002. Available online at www.christianitytoday.com/leaders/newsletter/2001/cln11212.html.

Miller, Kevin A. 2003. What We Have Uncommon: It's Our Differences That Make Our Churches Useful in the Kingdom. *Leadership,* January 16.

Miller, Sara. 2002. Global Gospel: Christianity Is Alive and Well in the Southern Hemisphere. *Christian Century,* 17-30 July, 20-27.

Miller, Vincent J. 2004. *Consuming Religion: Christian Faith and Practice in a Consumer Culture.* New York: Continuum.

Monahan, Susanne C. 1999. Role Ambiguity Among Protestant Clergy: Consequences of the Activated Laity. *Review of Religious Research* 41 (Fall): 79-94.

Moore, David W. 2004. Nurses Top List in Honesty and Ethic Poll. Princeton: The Gallup Organization.

Mueller, Charles W., and Elaine McDuff. 2004. Clergy-Congregation Mismatches and Clergy Job Satisfaction. *Journal for the Scientific Study of Religion* 43, no. 2, June: 261-73.

Murnion, Philip J., and David DeLambo. 1999. *Parishes and Parish Ministers: A Study of Parish Lay Ministry.* New York: National Parish Life Center.

National Vital Statistics Reports. 2004. Estimated Life Expectancy at Birth in Years. Washington: National Center for Health Statistics.

Nicolson, Adam. 2003. *God's Secretaries: The Making of the King James Bible.* New York: HarperCollins.

Niebuhr, H. Richard. 1957. *The Purpose of the Church and Its Ministry.* New York: Harper & Row.

Orsi, Robert A. 2005. *Between Heaven and Earth: The Religious Worlds People Make and the Scholars Who Study Them.* Princeton: Princeton University Press.

Pelusa-Verdend, Gary E. 2002. How Many Congregations Does It Take to Raise a Minister? *Circuit Rider,* January/February, 18-19.

Perl, Paul, and Bryan T. Froehle. 2002. *Priests in the United States: Satisfaction, Workload, and Support Structures,* CARA Working Paper no. 5. Washington D.C.: Center for Applied Research in the Apostolate.

Peters, Tom, and Robert Waterman. 1982. *In Search of Excellence.* New York: Warner.

Pohl, Christine. 2001. Reflections on Excellent Ministry. Paper presented at the Pulpit & Pew Theological Colloquium. Durham, N.C.: Duke Divinity School.

Porter, Eduardo. 2004. Coming Soon: The Vanishing Work Force. *The New York Times,* 29 August.

Price, Clay. 1977. A Brief Comparison of Small Rural Churches with Bi-Vocational Pastors with Small Rural Churches with Full-Time Pastors. Atlanta: Southern Baptist Convention Mission Surveys and Special Studies.

Price, Matthew J. 2001. Fear of Falling: Male Clergy in Financial Crisis. *The Christian Century,* 15-22 August.

Putnam, Robert D. 2000. *Bowling Alone: The Collapse and Revival of American Community.* New York: Simon and Schuster.

Ray, Julie. 2003. *Worlds Apart: Religion in Canada.* Princeton: The Gallup Organization.

Rendle, Gilbert R. 2002. Reclaiming Professional Jurisdiction: The Re-emergence of the Theological Task of Ministry. *Theology Today* 59, no. 3 (October): 408-20.

Robinson, Marilynne. 2004. *Gilead.* New York: Farrar, Straus, and Giroux.

Roof, Wade Clark, and William McKinney. 1987. *American Mainline Religion.* New Brunswick, N.J.: Rutgers University Press.

Roozen, David A. 2001. Findings Regarding Youth Involvement and Growth in Faith Communities Today. Hartford, Conn.: Hartford Institute for Religious Research.

Routhauge, Arlin J. 1995. *Sizing Up a Congregation for New Member Ministry.* New York: The Domestic and Foreign Missionary Society.

Ruger, Anthony, and Barbara G. Wheeler. 1995. *Manna from Heaven? Theological and Rabbinical Student Debt.* New York: Auburn Center for the Study of Theological Education.

Russell, Anthony. 1980. *The Clerical Profession.* London: SPCK.

Russell, Cheryl. 2000. *Demographics of the U.S.: Trends and Projections.* Ithaca, N.Y.: New Strategist Publications, Inc.

Saad, Lydia. 2003. Religion Is Very Important to Majority of Americans. Princeton: The Gallup Organization.

Schier, Tracy. 2002. Jack Wall: On Being a Pastor with Imagination. *Resources for American Christianity,* July 7. Available online at http://www.resourcingchristianity.org/down loads/interview_transcripts/Wall%20Interview.pdf.

————. n.d. Transition into Ministry: Programs Offer Hope for Revitalizing Congregational Leadership: An Interview with David Wood. Available online at http://www.resourcingchristianity.org/downloads/ministries_reshaped/Wood%20-%20Reshaping.%20pdf.pdf.

Schoenherr, Richard A. 2002. *Goodbye Father: The Celibate Male Priesthood and the Future of the Catholic Church.* Edited by David Yamane. New York: Oxford University Press.

Schoenherr, Richard A., and Lawrence A. Young. 1993. *Full Pews & Empty Altars: Demographics of the Priest Shortage in United States Catholic Dioceses.* Madison, Wis.: University of Wisconsin Press.

Schön, Donald. 1983. *The Reflective Practitioner.* New York: Basic Books.

Scott, Donald M. 1978. *From Office to Profession: The New England Ministry, 1750-1850.* Philadelphia: University of Pennsylvania Press.

Skinner, Jason. 1998. Bivocational Ministers' Role Crucial in Many Southern Baptist Churches. *BP News,* September 23.

Smith, Christian. 1998. *American Evangelicalism: Embattled and Thriving*. Chicago: University of Chicago Press.

Smith, H. Shelton, Robert Handy, and Lefferts A. Loetcher. 1960. *American Christianity: An Historical Interpretation with Representative Documents*. New York: Charles Scribner's Sons.

Smith, Tom W. 2000. *Changes in the Generation Gap, 1972-1998*. GSS Social Change Report No. 43. University of Chicago: National Opinion Research Center.

Stout, Harry S. 1986. *The New England Soul*. New York: Oxford University Press. Unpublished address.

Survey Results: Exploring Religious America. 2002. *Religion & Ethics Newsweekly*, June 7. Available online at http://www.pbs.org/wnet/religionandethics/week540/surveyresults.html.

Swicegood, Terry. N.d. Mammas, Don't Let Your Babies Grow Up to be Preachers. Unpublished address.

Swidler, Ann. 1986. Culture in Action: Symbols and Strategies. *American Sociological Review* 51: 273-86.

Theological Educators Speak to Religion Newswriters. 2004. Colloquy of the Association of Theological Schools, November-December.

Tseng, Timothy. 2005. *Pastoral Leadership in Asian American Congregations*. Pulpit & Pew: Research on Pastoral Leadership. Durham, N.C.: Duke Divinity School.

United States Census Bureau. 2000. *Statistical Abstract of the United States*. Washington: U.S. Census Bureau.

————. 2003. *Statistical Abstract of the United States*. Washington: U.S. Census Bureau.

Volf, Miroslav, and Dorothy C. Bass, eds. 2002. *Practicing Theology: Beliefs and Practices in Christian Life*. Grand Rapids: William B. Eerdmans Publishing Company.

Wagoner, Walter D. 1966. *The Seminary: Protestant and Catholic*. New York: Sheed and Ward.

Wallace, Ruth A. 1992. *They Call Her Pastor: A New Role for Catholic Women*. Albany: State University of New York Press.

Warner, R. Stephen. 1988. *New Wine in Old Wineskins: Evangelicals and Liberals in a Small-Town Church*. Berkeley: University of California Press.

————. 1994. The Place of the Congregation in the Contemporary American Religious Configuration. In *American Congregations*, edited by James P. Wind and James W. Lewis, Vol. 2: *New Perspectives in the Study of Congregations*. Chicago: University of Chicago Press.

————. 2004. Coming to America: Immigrants and the Faith They Bring. *Christian Century*, 10 February, 20-23.

Wells, Bob. 2002. Which Way to Clergy Health? Pulpit & Pew: Research on Pastoral Leadership. Durham, N.C.: Duke Divinity School. Available online at http://www.pulpitandpew.duke.edu/clergyhealth.html.

Wertheimer, Jack. 2003. The Rabbi Crisis. *Commentary*, May, 35-39.

Wheeler, Barbara G. 1984. The Educational Preferences and Practices of Talented Ministers: Report of an Exploratory Study. Report given at Auburn Theological Seminary, New York.

————. 2001. *Is There a Problem? Theological Students and Religious Leadership for the Future.* New York: Auburn Center for the Study of Theological Education.

Wiborg, Margaret S., and Elizabeth J. Collier. 1997. *United Methodist Clergywomen Retention Study.* Boston: Anna Howard Shaw Center, Boston University School of Theology.

Wilkes, Paul. 1999. Must Catholics Settle for Less? *Boston Sunday Globe,* 19 December.

————. 2001a. *Excellent Catholic Parishes: The Guide to Best Places and Practices.* New York: Paulist Press.

————. 2001b. *Excellent Protestant Congregations: The Guide to Best Places and Practices.* Louisville: Westminster John Knox Press.

Willimon, William H. 2002a. *Pastor: The Theology and Practice of Ordained Ministry.* Nashville: Abingdon Press.

Willimon, William H., ed. 2002b. *Pastor: A Reader for Ordained Ministry.* Nashville: Abingdon Press.

Wind, James P., and Gilbert R. Rendle. 2001. *The Leadership Situation Facing American Congregations.* Bethesda, Md.: The Alban Institute.

Wittberg, Patricia. 1993. Job Satisfaction Among Lay, Clergy and Religious Order Workers for the Catholic Church: A Preliminary Investigation. *Review of Religious Research* 35, No. 1, September: 19-39.

Wood, David. 2002. 'The Best Life': Eugene Peterson on Pastoral Ministry. *Christian Century,* 13-20 March, 18-25.

Wood, James R. 1981. *Leadership in Voluntary Organizations: The Controversy over Social Action in Protestant Churches.* New Brunswick, N.J.: Rutgers University Press.

Woolever, Cynthia, and Deborah Bruce. 2002. *A Field Guide to Congregations.* Louisville: Geneva Press.

———— 2004. *Beyond the Ordinary: 10 Strengths of U.S. Congregations.* Louisville: Westminster John Knox Press.

Wuthnow, Robert. 1987. *Restructuring American Protestantism.* Princeton: Princeton University Press.

Young, Lawrence A. 1998. Assessing and Updating the Schoenherr-Young Projections of Clergy Decline in the United States Roman Catholic Church. *Sociology of Religion* 59, no. 1 (Spring): 7-23.

Zikmund, Barbara Brown, Adair T. Lummis, and Patricia Mei Yin Chang. 1998. *Clergy Women: An Uphill Calling.* Louisville: Westminster John Knox Press.

Zondag, Hessel J. 2004. Knowing You Make A Difference: Result Awareness and Satisfaction in the Pastoral Profession. *Review of Religious Research* 45, no. 3, March: 254-69.

Index

burnout, 13, 103, 114, 160, 179, 212, 234
Burns, James MacGregor, 145-46, 201

calling: clergy commitment to, 159, 161-
63, 167, 169, 172-74, 185; clergy doubt
of, 162-69, 173-74, 181, 183, 207, 213,
220, 234; culture of, 223-25; Niebuhr
on, 22, 24, 223-24; ordained ministry
as, 22-24, 151, 154-57, 162
Calvary Chapel, 23, 200
Calvin, John, 22
Campbell, Alexander, 53
Campus Crusade for Christ, 227
campus ministry, 68n.13, 191, 224, 227
Canada, religious climate in, 37-38
Carder, Kenneth, 51
Carroll, Jackson W., 19n.12, 27n.17,
35n.4, 49, 50n.13, 92n.39, 145n.9,
147n.10
Catherine, 195
Catholic Church, 39, 45, 52, 55n.20, 59-
62, 65, 190, 204; large parish sizes of,
10, 59, 62-64, 106, 111, 115, 232; lay parish ministers of, 79, 81, 84; pedophilia
scandal in, 15, 24, 55n.20; redefinition
of clergy and lay roles in, 14, 18, 131,
223; and sacramental view of ordination, 18, 23-24, 155, 166; and tradition,
147, 149, 195
Catholic priests, 23-24, 85-86, 108-9, 115,
132, 142, 155-56; average age of, 71-73,
75; bivocational, 79, 81-82, 110; compensation for, 90-94; education of,
21, 23-24, 34, 77, 229, 230n.7; foreign,
45, 85n.31; health of, 124, 179; problems facing, 164, 166-67, 186n.9, 190,
213; recruitment of, 12, 16, 221; "sacredly male" image of, 66-67, 84; satisfaction of, 161-62, 174-75; second-
career, 73-74, 76-77; shortage of, 3, 7,
12, 14, 45, 63, 79, 81, 85n.31, 164, 167,
221-22, 229, 230n.7, 234; workweek of,
103, 106-7, 121-22, 234
celibacy, 46, 84, 166, 190, 213, 222

Center for Applied Research in the
Apostolate, 106n.9, 161
changes: in the church, 13-16, 28-29, 58,
72, 130, 148, 160-61, 169, 211; in society, 27, 128, 141-42, 147, 150, 207-8, 217
Chaves, Mark, 25n.16, 104n.8, 191
church: attendance, 38-39, 62-64; as
body of Christ, 11, 17, 97, 142-43, 194,
198-200; growth, 55-56; membership,
39, 55, 89, 233; programs, 143-46, 148-
49, 158; purpose of, 32-33, 56, 143; tradition and Scripture as guides for,
195-96, 205; as voluntary community,
52-55, 97, 129, 144, 146, 150
Churches of Christ, 53
clay jars. *See* pottery metaphor
clergy: commitment, 159, 161-63, 167,
169, 172-74, 179, 181, 185-86, 220; congregational assignments of, 52-53, 62,
80, 83, 128, 150, 217; cultural misalignment of, 32, 39, 56, 206, 237; as diverse, 9, 57, 204-5, 220, 227-28; leaving ministry, 160, 162-65, 167, 169,
172-74, 181, 183, 186n.9, 220; marital
and family lives of, 13, 36, 67, 69-70,
77, 94, 121-23, 165, 174, 176-77, 180, 213,
234-35; moral failures of, 15-16, 24, 39,
154, 177-78, 213-14; peer relationships
of, 53-54, 167, 171, 174-78, 212-14, 214,
230, 236-38; relationships of, with
congregations, 12, 26, 54-55, 179-80,
187, 200-201, 212; as role models, 24,
120, 224; roles of, 8-9, 12, 16-19, 97-98,
100, 118-20, 125-26, 177-78, 180, 219-20;
satisfaction, 13, 29, 108, 159-60, 169-
79, 181-82, 185, 212, 220; treated differently because of their pastoral role,
165-66, 177-80, 186
communal view of ministry, 198-201
community involvement, 104, 107-8, 120
compensation. *See* salaries of clergy
complaint, clerical culture of, 236-37
Confessing Movement, 46
conflict. *See* congregations: conflict in

Eck, Diana, 41, 43
education of clergy, 19-24, 77, 87-89, 215,
226-31; as basis of authority, 151, 154-
57; bivocational, 82-84; and debt, 75,
94, 225-26; history of, 20-21, 23-24; as
lifelong, 170-72, 214-17, 230, 236; suspicion of, 155, 205, 215. *See also* seminarians; seminaries
Eiesland, Nancy L., 34n.2
Episcopalians, 53, 82, 86, 155
Eucharist, 9, 17, 60, 106
Evangelical Lutheran Church in America, 80, 123, 226n.3, 230. *See also* Lutherans
evangelism, 55n.20, 100, 102, 137, 205
excellence, 192-94; business model of,
192-94, 196-98, 202; cruciform, 197-
98, 201-2, 205, 218, 221, 238; in Scripture, 195-96, 199, 201; in work for the
social good, 32, 85
excellent ministry, 29-30, 188-90, 192-96,
199-201, 220-21; characteristics of,
205-18; clergy responsibility for, 235-
38; as contextual, 195-96, 203-5; as
corporate and communal, 198-201;
education for, 226-31; and Jesus' cross
and resurrection, 196-202, 205; and
recruitment of clergy, 221-25

family life of clergy, 69, 121-23, 160-61,
165-66, 213; and clergy satisfaction,
170-71, 173-76, 178
Forsyth, P. T., 32
Free Church tradition, 18
Friedman, Edwin, 202n.6
friendships, 176-78, 212-14, 230, 236

Gardner, Howard, 32
Generations X and Y, 35, 49
gifts: for pastoral leadership, 17-18, 204-
5, 224; spiritual, 17-18, 200-201
Gilead (Robinson), 96, 98, 166, 167n.2
Glassie, Henry, 188
Gnosticism, 17

Good Work (Gardner et al.), 32n.1
GoodWork Project, 32, 85, 88, 183-84,
206
Great Awakening, 23
Great Britain, religious climate in, 20,
37-38
Greeley, Andrew, 14n.7, 190, 236-37
Gregory, 195
Gregory the Great, 7
Griswold, Wendy, 26-27, 194-95, 203, 219

Hahn, Scott, 109
Harris, Joseph Claude, 36n.6
Hartford Seminary study, 116
health care benefits, 80, 91, 93-94, 225,
232
health of clergy, 123-26, 160, 178-82, 185,
212, 220, 236
Healy, Anthony, 50n.14
Heifetz, Ronald, 151n.12, 207
Henry, Matthew, 109
hierarchical polities, 54, 61, 68n.13. *See
also* connectional polities
Hoge, Dean, 92n.39, 186n.9
Holifield, E. Brooks, 16n.9
Holmes, Urban, 24n.15
homosexuality, 44, 46, 209-10
Hope Chapel, 200
housing, 90-92, 94, 170-71, 173-74
Hutchison, William, 191-92
Hybels, Lynne and Bill, 190

identity, religious, 42-43, 48-49
imagination, pastoral, 208-10, 236
immigration, 37n.6, 39-41, 43-45, 65, 83,
98
Immigration and Nationality Act
Amendments, 40
innovation, 147-50, 158
In Search of Excellence (Peters and
Waterman), 192
Internet, and religion, 19, 50
internships for clergy, 76, 228-29
interreligious diversity, 41, 43